RICKETTS' BATTERY:

A HISTORY OF BATTERY F, 1ST PENNSYLVANIA LIGHT ARTILLERY

by

Dr. Richard A. Sauers
&
Peter Tomasak

PUBLISHED BY LUZERNE NATIONAL BANK
WILLIAM LEANDRI, PRESIDENT AND CEO

Copyright

Copyright © 2001

Dr. Richard A. Sauers & Peter Tomasak

Except as permitted under the United States Copyright Act of 1976, no part of this publication may be reproduced or distributed in any form or by any means, or stored in a data base or retrieval system, without the prior written permission of the publisher.

ISBN 0-9678561-1-6

Manufactured in the United States of America
Luzerne National Bank

Dedicated

To the memory of Chester Siegel

Table of Contents

List of Illustrations / viii

List of Maps / xi

Preface / xii

Introduction / xiv

Chapter One
1861 / 1

Chapter Two
Campaigning in Northern Virginia / 15

Chapter Three
The Army of Virginia / 29

Chapter Four
The Maryland Campaign / 47

Chapter Five
Fredericksburg and Chancellorsville / 59

Chapter Six
Gettysburg / 77

Chapter Seven
Autumn 1863 / 109

Chapter Eight
Veterans / 143

Chapter Nine
The Wilderness Campaign / 155

Chapter Ten
Petersburg / 175

Chapter Eleven
1865 / 199

Chapter Twelve
Postwar Memories / 217

Battery F Roster / 227

Bibliography / 271

Index / 279

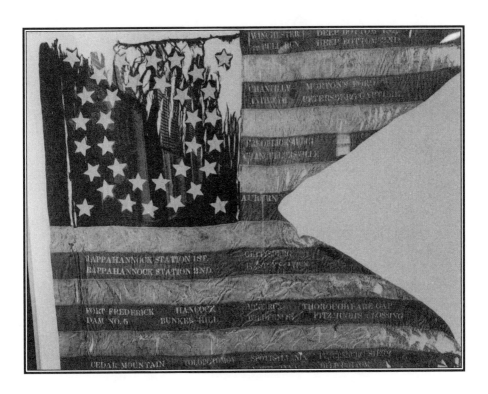

Battery F Guidon.

(LUZERNE COUNTY HISTORICAL SOCIETY)

Captain Ezra W. Matthews.

(PRIVATE COLLECTION)

Captain Robert Bruce Ricketts.

(USAMHI)

List of Illustrations

Battery Guidon / v

Captain Ezra W. Matthews / vi

Captain R. Bruce Ricketts / vii

Captain Matthews & Lieutenant Ricketts / 3

Lieutenant Charles B. Brockway / 4

Captain Matthews & Lieutenant Ricketts / 13

Pvt. Richard S. Stratford / 14

Lieutenant R. Bruce Ricketts / 20

Corporal Leon Eugene C. Moore / 26

Private Andrew Myers / 35

Corporal Hiram M. Pidcoe / 42

Private Thomas E. Frame / 46

Lieutenant Henry Godbold. / 51

QM Sergeant Stephen E. Ridgeway / 55

Musician William Morrison / 67

Lieutenant Charles B. Brockway / 79

Forbes Sketch of Cemetery Hill / 87

Contemporary Sketch of Cemetery Hill / 88

Forbes Sketch of Confederate Attack on Cemetery Hill / 92

Waud Drawing of 5th Maine Battery / 94

Woodcut Showing Fighting on Cemetery Hill / 95

Death of James H. Riggin / 98

Sergeant Myron French / 101

Waud Drawing Showing Charge on Cemetery Hill / 104

Lieutenant Francis H. Snider / 110

Corporal William Umberhower / 123

Lieutenant Truman L. Case / 131

Private Henry J. Carson / 132

Private James H. Phillips / 133

Private william G. Pinkerton / 134

Sergeant Charles G. Matthews / 135

Private George W. Ackerman / 136

Private William Frederick / 137

Lieutenant Franklin P. Brockway / 138

Private John Marquart / 139

Private Albert Herbine / 140

Private Henry J. Carson / 141

Captain John F. Campbell / 142

Waud Sketch of Battery F in March 1864 / 148

Corporal Ephraim Berger / 160

Sketches of Battery F at Mine Run and Cold Harbor / 171

Private Levi S. Bowers / 179

Private Samuel C. Torbett / 183

Private Charles Shipman / 188

Bugler William Warnick / 194

Four Members Playing Cards / 202

Corporal John W. Bullock / 205

Private Cyrus Jones / 211

Private Henry C. McClintock / 215

Monument Dedication at Gettysburg / 219

Veterans at Monument in 1894 / 223

Colonel Ricketts' Uniform and Sword / 226

List of Maps

Maryland-Northern Virginia / 8

Second Manassas / 39

Antietam / 50

Fredericksburg-Chancellorsville / 74

Gettysburg / 89

Bristoe Station / 110

Petersburg / 176

Preface

If you ever enjoyed Ricketts Glen State Park and forest in Luzerne County, Pennsylvania, give Colonel Robert Bruce Ricketts credit for keeping it the way it is today. The park is named in honor of the achievements of that famous Civil War veteran. The area of the park was his favorite getaway after the war. His fame is not just derived from his land of yesterday. Before making a career of purchasing land warrants he spent four years on the long road of making history during the Civil War.

The story behind the mysterious R. B. Ricketts has been silent for long enough. My study of the battle of Gettysburg began what seems like yesterday but seriously began in 1973. A year later, while visiting the Gettysburg battlefield, I met Colonel Jacob Sheads. Most people do not know his name, but Sheads is a scholar of the campaign and battle of Gettysburg. He is a native of the town, a retired school teacher and park guide, and among other things, a great friend to this author.

Colonel Sheads and I were discussing the battle during one of my many visits to the field. He asked me to do him a favor, a task that started a research project that has taken up a good fifteen years of my life's extra time. Sheads asked me, since I lived close to where Colonel Ricketts was from, to find out more about Battery Hell. I asked him what was Battery Hell? He replied that it referred to Ricketts' battery. Ricketts who? Robert Bruce Ricketts. I started out in 1985 to research Battery Hell and its commander. In the beginning it was tough to find any information about him. I found a few references in books and then a couple of stories on the battery itself. But I did not give up. Over the years, I found a few items from Battery F at Civil War relic shows. I shared what I found with Colonel Sheads.

A few years later, while going through a box of notes, I found an old notebook on Ricketts. The find revived my interest in his story. In the fall of 1990, I once again began to look for more on Ricketts. During that search I met the late Chester Siegel of Hillsgrove, Pennsylvania. He is the most important part in telling the history of Battery F. Chester had worked for the late William R. Ricketts for fifteen years; William was Colonel Ricketts' only son. When I interviewed Chester for this research I asked him how he knew so much about the colonel. "Bill liked to talk and I listened," was his concise answer. "Bill would talk about his dad and the war and all."

William Ricketts passed away in the fall of 1956. In 1959, his estate was sold. His twin daughters asked Chester to ready it for the new owners, empty the Ricketts Mansion and destroy what he did not want to keep. Chester told me that he kept most of Colonel Ricketts' Civil War papers and other pertinent related material. Over the two and a half years that I knew Chester, he shared his collection and knowledge with me. Within his collection were many answers needed in telling the full story of Robert Bruce Ricketts and his battery of artillery. What was missing here was found in other repositories. A mountain of material was growing.

My next question was what to do with it. My love of history said that since there is no battery history, one must be written to preserve the story. I decided to write one. Before tackling this, the only writing I had done previously was term papers and book reports in high school. Before trying to write a full history, I wrote an article on Battery F at Gettysburg that appeared in Issue 12 of *The Gettysburg Magazine*. It was received well by readers of the magazine.

Thus, the responsibility fell upon me to tell the full story of Ricketts and Battery F. However, I had so many other projects going that time was limited for me to do the job myself. So, I decided to contact a friend of mine and ask for help. Dr. Richard A. Sauers is the best person to ask for help on any Pennsylvania Civil War unit. He has over the years earned the reputation of being known for his vast knowledge of Pennsylvania Civil War history. He has written many books, one of which enticed me to contact him. That book was the letters of James B. Thomas of the 107th Pennsylvania. My great-great-grandfather, a Medal of Honor recipient, belonged to this unit. I called Dr. Sauers and we arranged a meeting to discuss the project. I quickly discovered that he had edited my *Gettysburg Magazine* article. After reviewing what material I had already assembled, we both knew that a great story was ready to be told. Rick knew it had special meaning also.

Sometimes facts have a way of getting blurred over time. To one, they are this, to another, they are something different. Many words. Many interpretations. No matter. After sorting through the research material there is something about the battles, the men, the memories that was missing long enough and ready to be told. This book is that story.

Peter Tomasak
Sweet Valley, Pennsylvania

Introduction

As a scholar of the campaign and battle of Gettysburg, I'm always looking for new material that adds to the already voluminous literature on America's greatest battle. Over the past several years, it has been an honor to be one of the editors for Bob Younger's successful The *Gettysburg Magazine*, which has featured fresh, new articles about the myriad events of this great military campaign. I am always glad to see articles that result from the introduction of unused manuscript material that provides fresh material on a battle that some historians mistakenly believe has been overworked as we start the twenty-first century.

One article drew my attention because it included previously unused material. When I read and edited Pete Tomasak's article on Ricketts' battery at Gettysburg, I was impressed by his use of "new" material, primarily the papers of then-Captain R. Bruce Ricketts. My special interest is in Pennsylvania Civil War history, and I was glad to see some new material on a battery about which little has been written.

And then, a couple of years later, Pete called me and told me that he wanted to write a complete battery history, but needed help. He came out to visit me in Pittsburgh, carrying along a file box crammed with material about Battery F. Manuscripts, military records, newspaper articles, and more! Here was the raw material which could be used to write a good, solid account of Battery F. I willingly agreed to co-author the book. Over the past few years, in between moves and job changes, I plowed ahead, until finally done earlier this year. Pete had done his research well and had found practically everything that could be located about Ricketts and his famous battery. Throughout this project, Pete unflaggingly answered questions, assisted with the writing, and did more research, tracking down leads I passed along and finding things I needed.

The result is this book. Here, under one cover, is the full story of a typical volunteer artillery battery of the Civil War. Originally recruited and organized by Captain Ezra A. Matthews, Battery F, 1st Pennsylvania Light Artillery drew into its ranks recruits and drafted men from 32 of the commonwealth's 66 counties, as well as the state of Maryland. Thus, the battery represented a wide cross-section of the commonwealth, but at the same time could call no one or two counties home. This resulted in postwar obscurity as the veterans answered the last call. By the time Colonel Ricketts' son William died in 1956, Battery F was known to only the serious Gettysburg buffs for its heroic action on East Cemetery Hill on the evening of July 2, 1863.

But there's more to the story than Gettysburg. Battery F served honorably throughout the war, seeing action at Second Manassas, Antietam, Fredericksburg, Chancellorsville, Gettysburg, Bristoe Station, Mine Run, the Wilderness, Spotsylvania, Cold Harbor, and several operations during the siege of Petersburg. There were no Medal of Honor winners in Battery F. There were also no executions for desertion or other crimes. The officers and men of Battery F saw the War for the Union to a successful conclusion and then went home to resume their lives. This is their wartime story.

Dr. Richard A. Sauers
Lake Nebagamon, Wisconsin

Acknowledgments

The authors have a number of people to thank for their generous help as this book went through all the stages from research to publication.

We owe a special debt of gratitude to Luzerne National Bank and William Leandri for being open-minded and providing us the opportunity to have this work published. Beverly Bittle, Gettysburg, PA, shared copies of several Battery F reunion documents that she found in the bottom of a box of books she purchased at an auction. Kenneth and Susan Boardman, Gettysburg, Pa., graciously shared the papers of the battery's last captain, John A. Campbell. Chris Calkins, Petersburg National Military Park, answered questions about geography and the locations of Battery F during various operations. Scott Hartwig of Gettysburg National Military Park, as always, was tremendously helpful in answering questions and identifying documents of interest from the park's collections. Harold Kashner, Bloomsburg, Pa., allowed us to use the Charles B. Brockway papers in his possession. Jeff Kowalis for use of the Ricketts monument photo. Garry Leister, Sunbury, Pa., generously shared the voluminous letters of William H. Thurston, which shed so much light on Battery F's actions in 1864 and 1865. We also appreciate his permission to use a number of Battery F photographs. The Luzerne County Historical Society allowed us to photograph Colonel Ricketts' uniform, sword, and battery guidon in its possession. Michael P. Musick, National Archives, patiently answered questions, checked some records, and guided us through the mass of 1st Pennsylvania Light Artillery material in Washington. Ronn Palm, Kittanning, PA, always the friend, shared Battery F images in his vast personal collection of Pennsylvania Civil War photographs. We are very grateful to Chester Siegel, Hillsgrove, PA, which made this book possible. Without his permission to copy the Ricketts papers in his possession, Battery F's story would be abject and weak. Frank Wright, Washington, D.C., donated a copy of Frank Brockway's 1865 diary to the project, which in itself made for an interesting reading.

In addition to the above folks, we also wish to thank Bill Gladstone, Andrew Hasco, Elaine Kline, and Gil Barrett for allowing us to use photographs from their private collections. To Michael Winey and Randy Hackenburg, both of the United States Army Military History Institute (abbreviated USAMHI in photo credits), we also say a hearty thanks for their help in securing copies of photographs in the Institute's vast holdings. Gettysburg National Military Park and the Library of Congress both contributed images to the book. To those we missed, thank you.

And last but certainly not the least, we owe our wives, Gina and Ayn, a debt of gratitude for their help and suffering over the years as we worked on this book.

Chapter One

1861

Following President Abraham Lincoln's call for seventy-five thousand militia to suppress the Southern rebellion, the Commonwealth of Pennsylvania raised twenty-five infantry regiments in only ten days. The twenty thousand soldiers in these units seriously depleted the state's pre-war militia organizations, many of which entered federal service. Many other companies were organized locally but were unable to enlist because the state's original quota was exceeded by far.

Governor Andrew G. Curtin was concerned about the militia shortage. Pennsylvania was bordered by Virginia and Maryland. Virginia had already seceded from the Union and Maryland kept loyal only by force of arms. Hence, the southern counties of the commonwealth were liable to attack at any time and needed protection. On May 15, Curtin signed into law the Reserve Volunteer Corps of the Commonwealth of Pennsylvania. The state would, at its own expense, raise and equip a force to consist of thirteen infantry regiments, one cavalry regiment, and one of artillery. The men would enlist in state service for three years. If the federal government needed more troops, Curtin was allowed by law to transfer the corps to federal service.[1]

Accordingly, the state organized the infantry regiments during the month of June 1861, with the 1st Pennsylvania Cavalry following in July. The 1st Pennsylvania Light Artillery was also formed in June, although its origins dated back to April, when Philadelphia citizen James Brady called for volunteers for a light artillery regiment. Brady managed to enroll well over a thousand men, but bureaucratic delays soured the recruits' enthusiasm; some companies joined other regiments and many recruits simply left camp for home.[2]

---

[1] Richard A. Sauers, Advance the Colors! Pennsylvania Civil War Battleflags, 2 volumes (Lebanon, PA: Sowers Printing Company for the PA Capitol Preservation Committee), 1:80.

[2] Samuel P. Bates, History of Pennsylvania Volunteers, 1861-5, 5 volumes (Harrisburg: B. Singerly, State Printer, 1869-1872), 1:944.

The nucleus of the 1st Artillery was rescued by the organization of the Reserve Corps. Brady, commanding one of the four remaining batteries, took all four companies to Camp Curtin at Harrisburg, where they were joined by four additional batteries. These eight batteries were organized as the 1st Pennsylvania Light Artillery. Command of the regiment was initially offered to Richard H. Rush of Philadelphia, with Lieutenant Colonel Charles T. Campbell and Majors Alfred E. Lewis and Henry T. Danforth. Rush declined the appointment and became colonel of the 6th Pennsylvania Cavalry, leaving Campbell in command of the recruits.[3]

The men who enlisted in what became Battery F were recruited in a number of Pennsylvania counties. One of the men instrumental in recruiting the battery was Ezra Wallace Matthews, a resident of Pine Grove, Schuylkill County. Born in Connecticut in 1835, Matthews was teaching school when the war erupted. He enlisted in the Pine Grove Light Infantry, which became Company D, 10th Pennsylvania, for three months. He was promoted to sergeant during this first enlistment. Immediately upon returning home, Matthews set about recruiting a battery.[4]

Matthews recruited men in Williamsport (Lycoming County), Danville (Montour County), and Harrisburg (Dauphin County). Men who were mustered in as commissioned officers brought recruits from Philadelphia, Columbia (Bloomsburg), Blair (Hollidaysburg and Williamsburg), and Susquehanna counties. More recruits came from a scattering of eleven Pennsylvania counties. Battery F truly was a conglomeration of eager young men from a wide variety of backgrounds.[5]

Battery F was mustered into state service on July 8. Captain Matthews had, under his command, 1st Lieutenants Elbridge McConkey and Robert B. Ricketts, 2nd Lieutenants Henry L. Godbold and Truman L. Case, 1st Sergeant William H. Trump, a quartermaster sergeant, four sergeants, eight

---

[3]Bates, *Pennsylvania Volunteers*, 1:944.

[4]*Military Order of the Loyal Legion of the United States. Commandery of Pennsylvania,* In Memoriam: Ezra Wallace Matthews *(Philadelphia, 1885); Sharman Meck Carroll to Peter Tomasak, October 22, 1992.*

[5]"Memoranda for reply to letter of August 28th [1915] from Col. John P. Nicholson, Chairman, Gettysburg National Park Commission," in Battery F Papers, Record Group 19, Department of Military Affairs, Pennsylvania State Archives (hereafter Battery F Papers). Ricketts objected to the War Department's listing that battery F was recruited in Schuylkill County, which is what was inscribed on the battery's monument at Gettysburg. Colonel Nicholson cited the Civil War-period register of the volunteer army as his source, which was the official guide issued by the War Department. In spite of Ricketts' protest, the inscription was never changed.

Captain Ezra W. Matthews (L) and 1st Lieutenant R. Bruce Ricketts (R).
(GIL BARRETT COLLECTION, USAMHI)

1st Lieutenant Charles B. Brockway. Next to Ricketts, Charles Brockway was perhaps the most influential man in Battery F until health concerns sidelined his military career.

(HAROLD KASHNER)

corporals, and sixty enlisted men.⁶ By the end of July, Matthews had gathered additional recruits to bring the strength of Battery F up to the required number. Lieutenant McConkey was soon detached from the battery and assigned to the staff of Brigadier General George W. McCall, commanding the Pennsylvania Reserves. McConkey served as an aide to the general.

While in Camp Curtin, the battery was drilled each day to familiarize the recruits with army life and discipline. The men started in squads. Then, when they had acquired the proper discipline and understood basic commands, the squads were doled out to form crews for individual cannon.

The men were then drilled as a gun crew and taught the rudimentary skills for loading and firing their cannon. Following this step, each battery was divided into sections, with two cannon per section. The section was then drilled as a unit and taught to work together. Finally, the captain assembled the entire battery and drilled the sections as a single unit. Thus, days were long and hard as the men learned new skills. In addition, each battery received horses to pull the cannon, limber chests, and caissons. Owing to a shortage of horses, Battery F, though, initially did not receive its allotment of horses; the men continued to drill on foot.⁷

Battery F was originally armed with four 6-pounder smoothbores supplied by the state. These Mexican War-vintage artillery pieces could throw a solid shot more than twelve hundred yards. Sometime in August, the 1st Pennsylvania Artillery batteries still at Camp Curtin finally were deemed ready to move. Together with other batteries, Battery F was

---

⁶*Instructions for Field Artillery (Philadelphia: J. B. Lippincott & Company, 1863), 7. One of the sergeants was Charles B. Brockway, a 21-year-old law student from Bloomsburg. Brockway, though a Democrat, was eager for war and joined the army in April 1861. His company, the Iron Guards, became Company A of the 6th Pennsylvania Reserves. Brockway, appointed a sergeant, aspired for a higher rank, but was rebuffed in his attempt to secure election as an officer. He wrote to his friend R. B. Ricketts to see about getting a transfer to Battery F. In one such letter, Brockway was near the point of begging to be transferred to the battery and would Ricketts help him in securing a position in the battery. Charles had his goal set on a commissioned rank. See Brockway to Ricketts, June 28, 1861, Battery F Papers.*

⁷*Instructions for Field Artillery was one of the basic manuals that the officers had to learn and was used as the primary instruction book by the drill instructors. Often, the officers were as ignorant as the men were in regard to artillery skills, and were expected to master the manuals more quickly then the men under their command. Regular Army officers were usually assigned to drill the officers and men of volunteer units.*

dispatched to join the Pennsylvania Reserves in camp at Tenallytown, just outside Washington.[8]

The 1st Pennsylvania Artillery batteries present at Camp Curtin were sworn into federal service on August 5, then paid through the end of July. That afternoon, the men sweated to load their artillery pieces onto railroad cars for the trip to Washington. It took far longer than anticipated to get everything ready, and it was not until ten o'clock that night when the train finally chugged out of Harrisburg.[9]

The long train lumbered through York shortly before daylight. After a brief halt, the regiment crossed the Mason-Dixon Line. "The men and women cheered us, and the darkies in Maryland waved their hats and showed their ivories," wrote Private John H. Christian. Indeed, Sergeant Brockway was surprised at Maryland. He, and many of his comrades, imagined that on crossing south, they would see "rags and filth, a desolate country and blighted crops"—the result of the scourge of slavery. Instead, the train passed by "a prosperous population, palatial residences, a beautiful country and well cultivated fields."[10]

The men detrained in Baltimore after a delay of several hours. Like many other regiments, the 1st Artillery marched through the city to the Baltimore & Ohio Railroad depot. Only a few children spewed forth secessionist sentiments. Most folks waved American flags at the passing Yankees. Another delay occurred before the troops boarded a B&O train, but local citizens plied the men with all sorts of goodies.[11]

The train steamed into Washington about ten o'clock in the morning of August 6. After leaving the cars, the men were herded into a large building near the depot, where they remained for a day. On the morning of the 8th, the entire regiment marched south through Washington. Since horses had not been sent yet, the men had to pull their cannon along the dusty streets. Camp was set up near the Washington Arsenal, on the banks of the Potomac River. From here, the men had a fine view of the country south of the river.[12]

---

[8]*Bates,* Pennsylvania Volunteers, *1:958.*

[9]*Charles B. Brockway letter of August 10 in the* Columbia Democrat, *September 17, 1861.*

[10]*Ibid.; John H. Christian letter of October 6, 1861, in the Danville* Intelligencer, *October 18, 1861.*

[11]*Brockway letter,* Columbia Democrat, *September 17, 1861.*

[12]*Ibid.; Christian letter, Danville* Intelligencer, *October 18, 1861. Christian wrote that the battery stayed in the Soldiers' Rest the first day after arriving in Washington; Brockway did not identify the building's name.*

While in camp near the Arsenal, Battery F finally received its share of horses and horse trappings. Less than three weeks later, the battery broke camp and marched through Washington to Tenallytown to join the Pennsylvania Reserves. Here the drilling continued as the battery successfully melded its men and horses into an efficient unit.

A full-strength battery of six cannon also included six caissons, twelve limbers, a traveling forge, a battery wagon, and perhaps two supply wagons. Batteries were divided into two-gun sections, each of which was under the command of one of the lieutenants. A sergeant was in charge of each cannon. Corporals commanded the gun during battle, and a corporal was in charge of the caisson and second limber, which were located to the rear of the battery's position. The unit's first sergeant was primarily responsible for the mundane army paperwork and any other duties assigned by the captain. The battery guidon bearer always remained near the captain to provide recognition of the location of the commander. The battery bugler also followed the captain closely. Finally, a specialized man called an artificer was attached to each battery. He was responsible for maintaing the forge and making repairs to equipment as needed. The officers, bugler, guidon bearer, and horse drivers rode horses; everyone else marched on foot with the battery.[13]

On September 12, Captain Matthews was ordered to report to Major General Nathaniel P. Banks for duty. Banks was in command of a division in the new Army of the Potomac. His command was deployed in central Maryland, guarding the Potomac River from Harper's Ferry to near Washington. Banks had three brigades of infantry as well as supporting artillery and cavalry.[14]

Battery F left Tenallytown and moved to Darnestown, Maryland, a small town west of Rockville. The batterymen pitched their new white tents in a clover field belonging to a planter. The plantation's slaves visited camp

---

[13]*The primary manual* Instruction for Field Artillery *details the composition of a battery and specifies how the limbers, forge, battery wagon, and caissons were to be packed. The manual also detailed all drills. For a brief capsule summary of the composition of a battery, see Ross M. Kimmel, "Men and Materiel,"* America's Civil War *14 #3 (July 2001): 12, 14, 16, 78.*

[14]*Ibid. Banks' command was organized as follows:*
>*First Brigade, Colonel George H. Gordon, Brig. Gen. Alpheus S. Williams (Oct. 18): 19th, 28th NY, 5th CT, 28th PA, 2nd MA, 1st MD*
>*Second Brigade, Brig. Gen. John J. Abercrombie: 12th MA, 12th, 16th IN*
>*Third Brigade, Colonel J. W. Stiles: 3rd WI, 29th PA, 13th MA, 83rd NY*
>*Artillery: Bty A, 1st RI; PA Bty F; Bty F, 4th US*
>*Cavalry: 3rd NY*

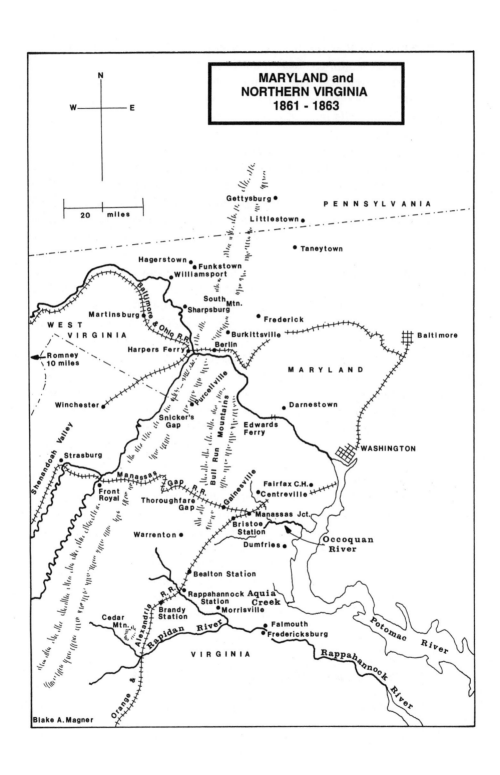

and encouraged the Yankees to steal their massa's chickens. The men in blue, however, were enjoined by their superiors not to steal anything belonging to civilians. "But when any pigs or chickens come into our camp," wrote Private Christian, "they are sure to forget the road out."[15]

After darkness fell on October 2, the long roll sounded and the battery was quickly in line. Orders came for the men to receive two days' cooked rations and to strike their tents. Sixty thousand Rebels, it was rumored, had crossed the Potomac and were marching to attack General Abercrombie's brigade. By six in the morning of the third of October, the entire brigade was ready to move. No sooner had the advance cavalry left camp, however, than the rumor was proven false and the men were ordered to pitch their tents.[16]

Three days later, on October 6, Battery F was strengthened by the arrival of two new 10-pounder Parrott rifled cannon. An election was held to appoint an officer to command this new section. At this time, the battery was short one officer, Lieutenant McConkey having been detached to serve as an aide on General McCall's staff. Captain Matthews informed Governor Curtin on October 24 that R. Bruce Ricketts was unanimously elected 1st Lieutenant, and Sergeant Charles B. Brockway was advanced over the heads of the other commissioned officers to be the junior 1st Lieutenant, in place of McConkey. Matthews placed Brockway in command of the first section, with the unanimous approval of the batterymen of the section.

However, Lieutenant McConkey got word of Brockway's promotion and complained about the illegality of Matthews' action. After all, McConkey had not resigned from Battery F; he had only been detached on other duty. As a result, Brockway tendered his resignation a month later, not wishing to test the legality of his promotion. Brockway resumed his former rank and continued to serve with Battery F.[17]

Battery F became more active in October, as Union troops probed across the Potomac River into enemy-held Virginia. On October 8, a Union force crossed the Potomac at Harper's Ferry to seize the local wheat crop. Eight days later, enemy troops pressured the Yankees, then stationed on Bolivar Heights. Both sides fed more troops into the area. In the end, the Yankees drove off the Rebels and held Harper's Ferry and vicinity.

As the action on Bolivar Heights progressed, Battery F was ordered

---

[15]*Christian letter, Danville* Intelligencer, *October 18, 1861.*

[16]*Ibid.*

[17]*Matthews to Governor Andrew G. Curtin, October 25, 1861, Battery F Papers; Charles B. Brockway to Lorenzo Thomas, November 25, 1861, Battery F Papers.*

into action as a support force. That night, Battery F followed the infantry of Abercrombie's brigade along the Hill Road from Darnestown via Poolesville toward the Potomac. Rain commenced falling after dark, causing a halt until late in the afternoon of the 17th, when the brigade again lurched forward through a ribbon of mud. The brigade reached Edwards' Ferry early in the morning of the 18th, completely worn out. Soon thereafter, one section of the battery was detached and stationed at Muddy Branch to guard a crossing over the river.[18]

The section at Muddy Branch remained there for a month. The rest of the battery soon moved to Williamsport, where Captain Matthews established headquarters. As colder weather came on, it reminded the soldiers that wood was needed for the winter. On October 24, a Union foraging party crossed the Potomac in search of winter fuel. The advance cavalry pushed on some six miles from the river, surprising and scattering a Rebel picket post. The cavalry neared Martinsburg and spied a lone rider heading their way. A Union officer rode forward to meet the oncoming man. The two halted several feet apart, the Yankee with his carbine trained on his opposite, who sported a horse pistol. They exchanged pleasantries and learned that they were enemies. The two men looked at each other and then decided to go their separate ways unharmed. The Yankees loaded forty cords of wood and recrossed the river.[19]

The remaining two sections of Battery F at first stayed near Williamsport. Sometime in mid-November, Brockway's section was sent west to Hancock to reinforce the infantry stationed at that Maryland town. The erstwhile lieutenant, while awaiting the decision on his resignation, was sent north on recruiting duty sometime in December. Matthews kept his headquarters near Williamsport, while one section remained at Muddy Run. By early December, the battery seems to have been suffering from a lack of proper clothing. Brockway thought his section looked like "ragged ass Pennsylvania Volunteers." The situation worsened when his section was suddenly dispatched to Hancock, leaving behind most of the camp equipage. Some discontent toward Captain Matthews surfaced at this time,

---

[18]*John H. Christian letter of November 5, 1861, in* Danville Intelligencer, *November 15, 1861.*

[19]*Charles B. Brockway letter of October 27, 1861, in* Columbia Democrat, *November 9, 1861; John H. Christian letter,* Danville Intelligencer, *November 15, 1861.*

the captain being blamed for the lack of proper attire and food.[20]

At the time Brockway left for home, events along the Potomac began to heat up. Major General Thomas J. Jackson, the new commander of the Confederate Department of the Shenandoah, began contemplating offensive maneuvers almost as soon as he took command of the department in November. Union troops had occupied Romney, a town of some importance on the South Branch of the Potomac, in late October, depriving the Confederacy of the branch's farms. Jackson, although commanding far fewer troops than those opposing him, decided that a bold thrust toward the Potomac might draw troops away from Romney and enable him to quickly move west to seize the town.

Accordingly, during the month of December, Jackson's forces moved north to the Potomac and attempted to destroy dams that were an integral part of the Chesapeake and Ohio Canal, a vital waterway that generally paralleled the Potomac. The Baltimore & Ohio Railroad had been shut down effectively ever since the Confederacy had occupied Harper's Ferry at the outset of war. Thus, Jackson reasoned that damaging the canal's commerce would distract the enemy long enough for him to be successful elsewhere.

Jackson's troops appeared at Dam Number Five on December 17. His men braved freezing water in a rash try to break the stone canal locks. Union troops on patrol soon saw the enemy and sent out the alert. Colonel Samuel H. Leonard, commanding the 13th Massachusetts, sent part of his regiment to drive off the Rebels. One of Ricketts' Parrott rifles went along and opened up on the enemy, assisting the infantry in driving the Secesh away from the dam. Sporadic skirmishing lasted through the 20th, when Jackson's men managed to damage the lock; it was soon repaired. Jackson reported the loss of one man killed. Lieutenant Ricketts wound up in bed, sick from exposure in the bitterly cold weather.[21]

---

[20]*Charles B. Brockway to Robert B. Ricketts, November 16, 29, December 9, 1861,* in Brockway Papers. *A notice about Brockway being home on recruiting duty appeared in the* Columbia Democrat, *December 21, 1861. Although Bates wrote that Brockway was in command of the Parrott section (Bates,* Pennsylvania Volunteers, *1:958), by the time of the action at Dam #5, Ricketts was supervising this section* (Ibid.).

[21]*On the action at Dam #5, see Thomas M. Rankin,* Stonewall Jackson's Romney Campaign, January 1-February 20, 1862 *(Lynchburg, VA: H. E. Howard, Inc., 1994), 73-76. For brief reports and telegrams concerning the actions around Dam #5, see United States War Department,* The War of the Rebellion: A Compilation of the Official Records of the Union and Confederate Armies, *70 volumes in 128 parts (Washington: Government Printing Office, 1880-1901), 5:390, 398-400 (hereafter all references to this set are abbreviated as* O.R. *with appropriate volume and part).*

After the unsuccessful action along the Potomac in December, Jackson returned to Winchester and marshaled his troops. On the 1st of January 1862, the general set out with about eighty-five hundred men, heading toward the Potomac. His advance drove Union troops from Bath (present-day Berkeley Springs) on January 4, then interdicted the B&O Railroad later that day, destroying track and several stations. Jackson's main force marched toward Hancock, which they spied late on the 4th.

Union reinforcements were rushed to Brigadier General Frederick W. Lander, in command at Hancock. On January 3, Ricketts was ordered to report to Colonel Leonard, who told him to patrol the Potomac and "pitch in wherever there is any fighting to do." Ricketts halted at Dam Number Five that night, but saw no enemy. His section continued to roll westward; their halt that night was cut short by General Lander himself, who told Ricketts that Hancock was threatened by fifteen thousand Confederates and that he must help defend the town. Ricketts' men roused themselves at two o'clock in the morning of January 5 and reached Hancock at daylight. During January 5 and 6, Ricketts' rifled cannon dueled with enemy batteries and shelled any visible infantry. Although Ricketts believed his guns caused damage to the enemy and compelled them to withdraw, the Rebels acknowledged only a single casualty from artillery fire.[22]

Jackson concluded that reinforcements in Hancock meant that it was impossible for his troops to cross the river and capture the town. Therefore, Jackson turned his column westward and marched for Romney. Union troops evacuated the strategic town and withdrew to Cumberland and New Creek. Jackson's men occupied Romney and remained there a month, until cold weather and discontent among his subordinates necessitated a withdrawal. In the meantime, Ricketts' section stayed in the Hancock area, occasionally moving out into the surrounding area to reinforce infantry patrols guarding the river. On February 12, Captain Matthews and Lieutenant Ricketts crossed the Potomac with a cavalry escort and scouted as far south as Unger's Store, locating no Rebel troops; Jackson's men had withdrawn to Winchester the week before.[23]

---

[22]*Robert B. Ricketts Diary, January 3-6, 1862, Ricketts Papers;* Rankin, Romney Campaign, *95-104.*

[23]*Ricketts Diary, February 12, 1862.*

1st Lieutenant R. Bruce Ricketts (L) and Captain Ezra W. Matthews (R).
(CHESTER SIEGEL)

Pvt. Richard S. Stratford - Captain R.B. Ricketts Orderly

(CHESTER SIEGEL)

Chapter Two

Campaigning in Northern Virginia

Following Stonewall Jackson's retreat from Romney to Winchester, General Banks concentrated his forces for an advance up the Shenandoah Valley. McClellan's strategy included the occupation of the Valley and the prevention of its defenders from joining the troops opposing the main body of the Army of the Potomac. Banks was placed in command of the Fifth Army Corps, which included Brigadier General Charles S. Hamilton's First Division (then concentrating in the Hagerstown area), and Lander's Second Division, which had reoccupied Romney. McClellan directed Banks to cross the Potomac and move on Winchester with Hamilton's men, to be reinforced by Lander's.[1]

As part of the concentration of forces, Banks assigned six new 3-inch ordnance rifles to Battery F, replacing the older 6-pounders. The battery's three sections were finally united and the battery prepared for action. On March 1, Ricketts' section accompanied the 13th Massachusetts to Williamsport, where General Williams' brigade began crossing the Potomac. The brigade pushed Lieutenant Colonel Turner Ashby's Confederate cavalry (7th Virginia) out of the way and marched into Martinsburg unopposed. Some of the population fled, but Lieutenant Brockway observed that the majority of the remaining population was delighted to see Yankee soldiers. Food was scarce and the town presented a dilapidated appearance. Martinsburg's economy was tied to the health of the Baltimore & Ohio Railroad. Jackson's men had burned all the engine houses and wrecked seventy-two locomotives that had been trapped in the town ever since the Confederates had first interdicted the B&O during the summer of 1861. The Confederates had removed some of the locomotives to work other lines farther south.[2]

---

[1] *Nathan Kimball, "Fighting Jackson at Kernstown," in Robert U. Johnson and Clarence C. Buel (editors),* Battles and Leaders of the Civil War, *4 volumes (New York: The Century Company, 1884-1888), 2:302.*

[2] *Brockway letter of March 4, 1862, in the* Columbia Democrat *of March 15, 1862; Ricketts Diary, March 1, 1862.*

On March 5, Hamilton's division left Martinsburg, heading south along the turnpike. Williams' Third Brigade led, with Ricketts' section accompanying the infantry. Williams hoped to reach the small town of Bunker Hill, some ten miles ahead. By mid-afternoon, Williams finally reached his goal, after skirmishing with Ashby's horsemen just north of the town. From here, Williams reported that his information sources said that Jackson was being reinforced and was entrenching Winchester, boasting that he would defeat any force the Yankees could throw against his formidable works.[3]

Two days later, Williams sent out a reconnaissance party to break up a camp of Southern horsemen who were said to be harassing loyalists in the area between Bunker Hill and Winchester. The 5th Connecticut and 46th Pennsylvania followed a company of Maryland cavalry and a section of Battery F on this mission. When contact was initiated, the Confederate main body deployed and held off the Union cavalry as the two infantry regiments, on parallel roads, attempted to maneuver across the enemy's line of retreat. Captain Matthews accompanied Ricketts, who loosed several rounds into the enemy as they retreated, having detected the Yankee infantry's approach. The Union column then returned to camp.[4]

Banks then concentrated Hamilton's division at Martinsburg and prepared to move on Winchester. Following Banks' request for reinforcements, the first of Lander's brigades arrived as well; General Lander had died and his division was now led by Brigadier General James Shields. On March 12, the Yankees started down the pike. Again, Matthews' guns followed the cavalry, shelling Rebel cavalry whenever they attempted to halt the advance. In one sharp exchange, the entire battery unlimbered to blast away at Ashby's horsemen, several of whom waved their sabers in defiance of the Union cannon. Banks' men slogged eight miles, encamping for the night within four miles of the town.[5]

As the Union troops approached, Jackson, badly outnumbered, withdrew to the south. Hence, surprised Federal skirmishers found the town's entrenchments empty as they cautiously approached the next day. Banks' infantry formed in column and marched into town, bands playing and colors flying, as Ashby's cavalry trotted out of the southern edge of town. Lieutenant Ricketts noticed that the inhabitants were cool to the

---

[3]O.R., *volume 5, 517-18; Ricketts Diary, March 5, 1862.*

[4]O.R., *volume 5, 520-23; Ricketts Diary, March 7, 1862.*

[5]Kimball, "Fighting Jackson," 302; Ricketts Diary, March 9-12, 1862; Brockway letter of March 14th in the Columbia Democrat, *March 29, 1862.*

invaders. "A few of the ladies waved their handkerchiefs, but only a very few."[6]

General Shields took his division and continued to follow Jackson up the Valley. His men skirmished with the enemy at Fisher's Hill on March 17, then ended the pursuit the next day, having reached Mount Jackson on the Shenandoah River. Shields then returned to Winchester, reporting to Banks that Jackson had fled south, leaving only Ashby's troopers to observe the Yankees. At this point, Banks felt the Valley situation was under control, enabling him to follow McClellan's March 16 order to make it his priority to rebuild the Manassas Gap Railroad, which ran from Washington to Strasburg. Once this was done, Banks was to post the majority of his corps in the vicinity of Manassas, leaving minimal forces in the Valley.[7]

With Winchester under Federal control and the enemy gone from his front, Banks began transferring his troops across the mountains toward Manassas. Shields' division remained in the Valley as the First Division, now under Alpheus Williams (following Hamilton's transfer to the Army of the Potomac) began its eastward trek on March 21, when the Second Brigade (now under the able command of Brigadier General John J. Abercrombie), accompanied by Matthews' guns, marched to Berryville. The next day, the brigade crossed the Shenandoah River on a pontoon bridge, then moved a further two miles and encamped on a beautiful plateau halfway up the Blue Ridge. On the twenty-third, the brigade marched seventeen miles to Aldie, "an old dilapidated Virginia village," wrote Lieutenant Ricketts.[8]

The march was hard on the battery. Said Lieutenant Brockway, "After descending the mountain we expected to find a level road, but were much deceived. Though the Valley looked level from the summit of Blue Ridge, experience proved it to be full [of] 'hilly holes and bunchy hollows.' The continual up and down hill nearly wearied out our horses."[9]

Even as Abercrombie's men approached Aldie, fighting erupted near Winchester. On March 22, Ashby's cavalry skirmished with the Yankees left behind. General Shields was wounded during the day and turned command

---

[6]*Ricketts Diary, March 13, 1862. Ricketts' Diary indicates that Winchester fell on March 13th, contrary to the majority of books which indicate a March 12 date.*

[7]*Kimball, "Fighting Jackson," 302-3; O.R. volume 12, part 1, 164.*

[8]*Ricketts Diary, March 21-23, 1862.*

[9]*Brockway letter of March 31, 1862, in April 5, 1862, edition of the* Columbia Democrat.

of his division over to his senior colonel, Nathan Kimball, commander of the First Brigade. On the twenty-third, Jackson's infantry approached Kimball's camps around the small village of Kernstown, each side unaware of the other. Kimball assumed he was facing only cavalry, and had instructions to move south and push them away from Winchester. Jackson had been erroneously informed that most of Banks' troops had left; he thus moved north to seize Winchester. The resulting fight at Kernstown left Kimball's men with 550 casualties and Jackson with 718. Outnumbered by Shields' troops, Jackson retreated.

As the battle opened, Kimball sent messengers for reinforcements. Williams received one of these couriers the next day and ordered his brigades to countermarch. The Second Brigade retraced its steps, hiked seventeen grueling miles, and made its camp two miles from the Shenandoah River. The night was bitterly cold and troops straggled in all night. Matthews' battery did not make camp until two o'clock in the morning of the twenty-fifth. After a short night, the command neared Berryville, only to learn that Jackson had retreated and Shields had the situation under control. Yet again the brigade crossed the river and encamped for a third time on familiar ground.[10]

On the twenty-sixth, the brigade struggled over the same "miserable roads" to Goose Creek. Along the way, the men glimpsed detachments of Colonel John W. Geary's 28th Pennsylvania, which was guarding the Manassas Gap Railroad in this vicinity. Enemy cavalry dogged the advance guard, so General Abercrombie ordered a detachment of troops out the next day to chase them away. A section of Matthews' battery accompanied the 28th New York and 13th Massachusetts to Middleburg, but enemy horsemen stayed out of their way and left the area without fighting.[11]

The brigade moved onward the next day (March 28), reaching the Chantilly area, where the tired and footsore troops bivouacked for the evening on the grounds of a fine old mansion, said by some to be the residence of Jeb Stuart. Lieutenant Brockway chronicled the physical destruction that occurred as Yankee soldiers took possession of the place:

> Dragoons ran their heavy spurs along the fine sofas, rich carpets were spread in tents, and ornaments and gildings were used as horse trappings. Books hundreds of years old were scattered around, while modern literature was picked up and stuffed into knapsacks. . . . Letters written generations ago were picked up and preserved. One

---

[10]*Ricketts Diary*, March 25, 1862; Brockway letter in April 5, 1862, edition of the Columbia Democrat.

[11]*Ricketts Diary*, March 26-27, 1862.

written nearly a century ago by Mrs. Stewart to her son David, urged him 'not to oppose the adoption of the Constitution, but to follow the example of her sister State Maryland.' . . . The poor old lady is spared the pang of knowing that one of her descendants is a leader in the destruction of the Constitution.[12]

From Chantilly, the column wound its way on March 29 towards Centreville. A blinding storm of mixed sleet and snow pelted the troops as they struggled over a corduroy road to Bull Run. Lieutenant Brockway saw numerous carcasses of dead horses lining the road. Half-buried skeletons from the July 1861 battle were also seen, some rooted out of the ground by wild pigs. Though the creek was swollen with water, the battery managed to get across and find a camping spot relatively free from the smell of dead animals. On March 30, the brigade reached Manassas Junction, viewing the remains left behind by retreating Confederates.[13]

Hopes of a rest here were dashed as the column trudged onward, reaching Warrenton Junction on April 2. Here, the brigade was only six miles from the Rappahannock River and was instructed to picket the area to watch for any enemy activity. McClellan's Army of the Potomac was in the process of being transferred from Alexandria to the Virginia Peninsula around Fort Monroe. From this position, McClellan expected to advance up the Peninsula to Richmond. In the meantime, Major General Irvin McDowell, commanding the army's First Corps, was withheld from McClellan and kept in northeastern Virginia to defend Washington. Banks' command, now called the Fifth Corps, was just beginning to advance down the Valley to pressure Jackson's troops. By moving on a number of fronts at once, McClellan hoped to keep General Joseph E. Johnston's Army of Northern Virginia from reinforcing the troops at Yorktown.

Accordingly, on the evening of April 6, Lieutenant Colonel Thomas J. Luczs of the 16th Indiana led a column of troops to reconnoiter Confederate positions along the Rappahannock in the vicinity of the burned bridge of the Orange & Alexandria Railroad . Lucas' force consisted of five companies of infantry, four of cavalry, and Lieutenant Ricketts' section of Battery F. Heavy rains had made the roads nearly impassable; the column left camp at 11 p.m. and did not reach the river until 11 a.m. on the seventh. Lucas deployed his troops under cover and examined the terrain on the opposite side of the river. He noted two earthworks, seemingly occupied only by pickets. Lucas brought up Ricketts' two guns,

---

[12]*Brockway letter of April 3, 1862, published in the April 12th edition of the* Columbia Democrat.

[13]*Ricketts Diary, March 29-30, 1862; Brockway letter in the April 12* Columbia Democrat.

1st Lieutenant R. Bruce Ricketts poses with hat and sword in hand.

(USAMHI)

which opened fire on the earthworks. The enemy evacuated in "great haste" without returning fire. Satisfied that there were no sizeable bodies of Confederates in the vicinity, Lucas withdrew after an hour and a half. On the way back, a storm of rain, sleet, and snow buffeted the soldiers.[14]

The storm that began on April 7 lasted until the tenth. Streams were swollen and roads turned to mud, making supply difficult at best. On the eleventh, Captain Matthews left camp for Washington, remaining there until the nineteenth. During his absence, Lieutenant Ricketts commanded Battery F. While in command of the battery, Ricketts participated in another reconnaissance to the Rappahannock on April 17-18. The purpose of this expedition was to support McDowell's advance on Fredericksburg. General Abercrombie accompanied the column, which was under the direct command of Lieutenant Colonel Timothy M. Bryan, Jr., of the 12th Massachusetts. His command consisted of seventeen companies of infantry from three regiments, four companies of the 1st Maine Cavalry,. and four sections of artillery from three batteries. Two sections of Battery F accounted for half the artillery. Lieutenants Godbold and Brockway took their sections, while Lieutenant Ricketts accompanied the general at his staff's request.[15]

The column reached the river in the same area as the April 6-7 action. Bryan deployed his infantry and artillery under cover of two hills, sent his cavalry to guard the flanks, then cautiously crept forward to reconnoiter. Bryan could see plainly several earthworks, a substantial addition to the strength of the position since the last expedition. Swarms of enemy soldiers were busy working on others. Bryan determined to use his artillery to draw fire and thus calculate how many Southern troops opposed his force. Godbold's two ordnance rifles, supported by a section of Parrotts from Captain James Thompson's Pennsylvania Independent Battery C, took position on a hill to the left, while Brockway's two guns deployed on a hill farther to the right. A section of New York artillery was left in reserve.

At least two Rebel bands were playing, perhaps signaling the end of the morning guard mounting, Brockway surmised. The whistle of busy locomotives could also be discerned in the morning air, suggesting that the enemy was busy bringing up reinforcements or supplies.

Colonel Bryan ordered Brockway to open fire with his right gun as the last strands of the bands died away. "This was a splendid shot," wrote Bryan. "The shell struck nearly the center of the large fort opposite, and

---

[14]*Ricketts Diary, April 6-7, 1862;* O.R., *volume 12, part 1, 422.*

[15]*Ricketts Diary, April 8-11, 17, 19, 1862;* O.R., *volume 12, part 1, 441.*

bursting, scattered the men on all sides, doubtless killing some." Brockway's next few shots went wide, giving the enemy some encouragement. A battery of 6-pounders opened a return fire, but their initial salvos fell short of Brockway's position.

By this time, Lieutenant John P. Barry's two guns of Thompson's Battery C joined the fight. Their fifth shot hit the fort's magazine; the resulting explosion scattered the enemy and silenced their cannon. However, a masked battery soon opened fire from an enfilading position, forcing Bryan to change Barry's and Godbold's positions. The colonel also observed a battery moving to the right in an effort to enfilade Brockway's position. He sent word to the Pennsylvania lieutenant, who also saw the enemy. Brockway changed his position slightly, then opened fire. "The case shot burnt at the proper distance, knocking the drivers from their horses, and sending the terrified and wounded animals frantically across the field, in an opposite direction. One poor fellow we saw get up and limp towards the neighbors woods."

Brockway then turned his attention to a large house within range, said to be the enemy headquarters. "Our first shot brought a man down near the house. A few more completely riddled the building, and if there were any in the earthworks they left suddenly." Additional enemy cannon opened fire on Brockway, forcing him again to change position. Recalled Brockway, "Though the shot whistled between the guns, and the shell burnt all around us, or, unexploded, buried themselves in the ground, not a man flinched but on the contrary kept cheering, each shot found its mark."

Colonel Bryan then ordered a retreat. He was worried that the enemy might try to cross the river and intercept his line of retreat, so he recalled Brockway and his infantry support. Even as the Yankees fell back, the Rebels opened fire, but soon ceased when it became apparent that the Federals had retired. Bryan's force reached its camps, the men and animals tired out from twenty-four hours of active operations. Bryan reported that his reconnaissance had perhaps convinced the enemy that they might be attacked and thus prevent them from sending troops to Fredericksburg. Bryan also noted that their position was too strong for a frontal attack, but could easily be flanked with the aid of local guides who could point out safe fords for Union infantry.[16]

---

[16] *O.R., volume 12, part 1, 441-45; Brockway letter of April 20,* Columbia Democrat, *May 3, 1862. In his letter, Brockway wrote that he fired on the headquarters building first, then turned his attention to the enemy artillery. Colonel Bryan reported that Brockway initially opened on the enemy earthworks, then silenced the opposing artillery before firing on the house.*

Troops from McDowell's Department of the Rappahannock occupied Falmouth on April 18, but retreating Southern troops burned the bridges over the Rappahannock, preventing McDowell's regiments from crossing in force. Content to keep the city under control of his artillery, McDowell brought up more troops and spread his men along the Rappahannock to patrol the countryside.

Meanwhile, there were changes elsewhere in northern Virginia that affected the men of Battery F. On April 30, General Abercrombie, in command of the Second Brigade, First Division, Department of the Shenandoah, was transferred to brigade command in the Army of the Potomac. His place was taken by Brigadier General George L. Hartsuff, whose brigade was in turn transferred, on May 10, to McDowell's department. Battery F broke camp near Catlett's Station and headed for Falmouth, reaching that village on May 14. Banks, at Strasburg, was left with two infantry brigades to guard the Valley; Shields' division was ordered to report to McDowell at Fredericksburg, leaving only the Harper's Ferry garrison within supporting distance of Banks' troops.[17]

McDowell's troops at Fredericksburg continued to grow and reorganize. In addition to Shields (First Division), McDowell's command included divisions led by Edward O. C. Ord (the Second Division), Rufus King, and George A. McCall (the Pennsylvania Reserves), a formidable collection of some 42,000 soldiers. Battery F was attached to Ord's division, which included the brigades of James B. Ricketts, Hartsuff, and George Bayard. Major Davis Tillson was placed in charge of the division's four batteries. McDowell was to advance south from Fredericksburg and link up with McClellan, who was nearing Richmond, following the retreating Southern army. McDowell's large corps would form the right flank of McClellan's Army of the Potomac and attack the Southern capital from the north, By mid-summer, the war in Virginia might be over.[18]

During this period, Battery F remained in camp near Falmouth, waiting for events to happen. On May 22, Lieutenant Ricketts took his two guns out about five miles from camp to engage the gunners in target practice. The

---

[17]*Hartsuff took command of the brigade on May 1 (Ricketts Diary, May 1, 1862). Battery F apparently began its march for Falmouth on May 12 and arrived on the fourteenth (Ricketts diary, May 12-14, 1862).*

[18]*See the organizational chart of the Department of the Rappahannock in O.R., volume 12, part 3, 309-12. Ord's division was organized on May 16 (O.R., volume 12, part 3, 196), and initially consisted of Ricketts' and Hartsuff's infantry brigades, Bayard's cavalry, and attached artillery. Abram Duryee's brigade was added about May 28, when the division reached Manassas.*

lieutenant pronounced the results "very satisfactory." The next day, President Lincoln, accompanied by several cabinet members and a host of dignitaries, arrived in camp and reviewed McDowell's corps. For the men of Battery F, the real event of the day was the later arrival of a government paymaster, who paid the company for the months of January through April, a boon to the cash-starved soldiers. Lincoln's visit was the culmination of McDowell's concentration of troops, for that night word filtered through the camps that it would be "on to Richmond" soon.[19]

But Major General Thomas J. Jackson, commanding Southern troops in the Valley, launched a surprise offensive that caught the Yankees off guard. When Shields' division began its march to join McDowell, Banks withdrew his infantry from New Market to Strasburg in order to be closer to his base at Winchester. Jackson's troops had fought an inconclusive battle with elements of Major General John C. Fremont's Mountain Department at McDowell on May 8th; even though Jackson's losses were higher, Fremont withdrew his two brigades into western Virginia, in effect neutralizing his force for the present.

Jackson then brought his army back into the Valley, where he received Richard S. Ewell's division as reinforcements, swelling his command to more than sixteen thousand men. On May 22, Jackson's united command left New Market, crossed the Massanutten Mountain into the Luray Valley, then moved north, hidden from Banks, yet cutting off communications with McDowell. The next day, May 23, Jackson's troops smashed Colonel John R. Kenly's Yankee detachment at Front Royal. Banks, now alerted to the danger, began a precipitous retreat toward Winchester. Jackson's troops caught up with the retreating Yankees just south of town early in the morning of May 25. Outnumbered, Banks' men could only continue their withdrawal. The survivors regrouped across the Potomac River by midday on the twenty-sixth. Casualties numbered more than three thousand, compared to a mere four hundred Confederates.[20]

Jackson's stunning victory provoked a crisis in Washington. President Lincoln himself took charge of the ensuing strategy that was needed to contain the victorious Southerners. Fremont received orders to move eastward into the Valley and ensure that Jackson could not retreat, while a reinforced Banks would drive south from Harper's Ferry. McDowell was ordered to part with some of his troops. Shields' division would retrace its steps to Catlett's Station, then head west and enter the Valley near Front

---

[19]*Ricketts Diary*, May 22-23, 1862.

[20]James I. Robertson, Jr., "Stonewall in the Shenandoah: The Valley Campaign of 1862," Civil War Times Illustrated *11 (May 1972): 17-32.*

Royal. Ord's division headed for Washington to reinforce the garrison in case the Rebels made at attempt on the capital. If events went as planned, Jackson could be netted by Fremont, Banks, and Shields, whose troops totalled some sixty-four thousand effectives.[21]

Accordingly, at first Ord was instructed to send his infantry via water from Acquia Creek to Alexandria, then overland to Catlett's Station to rendezvous with Shields. However, as the day wore on, one brigade was embarked and the other was ordered to follow Shields. The artillery and cavalry attached to the division were ordered to get underway immediately and head north.[22]

For the men of Battery F, the northward march was terrible. "The roads were in an awful condition," wrote Lieutenant Brockway, "and we were frequently obliged to double teams." Ricketts noted that the battery made a mere five miles on the twenty-fifth before camping for the night. The column passed through Stafford Court House that day. Wrote Brockway:

> Stafford Court House stands almost alone in the woods. It is a quaint old building, and contains many curious records. Some date back over 200 years. Our men immediately seized them. I regretted it, as it smacks of vandalism to deface or destroy the records of a court; yet as I saw everything going I seized a few old documents. . . . The gibbet and jail were the only surroundings.[23]

On the twenty-sixth, the battery reached the village of Dumfries before halting. Ricketts described the village as "an old dilapidated broken down place. Inhabitants ditto." Rain set in that night as the men found shelter in huts constructed by the Rebels the previous winter as they guarded the Potomac River.[24]

At noon on May 27, the battery received orders to head for Manassas instead of Alexandria, When the battery reached the junction the next day, the men finally learned of Jackson's advance and Banks' precipitate retreat, and of the "consternation" and "excitement" that resulted. Here, Brigadier General Abram Duryee's brigade was assigned to Ord's division as the Second Brigade. Shields' troops were already heading for the Valley in an effort to trap Jackson. His advance camped at Rectortown, having passed

---

[21] Ibid., *32-33;* O.R., *volume 12, part 3, 235.*

[22] O.R., *volume 12, part 3, 229-34.*

[23] Brockway letter of June 3, published in the June 14, 1862, edition of the Columbia Democrat; *Ricketts Diary, May 25, 1862.*

[24] *Ricketts Diary, May 26, 1862.*

A youthful-looking Corporal Leon Eugene C. Moore. He was born in 1844 and died in Los Angeles in 1927.

(RONN PALM)

through Thoroughfare Gap in the Bull Run Mountains, on the evening of May 28.[25]

Ord's regiments headed west on May 29. Traveling rapidly over a "beautiful and level country," the entire division encamped at Thoroughfare Gap that evening. As the command pushed on the next day, the level country became more mountainous, allowing the column to make only fifteen miles before nightfall. The rainfall that began on the afternoon of the thirtieth contributed to the slow progress, as did the horrible condition of the roads, already cut to ribbons by the troops in Shields' regiments.[26]

Shields' troops had already marched through Manassas Gap. On the thirtieth, his lead brigade deployed in the hills around Front Royal, but the Yankees were discovered before they could surround the detachment of Confederates in the town. The enemy set fire to the depots and other supplies before fleeing. Union troops rushed into Front Royal and managed to save some loaded freight cars on the railroad, but the depots were a complete loss. By nightfall, Shields had his entire division concentrated at Front Royal, poised to strike at Jackson's rear.

That same night, Jackson, now alerted to the danger, began a harried retreat from Winchester. The Stonewall Brigade, camped near Harper's Ferry, had the longest march to make. Jackson hoped to get his army south past Strasburg before Fremont's column arrived to close the door; otherwise, Shields and Fremont would have Jackson's divisions at their mercy. But the Union generals failed to close the trap. Shields, instead of advancing, chose to await Ord's arrival and contented himself with skirmishing with enemy cavalry opposing his division. Fremont, even though he saw Jackson's retreating column spread along the Valley Turnpike, chose to entrench instead of boldly attack. By the time he launched a timid probe, most of Jackson's column had passed.[27]

Ord's march was delayed, in part because of the wretched condition of the roads, and then, soon after the column had left Piedmont, Ord found that the men were out of rations. General McDowell, who had personally come to Manassas to superintend the movements of his divisions, had neglected to issue the necessary orders to ensure that his men were properly rationed. As a result, Ord called a halt, sent wagons to bring up

---

[25]*Brockway letter of June 3,* Columbia Democrat, *June 14; Ricketts Diary, May 27-28, 1862; Kimball, "Fighting Jackson," 311.*

[26]*Brockway letter of June 3; Ricketts Diary, May 30, 1862.*

[27]*Kimball, "Fighting Jackson," 311; Robertson, "Stonewall in the Shenandoah," 33-34.*

the supplies, then personally assisted in doling out the food, informing his adoring men to take all that they could carry. Ord's brigades finally reached Front Royal on the thirty-first, the men tired out and soaking wet from the heavy downpours of rain.[28]

As Jackson retired, Fremont's troops pursued up the Valley, while Shields sent his brigades up the Luray Valley, both commanders expecting to unite their forces at the southern end of the Massanutten Mountain. The rains interfered with rapid movement, and pursuit was slowed. Jackson accepted the challenge posed by the two Union generals. He engaged Fremont's troops at Cross Keys on June 8; the battle stopped the Union advance after a day's hard fighting. Leaving a brigade to watch Fremont, Jackson then marched his troops across the south fork of the Shenandoah River and on June 9 assailed two brigades of Shields' division, inflicting casualties totaling one quarter of the Yankees engaged, but suffering equally high losses himself. Shields' men fell back, and the Valley campaign was effectively over.

The men of Battery F remained in Front Royal during the latter stages of the campaign. Duryee's brigade was deployed to guard railroad bridges between Front Royal and Strasburg, while the other two brigades were held in readiness to support Shields. Lieutenant Ricketts and his two cannon accompanied Hartsuff's brigade to Strasburg for garrison duty. Ord, disgusted by McDowell's actions against him while on the march into the Valley, asked for a transfer and on June 8 was ordered to report to Corinth, Mississippi, for duty with the army there. General Ricketts assumed command of the division.[29]

---

[28]*Brockway letter of June 3 in* Columbia Democrat, *June 14, 1862; Ricketts Diary, May 31, 1862. For details on the ration problems, see James B. Thomas to father, June 23, 1862, in Mary W. Thomas and Richard A. Sauers (editors),* The Civil War Letters of First Lieutenant James B. Thomas, Adjutant, 107th Pennsylvania *(Baltimore: Butternut & Blue, 1995), 54-55. Ord and McDowell got into an argument and for a time, General Ricketts led the division during this march.*

[29]*O.R., volume 12, part 3, 355 (Ord's transfer); Ricketts Diary, June 1-4, 7, 1862.*

Chapter Three

The Army of Virginia

At the conclusion of the Valley Campaign, Jackson marched most of his troops to Charlottesville, put them aboard railroad cars, and disembarked the men near Richmond, arriving in time to assist Lee's troops against McClellan at the opening of the Seven Days' Battles. Meanwhile, in order to develop better effectiveness and coordination among the Union troops in northern Virginia, on June 26 the new Army of Virginia was created. Major General John Pope, a veteran officer of service in the western theater, was assigned to command this new three-corps army.

Pope's army unified the former independent commands operating against Jackson. Rather than serve under Pope, whom he despised, Fremont resigned. Major General Franz Sigel, one of the leading German-Americans of the day, replaced Fremont as commander of the First Corps. General Banks' troops were designated the Second Corps, while McDowell's two available divisions became the Third Corps. Shields' old division was broken up and most of its troops assigned to McDowell's divisions, led by Rufus King and James Ricketts. Battery F remained in Ricketts' Second Division.[1]

General Ricketts' brigades left Front Royal on June 18, the infantry and artillery pieces having the good fortune to ride the cars of the Manassas Gap Railroad all the way to Manassas Junction, where the troops went into camp to rest and refit after the late campaign. Bayard's cavalry brigade, accompanied by the corps baggage trains and all the artillery horses,

---

[1]Ricketts' division was organized as follows:
    First Brigade, Brig. Gen. Abram Duryee: 97th, 104th, 105th NY, 107th PA
    Second Brigade, Brig. Gen. Zealous B. Tower: 26th, 94th NY, 88th, 90th PA
    Third Brigade, Brig. Gen. George L. Hartsuff: 12th, 13th MA, 83rd NY, 11th PA
    Fourth Brigade, Col. Samuel S. Carroll: 7th IN, 84th, 110th PA, 1st WV
    Artillery, Major Davis Tillson: 2nd, 5th ME Btys; Bty F,1st PA; PA Bty C

followed by road. The column arrived at camp three days later after an uneventful march.[2]

By the time Pope arrived in Washington, McClellan had withdrawn to Harrison's Landing, altering the administration's hopes that the Army of Virginia could advance south toward Richmond to divert Southern troops away from McClellan. Pope therefore decided to remain on the defensive and concentrated his army in a line from Fredericksburg westward to Culpeper and Sperryville. The exhausted and demoralized troops needed fresh uniforms, equipment, and food. Thus, while Pope delayed in Washington, the army was left to fend for itself until late July. By that time, Lee had sent Jackson's corps to keep Pope's army under surveillance. Jackson and two divisions arrived in Gordonsville on July 19, just in time to fend off a Yankee cavalry foray against the Virginia Central Railroad, Richmond's link to the Valley. Other mounted reconnaissances revealed Jackson's presence to Pope. On July 29, A. P. Hill's large division joined Jackson, giving the general enough men to launch a limited offensive.[3]

Pope joined the army in the field in late July and prepared for offensive operations. He decided to concentrate his army at Culpeper and move against Jackson's left flank. Jackson, intending to attack himself, learned that only Banks' small corps was near Culpeper. Rather than wait for Pope to mass his forces in front of him, Stonewall took the initiative. On August 8, his brigades crossed the Rapidan and headed north toward Banks. The Union general, hearing of the enemy approach, moved south and on August 9 struck Jackson's troops, deployed near Cedar Mountain. Banks' initial attack caught Jackson's troops off guard and punished the grayclad soldiers. Jackson rallied his troops, brought up A. P. Hill, and repulsed Banks' outnumbered men. By day's end, Banks had suffered almost twenty-four hundred casualties, as opposed to twelve hundred Southern boys killed and wounded.

The men of Battery F heard the distant sounds of battle that day. Ricketts' troops had left their camps near Manassas Junction in July, minus Lieutenant Ricketts, ordered home on recruiting service in late June. The division marched to Warrenton, then to Waterloo Bridge, on the Rappahannock River between Warrenton and Sperryville. On August 7, it headed south toward Culpeper. King's division of the Third Corps was opposite Fredericksburg, with orders to patrol the river until the arrival of

---

[2]*Ricketts Diary, June 17-20, 1862;* Brockway letter of June 23, 1862, in Columbia Democrat, *June 28, 1862.*

[3]*John J. Hennessy,* Return to Bull Run: The Campaign and Battle of Second Manassas *(New York: Simon & Schuster, 1993), 8-10, 21-26.*

expected reinforcements from the Army of the Potomac. McClellan had been ordered to leave the Peninsula and bring the army north to unite with Pope. The combined armies would then face Lee's badly outnumbered Army of Northern Virginia.[4]

Ricketts' soldiers heard the rumor that Jackson had crossed the Rapidan and was heading north. Sergeant Major James B. Thomas of the 107th Pennsylvania, part of Duryee's brigade, echoed his comrades when he wrote home early on August 9 that "we will have a fight by tomorrow night. Our boys are all in good spirits and anxious for it."[5]

But most of the division was disappointed. General Pope heard the artillery fire that announced the start of the late afternoon battle, but was kept in the dark about the severe fighting as a result of Banks' messages that no enemy attack was expected. At last, when the cannon fire increased in severity, Pope acted to reinforce Banks. He instructed McDowell to push Ricketts forward and ordered Sigel to bring his entire corps. Lieutenant Brockway noted that by the time the division started forward, there was a "perfect roar" of artillery, "while ever and anon we could catch the rattle of musketry."[6]

"On getting nearer we saw the wounded scattered along the road, those able to speak representing our position as desperate in the extreme," penned Brockway. "However, many more sound men than wounded passed to the rear." It was growing dark by the time the division reached the battlefield. Ricketts formed a line of battle to cover the withdrawal of Banks' shattered regiments. Matthews unlimbered the guns of Battery F next to Captain George F. Leppien's 5th Maine Battery on the right flank of the infantry line. The other two batteries, Captain Thompson's Pennsylvania Battery C and Captain James A. Hall's 2nd Maine Battery, formed on the left. Shortly afterwards, a Rebel battery rolled out of a nearby woods on the division's left and opened fire. Hall and Thompson both replied, effectively smothering the enemy and forcing the battery to retreat.[7]

---

[4]*Ricketts Diary, June 28-30, 1862;* O.R., *volume 12, part 2, 24-25.*

[5]*Thomas to Lucy, August 9, 1862, in Thomas and Sauers,* Civil War Letters of James B. Thomas, *67-68.*

[6]*Brockway letter of August 12 in* Columbia Democrat, *August 23, 1862.*

[7]O.R., *volume 12, part 2, 170-172; Brockway letter in Columbia* Democrat, *August 23, 1862. The Southern battery was the Purcell Artillery, Captain Willis J. Pegram commanding.*

The next morning, Lieutenant Brockway walked over the battlefield. He was gratified to see thirteen dead horses, three dead artillerists–two of them officers–plus other wreckage, where the enemy battery had been located. "Further along in the woods were dead men, horses, ruins of wagons, etc." Jackson withdrew across the Rapidan, while Pope concentrated his army in the vicinity of Culpeper.[8]

While Pope's army rested and grumbled in the Culpeper area, General James Longstreet and most of his corps joined Jackson, along with Lee himself. Lee wanted to advance against Pope before McClellan's soldiers moved to join Pope; the combined Union armies would seriously outnumber the Army of Northern Virginia. Lee planned an offensive against Pope's left flank that would drive a wedge between Pope and reinforcements from McClellan, which would land at Aquia Creek (near Fredericksburg), then march to Culpeper along the roads north of the Rappahannock.

The Confederate advance was scheduled for August 16. That morning, Southern infantry broke camp around Gordonsville and headed for the fords over the Rapidan. Lee had planned for the army to cross on August 18, but soon learned that Longstreet's troops were not well provisioned and that Stuart's cavalry was not ready to cover the advance. Also, a succession of errors led to the failure to picket Raccoon Ford. On the evening of the seventeenth, two regiments of Federal cavalry crossed the river, eluded enemy infantry, and managed to seize one of Stuart's officers and two satchels full of orders and associated papers. Then, the column almost captured Stuart himself when the advancing Yankees surprised the incredulous Stuart and his staff at the house where they were sleeping. Gleeful cavalrymen did take their enemy's plumed hat and other personal effects before retiring across the Rapidan.

Upon reading Lee's orders, Pope suddenly became aware of the danger facing his army. After dark on August 18, the Army of Virginia began its withdrawal across the Rappahannock. Lee did not learn of the retreat until the next day, when he and Longstreet, having ridden to the top of Clark's Mountain to survey the Union positions, saw the dust of retreating infantry columns and the white tops of columns of supply wagons, all heading for the rear. The disappointed chieftain issued orders for an immediate pursuit, but except for some cavalry clashes, the Yankees reached the opposite side of the Rappahannock without any interference from the enemy.[9]

---

[8]*Brockway letter in* Columbia Democrat, *August 23, 1862.*

[9]*Hennessy,* Return to Bull Run, *33-57.*

Ricketts' division crossed the Rappahannock at Rappahannock Station, where the Orange & Alexandria Railroad crossed the stream via bridge, the same area where the men of Battery F had opened on the Rebels back in April. The infantry and artillery took up positions to cover the bridge. Then, on August 20, McDowell ordered Ricketts to send a force back across the river to cover the southern approaches to the bridge. Ricketts detailed two regiments from Hartsuff's brigade, accompanied by a section of Matthews' battery, to occupy a knoll about five hundred yards from the river.[10]

To reinforce the position at Rappahannock Station, Pope's engineers, on the evening of August 20, constructed a pontoon bridge across the river some eight hundred yards north of the railroad trestle bridge. This new structure was hidden from enemy view by a point of woods that reached to the water's edge. The next morning, the rest of Hartsuff's brigade crossed to the south side, accompanied by Matthews' four remaining guns and Thompson's entire battery. The Yankees spent the day firing occasional shots at passing Southern infantry columns that were occasionally visible in the distance. August 22 was spent in similar style, as Lee's Confederates sidled north along the river, looking for a place to cross.[11]

During the late afternoon of the twenty-second, a series of tremendous thunderstorms deluged the Rappahannock River area, causing a rapid rise in the water level that left some of Jackson's men stranded near Sulphur Springs. The swirling river channel loosened the new pontoon bridge at Rappahannock Station and sent it downstream to lodge against the trestles of the railroad span, threatening the bridge's integrity. Worried about the situation, McDowell the next morning withdrew Hartsuff's infantry and all the artillery except a section of Thompson's battery.[12]

As the withdrawal was in progress, Confederates approached the bridgehead. Lee, in the process of moving north to flank Pope's right, ordered Longstreet to drive the enemy across the river at Rappahannock Station, in order to ensure that Pope would not in turn attack Lee's rear. A two-hour artillery clash, described by a modern historian as "one of the fiercest small artillery duels of the war," preceded the infantry attack. Major Davis Tillson, commanding the divisional artillery, recorded that

---

[10] O.R., *volume 12, part 2, 383.*

[11] Ibid.; *Hennessy,* Return to Bull Run, *60-65;* Supplement to the Official Records of the Union and Confederate Armies *(Wilmington, NC: Broadfoot Publishing Company, 1994-1999), volume 2, 724 (hereafter cited as* O.R. Supplement).

[12] O.R., *volume 12, part 2, 383;* O.R. Supplement, *volume 2, 725.*

"the enemy kept up a sharp and well directed fire on the bridge and batteries near it, several times hitting the bridge and occasioning some casualties among men and horses." A non-commissioned officer of the 107th Pennsylvania wrote that his regiment lay under this intense artillery fire for perhaps five hours, "the first 2 or 3 kept us busy dodging untill we all got tired and paid but little attention to them the last 2 hours."[13]

Battery F was in the middle of this artillery fighting, and paid dearly for it. Two of the battery's cannon were disabled during the shelling. Lieutenant Godbold, commanding the left section, was hit in the left leg by a shell and taken from the field. He was sent to Armory Square Hospital in Washington, where his leg was amputated. The wound proved mortal however and the young lieutenant died on September 22.[14]

Longstreet sent the brigades of George T. Anderson and Nathan G. Evans to attack the Yankees. Thompson's gunners saw them coming and fired several rounds of grape and canister before limbering up and dashing back across the bridge. When the Rebels reached the top of the knoll, Union batteries across the river opened a heavy fire, driving them back under cover. General Evans brought up his own battery, but the weight of metal thrown at it forced a hasty retreat. By this time, most of Ricketts' division had marched away, heading north to reinforce the Union right flank. General Tower's brigade remained, supporting the divisional artillery. Once Thompson had crossed the bridge, Tower had orders to destroy the bridge, which was accomplished after an afternoon thunderstorm drenched the area. As the last of the rearguard headed away from the river, Southern artillery unlimbered and lobbed a few shells at the Yankees, but none struck the bluecoats.[15]

During the day on August 24th, Ricketts' division marched north to Warrenton, then headed west on the road toward Sulphur Springs, bivouacking four miles from Warrenton. Pope still remained behind the Rappahannock River, having parried the Confederates thus far while waiting for the Army of the Potomac to link up with his three corps. Lee,

---

[13]Hennessy, Return to Bull Run, *85;* O.R. Supplement, *volume 2, 725; James B. Thomas to father, September 5, 1862, in Thomas and Sauers,* Civil War Letters of James B. Thomas, *79-80.*

[14]Bates, History of Pennsylvania Volunteers, *1:959-960; Godbold compiled service record, Record Group 94, Records of the Office of the Adjutant General, National Archives.*

[15]Hennessy, Return to Bull Run, *85-86;* O.R. Supplement, *volume 2, 725-726;* O.R., *volume 12, part 2, 383.*

Private Andrew Myers transferred from Battery G.
(ANDREW HASCO COLLECTION, USAMHI)

frustrated, worried that the arriving Yankee troops would shift the balance beyond his army's capability to defend, so the general devised a risky plan. Jackson's corps would withdraw from the Rappahannock, along which Longstreet's divisions would continue to attract Pope's attention. Jackson would take his twenty-five thousand men and strike north, then march in behind Pope's army to interdict his line of supplies. If, as Lee believed, McClellan's men would move from Aquia Creek and Fredericksburg toward Pope, by drawing Pope away from his reinforcements, the Confederates might be able to defeat him before both Union armies combined their numbers.[16]

Jackson's regiments began their march early in the morning of August 25. By midnight, Confederates were bivouacked in the fields around Salem, a small village on the Manassas Gap Railroad, some twelve miles beyond Pope's right flank. The next day, August 26, Jackson's column trekked eastward, through the Bull Run Mountains at Thoroughfare Gap, then turned south to reach the Orange & Alexandria Railroad at Bristoe Station. After seizing the station, the Confederates learned that Pope's major supply depot, five miles away at Manassas Junction, was guarded by only a few hundred men. After darkness fell, so did Manassas Junction.[17]

Jackson's strategic success forced Pope to act. Realizing that the Confederate army was in two parts, Pope, now reinforced by the Third Army Corps, Army of the Potomac, and by Fitz-John Porter's Fifth Army Corps, decided to reverse direction and attempt to snare Jackson before Longstreet's corps could come to his assistance. Thus, on August 27, Ricketts' division marched eastward through Warrenton toward Gainesville, as part of the left flank of Pope's army, following Sigel's corps. Lee, accompanying Longstreet, followed Jackson's route toward Thoroughfare Gap, while Jackson spent the day on August 27 sacking Manassas Junction before heading north to take position behind an unfinished railroad bed just north of the old Manassas battlefield of July 1861.

Pope, hoping that Jackson would remain in the Manassas Junction area, issued orders for his columns of troops to close in on the junction on August 28 to fight Jackson before Longstreet arrived. McDowell, in transmitting Pope's marching orders, decided to vary them slightly. As Sigel's corps, followed by King's division, headed for the junction, McDowell instructed Ricketts to halt at Gainesville and be prepared to defend Thoroughfare Gap against Longstreet.

---

[16]O.R., *volume 12, part 2, 383.*

[17]*Hennessy,* Return to Bull Run, *96-115.*

Ricketts' men bivouacked on the night of the twenty-seventh along the road to Gainesville. Off in the distance, his tired soldiers could see the lights of the burning supplies at Manassas Junction. The next morning, Ricketts continued his march, only to encounter a courier from the 1st New Jersey Cavalry. Longstreet's men had been sighted west of Thoroughfare Gap, and the cavalry would attempt to delay their march until Ricketts came to their aid. Hearing the news, Ricketts turned the division off the pike and marched overland to Haymarket, a small village about three miles from the gap. The lead elements of the division reached the village around 2:00 p.m., to find the Jerseymen retiring toward the village, reporting that the enemy was in the gap.[18]

Ricketts sent Hartsuff's brigade, now under the command of Colonel John Stiles (Hartsuff was sick) into the gap. Slowed by the fallen trees that the cavalry had felled across the road, the Yankees nevertheless made good progress and soon encountered the lead regiments of Longstreet's command, Georgians of George T. Anderson's Brigade. Stiles' men pushed the enemy back into the gap. As they advanced slowly, Ricketts brought up Battery F and Captain Thompson's Independent Pennsylvania Battery C to support the attack. Lieutenant Brockway unlimbered his section and opened fire on some Georgians who had taken possession of an old grist mill and some other stone buildings north of the Manassas Gap Railroad. A few shots chased the enemy away. A second Georgia brigade joined the fray, while Ricketts deployed two more brigades to support Stiles, who had occupied a ridge that commanded the entrance to the gap.

Ricketts, however, was outnumbered, and Southern troops scaled the mountains on both sides of the gap and threatened both Yankee flanks. Ricketts, who had hoped to delay the enemy as long as possible, finally realized that he had to withdraw. As the artillery banged away with redoubled fury, Ricketts withdrew his infantry and headed east to Gainesville, where his men sometime around midnight.[19]

After a short rest, Ricketts had the men on their feet and heading away from Longstreet's troops, who were nearby but hidden by fog. The retreating brigades reached Bristoe Station about seven in the morning of Friday, August 29. Here, the column halted so the men could draw rations, then continued, following the Orange & Alexandria Railroad to Manassas

---

[18]Hennessy, Return to Bull Run, *154-55;* O.R., *volume 12, part 2, 383-84.*

[19]Hennessy, Return to Bull Run, *155-60;* O.R., *volume 12, part 2, 384;* Bates, Pennsylvania Volunteers, *1:960;* William H. Locke, The Story of the Regiment *(New York: James Miller, Publisher, 1872), 102-4;* James Thomas to father, September 5, 1862, in Thomas and Sauers, Civil War Letters of James B. Thomas, *81.*

Junction, where the men saw the damage done by Jackson's troops. The division then moved on, guided by the sound of gunfire. While Ricketts had been engaged at Thoroughfare Gap, Jackson had revealed his position by attacking King's division at Brawner Farm. His action drew the Yankee columns toward the old Manassas battlefield, and throughout the day on August 29, Pope launched a series of assaults on Jackson's line as Longstreet headed to the field. By nightfall, Longstreet had arrived and the battle still continued.[20]

Marching up the Manassas-Sudley Spring Road, Ricketts' brigades reached the battlefield after dark, bivouacking along the road from the Stone House to near the New Market Crossroads. Early in the morning, the battle again erupted with renewed fury. Ricketts' division was soon involved. McDowell ordered Ricketts to send two brigades to report to Major General Phil Kearny, commanding one of the Third Army Corps' divisions opposing Jackson's line. Ricketts personally took Duryee's and Colonel Joseph Thoburn's brigades, which took position on the battleline. Duryee soon engaged the enemy, but fell back and supported Thompson's battery, which arrived to bolster the Union line. Tower's and Stiles' brigades remained behind, near their bivouac, to act as a reserve if needed.[21]

Captain Matthews soon received orders to follow Duryee and Thoburn and assist the infantry. When Matthews' four guns unlimbered, they joined a growing line of Union batteries that faced Jackson's men, still in position behind the unfinished railroad cut. Lieutenant Brockway described the terrain:

> An almost level plain ran along in front of the ridge, woods were on our right and rear, and about 500 yards in front of us was another strip of woods. In this lay Gen. Duryea's brigade and Gen. Carroll was on his right. In the afternoon the enemy opened on us from their extreme left, but owing to the woods in front their aim was inaccurate.[22]

---

[20]O.R., *volume 12, part 2, 384;* O.R. Supplement, *volume 2, 735, Thomas to father, September 5, 1862,* in Thomas and Sauers, Civil War Letters of James B. Thomas, *81.*

[21]John Hennessy, Historical Report on the Troop Movements for the Second Battle of Manassas, August 28 Through 30, 1862 *(Denver Service Center, National Park Service, 1985), 241, 268-69. Colonel Thoburn now led the brigade formerly under the command of Colonel Samuel S. Carroll, who was absent wounded since August 14.*

[22]Brockway to Matthews, October 18, 1862, Brockway Papers. *A slightly different version of this letter was dated October 24 and published in the* Columbia Democrat, *November 22, 1862.*

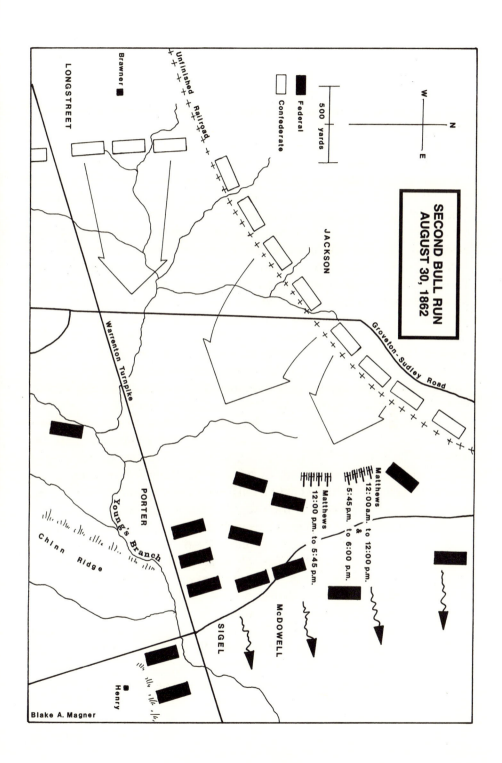

Duryee's four regiments deployed in a wood facing Jackson's men behind the unfinished railroad embankment. To Duryee's left were Thompson's four guns, followed by Matthews' four cannon, then four more batteries. Matthews' gunners remained quiet most of the afternoon, firing only an occasional shot toward the enemy. During the day, Pope hurled his infantry against Jackson's bending but unbroken line. At three o'clock, Porter's Fifth Corps launched a massive assault. Although Union soldiers reached the embankment and fought hand-to-hand, Jackson's men held and Porter's units fell back.

Following Pope's repulse, about 4:00 p.m. General Lee authorized Longstreet to charge the Union line. As a support, Colonel Stephen D. Lee assembled a number of batteries that were able to enfilade the Union troops fronting Jackson's position. To counter the hot Southern fire, some Union batteries changed position in an effort to obtain a better field of fire. Thompson pivoted his four guns to the left and opened on the enemy, but the Confederate shelling was so intense that Thomspon soon withdrew to his former position on Duryee's left and ceased fire.[23]

As Thompson moved into his firing position, Captain Matthews ordered Lieutenant Case to move his section more toward the left and report to Brigadier General Isaac I. Stevens, commanding a Ninth Corps division. Lieutenant Brockway then limbered his two guns and moved out into the field, wheeling to the left to fire on Colonel Lee's distant artillery. "We fired about fifteen minutes," recalled Brockway, "when the smoke became so dense as to make objects indistinguishable 300 yards from us. Although the enemy fire also slackened, Brockway complained that a Rebel battery in position to his right also fired on Battery F, enfilading his position. Fortunately, the enemy shells were defective and few of them burst, thus saving the battery from serious loss at this time.[24]

In the meantime, Longstreet's assault drove several Union regiments from the field and threatened the integrity of the entire Union army. Fortunately, McDowell rushed two of Ricketts' brigades into action on Chinn Ridge as other troops moved to protect the Union left. An obstinate defense slowed Longstreet's brigades and allowed Pope time to begin withdrawing the army toward Washington.

As the battle raged on the Union left and progressed along the line toward the right, Ricketts' men could hear the sounds of fighting drawing closer. At 6:00 p.m., General Ricketts was standing next to General Stevens, watching the smoke come closer, when a staff officer rode up and said the

---

[23]*Hennessy,* Historical Report, *336.*

[24]*Brockway to Matthews, October 18, 1862.*

left was turned and that the army was retreating. Immediately, both generals went to their commands and issued orders for a withdrawal.[25]

The Union line soon degenerated into a confused mass of units attempting to withdraw under heavy enemy pressure. To Matthews' left, two Ninth Corps batteries limbered and retreated, leaving a gap in the line. Then, Brockway noticed a Rebel battleflag coming out of the woods on his right, the men beneath it invisible in the acrid-smelling smoke. "As soon as I discovered the enemy I opened fire on them with canister and I believe Thompson's Battery did the same," penned Brockway. "Our first fire checked them, they then halted and fell back to the woods. . . . They again came steadily forward, though their men fell in scores before our fire."[26]

This enemy brigade was composed of Mississippi units led by Brigadier General Winfield S. Featherston. His line crashed into Duryee's brigade and dislodged two New York regiments, leading to a disorganized retreat by the entire brigade. With the Yankee infantry running back through the woods, some of Featherston's men turned and charged into Thompson's guns, shooting down men and horses and capturing three of the cannon before they could be limbered and withdrawn.[27]

Farther to the left, Brigadier General William D. Pender's brigade of A. P. Hill's division captured two guns of the 6th Maine Battery. Then it was Matthews' turn to face the oncoming enemy. They turned out to be the Alabama, Georgia, and Tennessee regiments led by Brigadier General James J. Archer, another of Hill's brigades. Captain Matthews ordered his battery to retire to its original position, there to halt and open fire on the enemy. Brockway reported doing so, and was able to see Pender's capture of the 6th Maine. Then, wrote the lieutenant, he sent his caissons to the rear.

> The enemy came on with loud cheers, and after placing their colors on the deserted guns [6th Maine] made a left half wheel and with renewed confidence came yelling on. Thompson fell back to the rear and my guns were the only ones left on the field. Nearer and nearer they came, many of my men were scattered, three of my horses were shot, and to my dismay I learned that our infantry support had left the woods in our rear. The enemy already held the Sudley Church road so that my only chance of escape lay in getting through the woods. We had only time to limber up one piece, and got into the woods but found it impossible to get through. While there one of the wheel horses was

---

[25]Hennessy, Historical Report, *440*.

[26]Brockway to Matthews, October 18, 1862.

[27]Hennessy, Return to Bull Run, *428*.

Corporal Hiram M. Pidcoe transferred from Battery G. Service stripes are visible on his sleeves, as well as a Second Corps badge on his left breast area of his artillery jacket.

(GARRY LEISTER COLLECTION, USAMHI)

shot dead, and others severely wounded. One wheel horse would not pull the pieces, and the enemy were behind the trees picking off men and horses, so I told the few men left to save themselves."[28]

Lieutenant Brockway got through the woods and rallied some infantrymen to help him retake his guns, but an unidentified general ordered him not to make the attempt. Dejected, Brockway rode to the rear with the three men who remained with him. Near an old estate known as Pittsylvania, the lieutenant came upon Captain Matthews and General Ricketts, with what was left of Case's section. Matthews "loaned" Brockway one of Case's guns and some more men, with orders to "use it as I saw best." Brockway unlimbered the cannon in front of a hospital filled with wounded Yankees and began firing away until darkness, when Major General Samuel P. Heintzelman rode up and ordered Brockway to cease firing until further orders.[29]

Brockway then dismounted and began speaking with his men. At this time, a Southerner belonging to the 16th Mississippi of Featherston's brigade wandered into the Yankee line and was taken prisoner. "He told me that I had better yield myself as prisoner to him as their Brigade was stretched along in my front and Pender's Brigade in my rear," recalled Brockway. The lieutenant, supposing he was supported by infantry, turned to locate Heintzelman but could not find the general. Brockway recalled seeing Carroll's brigade drawn up nearby, and so decided to limber the piece and fall back.

As Brockway steered the gun through the yard filled with wounded, he spied an advancing line of battle. Brockway challenged the infantry with the familiar "who comes there?" "Pender" was the answer. One of the artillerists, thinking the reply was "Patrick," called out, "all right, we're Union." In reply, the Confederates fired a volley, then charged. The firing felled two horses. Brockway, realizing that he could not unlimber his gun among the wounded, ordered his men into the cellar of the house to escape the minie balls flying about in the darkness. Union infantry nearby melted into the woods in retreat, stranding Brockway, who surrendered to a lieutenant of the 49th Georgia. Before giving up, Brockway threw away any

---

[28]*Brockway to Matthews, October 18, 1862.*

[29]*Brockway to Matthews, October 18, 1862. Bates,* Pennsylvania Volunteers, *1:960, wrote that Brockway took position near the Henry House, apparently basing his text on information supplied by Brockway. However, a number of contemporary sources all place both A. P. Hill's brigades and Ricketts' two brigades in the vicinity of Pittsylvania. See Hennessy,* Historical Report, *511-12. General Heintzelman was in command of the Third Army Corps, Army of the Potomac.*

remaining friction primers, pocketed the fuses, and used his pocket knife to cut open the cartridge bags full of powder, to prevent the enemy from using the cannon.[30]

Of Matthews' four guns, only one of Case's got off the field safely. The battery's loss for the day of fighting was eight killed, fifteen wounded, and five captured. As the retreating column reached Centreville, Captain Matthews received the guns and equipment of an Indiana battery to replace the captured cannon. Pope's army continued to retreat into the defenses of Washington, where he was relieved of command and George McClellan again given control of the combined Union armies.[31]

Following Brockway's capture, he and other prisoners were herded together and marched back through the woods to the area where his section was captured. Officers were separated from enlisted men and placed on the side of a stony hill near Young's Branch, where they remained in the rain that fell on the thirty-first. On September 1, wounded prisoners were cared for under a flag of truce. Later that day, unwounded prisoners were paroled, but the officers, Virginia troops, and two hundred black refugees, were kept under guard, and started marching south the next day.

Brockway recalled with indignation the insults and slurs hurled at the prisoners from Confederate troops heading north. Near the village of Haymarket, Brockway, exhausted from lack of food, fell down and could not get up, even when threatened with a bayonet. His captors, however, permitted him to ride a horse for about a mile. The column reached Thoroughfare Gap that evening, where the men were allowed four ounces of meat each. The weary, hungry prisoners continued to trudge southward, sleeping at night without blankets and largely deprived of food. Upon reaching the Rapidan River, the Yankees were loaded into railroad cars and shipped to Gordonsville, where they were thrown into a "filthy shop, the

---

[30]*Brockway to Matthews, October 18, 1862;* Hennessy, *Return to Bull Run, 436-37.* Brockway, in his October 18 letter, wrote that he surrendered to a lieutenant of the 49th Alabama. However, there was no 49th Alabama engaged at Bull Run; there was a 49th Georgia in Thomas' Brigade of Hill's Division, and these authors believe that Brockway surrendered to this regiment. Opposed to this view, Hennessy, *Historical Report, 518,* concluded that only Pender's and Archer's brigades were engaged after dark, and thus it is possible that Brockway was completely mistaken as to the identity of the man to whom he surrendered.

[31]*Casualty figures are from Bates,* Pennsylvania Volunteers, *1:960.* The figures included in O.R., volume 12, part 2, 255, total one killed, eight wounded, and ten captured. Bates, ibid., also includes the information about the Indiana battery. The only Indiana battery present at the battle was the 16th Indiana Battery, a part of McDowell's corps.

floor of which was so filled with dirt and excrement as to cause disgust among the Negroes.

On Saturday, September 6, Brockway and his comrades entered Richmond and found themselves locked up in Libby Prison, an old tobacco warehouse near the James River. Brockway wrote that the prison floor was covered with drainings from molasses barrels, never having been cleaned even after eighteen months of use as a prison. "The sink was a small box on the same floor, and gave forth a horrible stench," wrote the lieutenant. "We were not allowed to look out of the windows; one man was killed for doing so the day we got there." A swill soup was issued twice a day, for which the men split their canteens to use as bowls, and whittled spoons from sticks. Some "doubtful beef" was issued, as was cockroach-filled bread.

The Confederates especially hated Pope's officers, who were not paroled as quickly as men from the Army of the Potomac. Finally, after five demands for parole, Brockway was one of those set free on September 24. The lieutenant was granted a twenty-day furlough and hastened to visit his parents in Luzerne County before reporting to Camp Parole outside Annapolis, Maryland.[32]

---

[32]*Brockway to Matthews, October 18, 1862;* untitled letter about Brockway's return home in the Columbia Democrat, *October 4, 1862.*

Private Thomas E. Frame strikes a popular Napoleonic stance, hand in jacket, cap jauntily askew.

(GARRY LEISTER COLLECTION, USAMHI)

Chapter Four

The Maryland Campaign

The defeated Army of Virginia and attached corps from the Army of the Potomac retreated from the Manassas and Chantilly battlefields into the defenses of Washington. General Pope was relieved from command on September 5 and McClellan placed in command of the defenses of the city. Given the power to consolidate the troops defending the city, McClellan began replacing the three hapless corps commanders of the Army of Virginia. On September 7, McDowell was relieved from command of the Third Corps and superseded by Major General Joseph Hooker, a capable division commander in the Third Army Corps of the Army of the Potomac. On the twelfth of September, the three corps were renumbered and consolidated with the Army of the Potomac. Hooker's corps was designated the First Army Corps, Banks' old command became the Twelfth Army Corps, and Sigel's was designated the Eleventh Army Corps.[1]

Hooker's corps underwent few changes. General King remained in command of the First Division, General Ricketts retained control of the Second Division, and a new Third Division, the Pennsylvania Reserves under Brigadier General George G. Meade, was attached to the corps. Battery F continued to support the infantry of Ricketts' Second Division.[2] The battery had suffered severely at Second Manassas. Captain Matthews was still in command, but his lieutenants were gone. Brockway had been captured, Ricketts was still in Pennsylvania on recruiting service, and Case went home on sick leave shortly after Second Manassas. Sergeant Francis H. Snider was the senior non-commissioned officer of the battery still

---

[1] *O.R., volume 19, part 1, 157.*

[2] *Ricketts' division was organized as follows:*
   First Brigade, Brig. Gen. Abram Duryee: 97th, 104th, 105th NY, 107th PA
   Second Brigade, Col. William A. Christian: 26th, 94th NY, 88th, 90th PA
   Third Brigade, Brig. Gen. George L. Hartsuff: 12th, 13th MA, 83rd NY, 11th PA
   Artillery: Bty F, 1st PA; PA Ind Bty C

present for duty. The battery was now equipped with four 3-inch ordnance rifles.[3]

McClellan had barely organized the army when Lee invaded Maryland. His victorious legions crossed the Potomac and moved into central Maryland. Lee had divided his army into several columns. Three of these, under the overall command of Stonewall Jackson, moved to surround the thirteen thousand-man garrison of Harper's Ferry. To counter the Rebels, McClellan moved out of Washington with most of the reorganized army. Hooker's First Corps and Jesse Reno's Ninth Corps comprised the Right Wing, led by General Burnside. Major General Edwin V. Sumner led the Centre, composed of the Second and Twelfth Corps, and Major General William B. Franklin commanded the Left, composed of the Sixth and one division of the Fourth Corps. The Third and Eleventh Corps remained behind to augment the Washington garrison.

McClellan's bluecoats swept forward and entered Frederick on September 12, the same day that Harper's Ferry was surrounded by Jackson's columns. The next day, September 13, a soldier of the 27th Indiana found a copy of one of Lee's orders, wrapped around three cigars, in an abandoned campsite near Frederick. The order soon found its way to army headquarters, where McClellan was dumbfounded. Here was the entire enemy plan, outlining the positions of each column. The general now decided to move on and attempt to defeat the Army of Northern Virginia in detail. The Battle of South Mountain took place on the fourteenth, when the Army of the Potomac hammered Rebels defending key passes across the mountain. Hooker's First Corps engaged the enemy at Turner's Gap, driving back the gray defenders by the time darkness fell. In this sharp encounter, Matthews' battery was not engaged.

Lee, worried about the Union preponderance in numbers, withdrew Longstreet's troops behind Antietam Creek in the vicinity of Sharpsburg. He decided to await the Union attack while at the same time hoping Jackson would capture Harper's Ferry and rejoin him in time to stave off the Yankees. The Union garrison surrendered on September 15, allowing Jackson the time to begin sending his divisions north to reinforce Lee at Sharpsburg. McClellan, meanwhile, moved over South Mountain and took position east of Antietam Creek facing the enemy positions. On the sixteenth, troops on the Union right flank, comprising Hooker's First Corps, Mansfield's Twelfth Corps, and some cavalry, crossed Antietam Creek and at dark, Meade's Pennsylvanians fought a number of Confederate regiments for control of a woodlot that would become known as East Woods. McClellan planned to attack the next day, starting on the right and left,

---

[3]Snider to Andrew G. Curtin, August 5, 1863, Battery F Papers, PSA.

followed by an attack across the Middle Bridge against Lee's center.

Battery F followed Ricketts' division across the creek that afternoon and parked for the night in a field that was "considerably grown up with underbrush." Matthews received orders to make sure his men stayed near their guns, with drivers sleeping near their horses. This field was located north and slightly west of a woodlot belonging to farmer David R. Miller; this woods would later become known as the North Woods. Two brigades of Meade's division rested just north of these woods, with one of his brigades occupying the East Woods. Abner Doubleday's First Division deployed along the Hagerstown Turnpike, while Ricketts' infantry extended Meade's line to the east.[4]

Hooker's First Corps was the first of McClellan's corps to attack Lee's Confederates on September 17. Doubleday's First Division moved south astride the Hagerstown Pike, heading for the whitewashed Dunker Church, visible against the trees of the West Woods to the south. The church was situated on some high ground, which would be the focal point of Union assaults on the Confederate left flank, which was held by Stonewall Jackson's divisions.

General Ricketts was ordered to move his three brigades southward and assail the enemy in conjunction with Doubleday's advance. Hooker instructed Ricketts to sweep through the East Woods, then continue on and strike the enemy line. Meade's Pennsylvania Reserves would provide support in the center as needed; one of his brigades still occupied much of the East Woods after the fighting of the previous night.[5]

Abram Duryee's First brigade moved diagonally through the northern end of the East Woods and entered a thirty-acre cornfield, which stretched from the woods west to the Hagerstown Pike. The brigade's four regiments swept through the tall corn and came to the southern edge of the field. As they entered a rolling pasture field, Confederate troops arose and poured a destructive fire into the oncoming Yankees. These Rebels–two brigades of Ewell's Division (now led by Brigadier General Alexander R. Lawton)–brought the Union advance to a standstill.[6]

As Duryee's brigade advanced, Ricketts sent his two batteries into action. Both Thompson and Matthews moved their guns into position in a

---

[4]Henry Wireman to Ezra A. Carman, March 13, 1898, Antietam Studies, RG 94. General Doubleday took over for King, who was sick.

[5]O.R., volume 19, part 1, 259.

[6]Stephen W. Sears, Landscape Turned Red: The Battle of Antietam (New Haven, CT: Ticknor & Fields, 1983), 185-86.

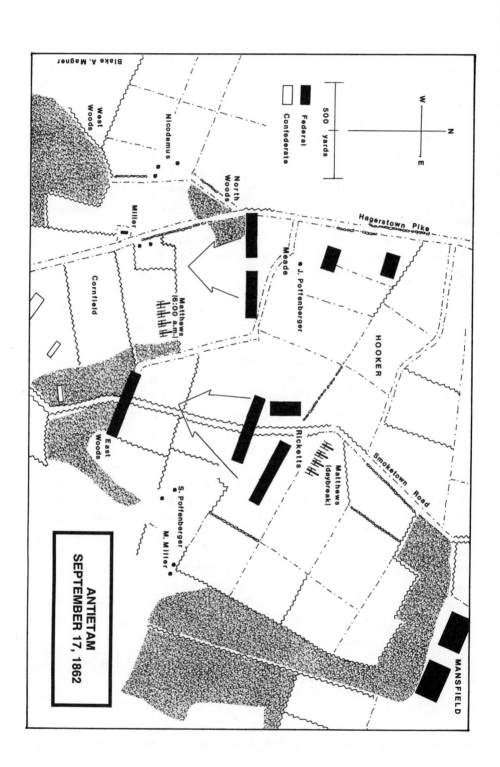

1st Lieutenant Henry Godbold holds a model 1840 artillery officer's saber.
(USAMHI)

clover field north of the corn. "Taking advantage of the ground," penned Ricketts, "both batteries opened with destructive effect, officers and men displaying great coolness while exposed to a severe fire of artillery and infantry."[7]

Matthews brought his four ordnance rifles into position with the command "Forward on the right into line gallop." Survivors later recalled that the left piece of the battery was not more than ten feet from the edge of the East Woods. As soon as the guns were unlimbered, they became the targets of Rebel artillery located at the Dunker Church, some three-fourths of a mile straight ahead. Here, Colonel Stephen D. Lee had four batteries in line, and they began firing at Thompson and Matthews. Sergeant Henry Wireman wrote that the resulting "lively" artillery duel lasted for some time. In the mean time, Duryee's brigade gave ground and withdrew north across the cornfield, ammunition in short supply and no sign of support.[8]

Ricketts had intended to send his remaining two brigades to support Duryee's attack. However, General Hartsuff was wounded by a shell fragment as he reconnoitered; the resulting confusion while Colonel Richard Coulter was notified that he was in command meant that the brigade remained motionless. Colonel William A. Christian, leading the Second Brigade onto the field, lost his nerve as Confederate artillery projectiles rained down on his approaching line. The colonel beat a hasty retreat to the rear and resigned two days later. Colonel Peter Lyle of the 90th Pennsylvania took over and pushed his men forward.[9]

Coulter's men swept through the East Woods and into the Cornfield before grinding to a halt amid the debris of bodies from Duryee's earlier attack. Fresh Confederate troops braved the Federal artillery fire to crash into Coulter's brigade, sending it back into the East Woods. Then Lyle's regiments entered the Cornfield just as Doubleday's attack to the right surged into the western half of the field. The oncoming Yankees drove through the field and beyond. Captain Thompson limbered his guns and moved forward to a small knoll in the midst of the Cornfield. From here, they opened fire on the enemy at the Dunker Church.[10]

---

[7]O.R., *volume 19, part 1, 259.*

[8]*Wireman to Carman, March 13, 1898; Wireman to A. J. Sellers, February 22, 1895, Antietam Studies, NA.*

[9]*Sears,* Landscape Turned Red, *187-88.*

[10]Ibid., *188-90.*

The Union success was shortlived, for Brigadier General John B. Hood's two brigades were called from reserve and flung into the maelstrom in the Cornfield. The fresh Rebel troops shattered the spent Union attack and forced a disorganized withdrawal. Hood's victorious men followed, threatening Thompson's guns with capture. The artillery was saved and hastily retired to the rear. Hood's men followed, sweeping through the cornfield to the fence beyond. Their ardor unquenchable, the Rebels continued on.[11]

Matthews saw them coming and changed position slightly to enable his four cannon to rake the oncoming enemy with grapeshot and canister at point blank range. General Meade fed his two available brigades into the fight and the fresh infantry forced Hood's outnumbered men to fall back across the cornfield, now largely trampled and littered with dead and wounded soldiers in blue and gray. It was now only about 7:30 in the morning, and the battle continued to rage as more Union infantry approached. This was Mansfield's Twelfth Corps, finally entering the battle to relieve Hooker's battered corps. Hooker himself was wounded as he accompanied Doubleday's division in a fresh charge in pursuit of Hood's "fugitives."[12]

Meade took command of the corps and attempted to reorganize the survivors as Mansfield's two divisions swept forward. Casualties were high. Ricketts lost one-third of his division. The general himself had two horses killed under him. Ricketts was injured when the second fell on him. Captain Matthews reported casualties of three killed and eight wounded. Many horses had been killed, including Matthews' own mount. When his steed fell, Matthews injured a knee, which would incapacitate him for further active duty.[13]

---

[11]Ibid., *197-99.*

[12]O.R., *volume 19, part 1, 219; Wireman to Carman, March 13, 1898;* Sears, Landscape Turned Red, *199-203.*

[13]O.R., *volume 19, part 1, 190;* Bates, Pennsylvania Volunteers, *961;* Ezra J. Warner, Generals in Blue *(Baton Rouge: Louisiana State University Press, 1964), 404. The paucity of sources for Battery F's role at Antietam leaves many questions unanswered. In an 1895 letter, William H. Thurston recalled that when Confederate infantry charged the battery, they came within a few yards, "compelling us to make an effort to save our guns, but owing to the loss of horses and drivers we were obliged to leave part on the field for a time." Thurston to John M. Gould, February 6, 1895, Antietam Papers, Dartmouth College. This passage suggests that the battery was abandoned for a few moments until Union infantry came up to drive Hood's men back across the Cornfield.*

Indeed, on September 26, Brigadier General George G. Meade, then in command of the First Corps, issued Special Orders Number 17. Paragraph three of this order sent Captain Matthews and Private John C. Truman of Battery F to Harrisburg on recruiting service. Upon arrival at Harrisburg, the two Pennsylvanians were to report to Captain Dodge, the government recruiting agent at that city. Lieutenant Ricketts had rejoined Battery F on September 23, and when Matthews departed, Ricketts was placed in charge of the battery. The lieutenant remarked in his diary on September 25 "myself alone and in command of the battery." Lieutenant Case was still home, sick. Brockway had been captured, and Godbold, wounded at Rappahannock Station, died in a Washington hospital on September 22. As a result, Ricketts was the only commissioned officer on duty with Battery F.[14]

The Army of the Potomac remained encamped in the vicinity of Antietam battlefield. The boys in blue had something to talk about around the campfires when they heard about Lincoln's notice that an emancipation proclamation would be formally issued on January 1, 1863, stating that if the Southern states did not cease the rebellion and return to the Union by year's end, then any slaves within their borders would be forever free on New Year's Day 1863.[15]

Lincoln himself, disappointed with McClellan's inactivity after the battle, left Washington and appeared unannounced at McClellan's headquarters on October 1. For the next four days, the president and McClellan had a series of meetings, after which the chief reviewed various army units. The First Corps assembled for a grand review on October 2, but the president was delayed elsewhere and the disgusted soldiers finally returned to camp after dark. The review went off as planned the next day, but only after the corps waited "under a scorching sun until after 5 p.m."[16]

By the time Lincoln visited the army, changes were beginning to take place in the First Corps. On September 29, Major General John F. Reynolds returned from Pennsylvania and was assigned to corps command, relieving Meade, who returned to his Third Division. On the fourth of October, Brigadier General Nelson Taylor arrived in camp and was assigned to Ricketts' division. Ricketts placed him in command of the Third Brigade, replacing the badly-wounded Hartsuff.[17]

---

[14]*Special Orders #17, September 26, 1862*, copy in Ricketts Papers. Ricketts recorded in his diary on September 25th that Captain Matthews left for recruiting duty.

[15]Sears, *Landscape Turned Red, 317-21.*

[16]Ibid., *323-25; Ricketts Diary, October 2-3, 1862.*

[17]O.R., *volume 19, part 2, 367, 381.*

Quartermaster Sergeant Stephen E. Ridgeway enlisted at Danville and was promoted to sergeant at war's end.

(GARRY LEISTER COLLECTION, USAMHI)

The Army of the Potomac remained in the Sharpsburg area as October waned. McClellan continually called for reinforcements and resisted the president's repeated calls for action, blaming the lack of adequate supplies as the primary reason for not moving against Lee's troops, then located in the Shenandoah Valley. While the Yankees remained in camp, the army grew stronger as efficiency was improved and battered units recovered from the ordeal of the last campaigns. On October 8, Colonel Charles P. Wainwright, in command of the First Corps artillery, issued an order to all battery commanders, instructing each to furnish a list of absentees as well as an exact statement as to the number of guns and artillerists present for duty. If a battery did not have enough men, each commander was to fill up the deficiency by asking the infantry of the corps to supply the number of men needed.[18]

For Captain Ricketts, October was a sometimes trying month. Since both his own battery and Captain Thompson's had been reduced in size owing to battle losses, Colonel Henry J. Hunt, the army's Chief of Artillery, examined the possibility of consolidating the two batteries into one. Ricketts approached General Ricketts and Colonel Wainwright for help and succeeded in preventing the plan. Then, on October 16, Lieutenant C. R. Denning, the division's artillery quartermaster, was sent to Washington with a detachment of men from the two Pennsylvania batteries with orders to bring back a two-gun section of 3-inch rifles for each battery.[19]

While Battery F reorganized and McClellan fretted about supplies, Lincoln became more and more exasperated with the army's inactivity. The situation worsened on October 10, when eighteen hundred Rebel horsemen led by Jeb Stuart splashed across the Potomac and swept north on a raid. The Southern horsemen rode into Chambersburg, Pennsylvania, seizing horses, burning government supplies, and evading frantic efforts from blueclad horsemen to catch up with them. Stuart's tired but jubilant men recrossed the river near Leesburg on October 12, having lost only one man wounded and two captured.[20]

Finally, by late October, McClellan was ready to move the Army of the Potomac from its Sharpsburg camps. A flurry of general orders from headquarters preceded the movement. On the seventh, General Reynolds issued instructions that each regiment in the corps was to keep on hand at

---

[18]*General Orders #13, First Corps, October 8, 1862,* copy in Ricketts Papers.

[19]*Ricketts Diary, October13, 17, 1862; Special Orders #31, First Corps, October 16, 1862,* copy in Ricketts Papers.

[20]Sears, *Landscape Turned Red, 325-28.*

all times five days' cooked rations. Two days later, artillery battery commanders were ordered to make sure that each gun was supplied with 250 rounds of ammunition. On October 22nd, army headquarters mandated that each battery would be restricted to three wagons, a two-horse ambulance, and three wall tents for officers. The same day, Reynolds reduced the amount of cooked rations on hand to three days. Finally, on October 25, Captain George F. Leppien of the 5th Maine Battery was announced as the Second Division's Chief of Artillery.[21]

The Army of the Potomac began to move from its camps on October 26, slowly making its way to the Potomac, crossing below Harper's Ferry. Battery F left camp at 4:00 a.m. on the twenty-sixth, crossed South Mountain at Crampton's Pass, all the while toiling under rainy skies. That night the disgruntled men encamped on the east side of the mountain. The next day, the battery rolled only a few miles to Burkittsville and went into camp. The end of day on October 28 found Battery F at Berlin, a small town on the Potomac River east of Harper's Ferry. Here, the men waited while other units crossed the river on a series of pontoon bridges.[22]

Battery F crossed the Potomac at Berlin on October 30 and moved south to Lovettsville. "The day was superb," wrote Colonel Wainwright, "the first of Indian summer; the air soft and balmy, the smoky mist hanging on the mountains, and the country rolling beautifully into rich knolls." Lead elements of the army were continuing south to seize passes across the Blue Ridge Mountains in order to prevent Rebel attacks on the army's supply line from Harper's Ferry as the troops moved south. By nightfall on November 1st, Battery F had reached the small village of Purcellville. Off to the southwest, the sounds of firing could be heard at Snicker's Gap, where units of both armies skirmished over control of this gap. Lee, in an effort to remain between the Yankee advance and Richmond, sent Longstreet's Corps to Culpeper, squarely in the path of the Army of the Potomac. Stonewall Jackson's Corps remained in the Shenandoah Valley, poised to strike McClellan's communications should the opportunity present itself.[23]

---

[21]*General Orders #12, First Corps, October 7, 1862; Circular, October 9, 1862; Extract from Quartermaster's Office Orders, October 22, 1862; General Orders #21, First Corps, October 22, 1862; Special Orders #127, First Corps, October 25, 1862*, copies in Ricketts Papers.

[22]*Ricketts Diary, October 26-29, 1862*.

[23]Ibid., *October 31-November 1, 1862;* Sears, Landscape Turned Red, *336-38;* Allan Nevins (editor), A Diary of Battle: The Personal Journals of Colonel Charles S. Wainwright, 1861-1865 *(reprint edition, New York: Da Capo Press, 1998), 119.*

On November 2, General Ricketts was relieved from duty with the corps and ordered to report to Harper's Ferry for further orders. Ricketts' Antietam wound apparently still bothered the general enough to incapacitate him from active duty. Ricketts was replaced by Brigadier General John Gibbon, commander of the now-famed Iron Brigade in the First Division of the corps.[24]

By nightfall on November 5, Battery F had moved through Bloomfield and reached Rectortown, where McClellan had his headquarters. Two days later, the battery reached Warrenton. "Snowed all day," Lieutenant Ricketts penned in his diary. The storm was presaged by colder weather. Colonel Wainwright found the water in his tent coated with ice when he arose early in the morning. The colonel wrote that the snow began after nine o'clock, and continued until late afternoon. That evening, Brigadier General Catharinus P. Buckingham came out from Washington with an order relieving McClellan and assigning Major General Ambrose E. Burnside to the command of the Army of the Potomac.[25]

---

[24]O.R., *volume 19, part 2, 533;* Nevins, Diary of Battle, *121. Gibbon was transferred to the Second Division on November 4 via Special Orders #44, First Corps, copy in Ricketts Papers.*

[25]*Ricketts Diary, November 2-7, 1862;* Sears, Landscape Turned Red, *338-41.*

  On November 8, Lieutenant Colonel James S. Fillebrown reported that Lieutenant Denning, the division's artillery quartermaster, commanding a section each from Matthews' and Thompson's batteries, accompanied by four wagons and an ambulance, was attacked near Snickersville and forced to retreat to Fillebrown's camp. The lieutenant colonel was in command of the 10th Maine of the Twelfth Army Corps, which was guarding the army's rear as it moved forward. Curiously, none of the extant papers from Battery F mention this action. For Fillebrown's report, see O.R., volume 19, part 2, 139-40.

Chapter Five

Fredericksburg and Chancellorsville

When General Burnside took command of the Army of the Potomac, he did so hesitatingly, unwilling to command an army, but forced to do so by the administration. The new army commander was briefed by McClellan before that general departed. On November 10, McClellan visited each corps before taking leave, receiving thunderous accolades from most units. The next day, the general boarded a train and left he army he had created.[1]

By the time McClellan departed, Burnside had developed a plan of operations that he submitted to General in Chief Henry W. Halleck for approval. Instead of continuing south toward Culpeper and Longstreet's Corps, Burnside proposed shifting his base of operations from Warrenton to Fredericksburg, giving up the overworked Orange & Alexandria Railroad in favor of the Richmond, Fredericksburg, and Potomac Railroad and a base at Aquia Creek. Burnside proposed feinting south to hold the enemy's attention, then move the bulk of the army rapidly to Fredericksburg, cross the Rappahannock, and head toward Richmond before Lee could unite his army. Since Jackson was still in the Shenandoah Valley, Burnside felt that by shifting the base of operations east he would compel Jackson to leave the Valley as well as alleviate any risk to the Union supply lines from Confederates in the Valley.[2]

Burnside also shifted the command structure of the Army of the Potomac by creating three "Grand Divisions," each composed of two corps. Major General Edwin V. Sumner led the Right Grand Division, which included the Second and Ninth Army Corps. The Centre, under the command of General Hooker, was composed of the Third and Fifth Army Corps. The First and Sixth Army Corps formed the Left Grand Division,

---

[1]*Sears,* Landscape Turned Red, *340-45.*

[2]*Vorin E. Whan, Jr.,* Fiasco at Fredericksburg *(University Park: Pennsylvania State University Press, 1961), 18.*

Major General William B. Franklin commanding. Cavalry was attached to each grand division.

Battery F moved to Bealton Station on November 11, remaining there near division headquarters for six days. Lieutenant Ricketts used the time to catch up on correspondence and send in his monthly return for October to regimental headquarters. On the thirteenth, General Gibbon reviewed the batteries attached to his command. Captain Leppien reviewed the batteries on the fourteenth. That evening, Ricketts and Leppien left camp and rode down the rail line to Rappahannock Station, probably to see the present condition of the area where their batteries engaged the enemy almost three months before.[3]

Monday, November 17 brought good weather and the beginning of the First Corps' march toward Fredericksburg. Colonel Wainwright wrote that the march that day was a "pleasant one; but through a most wretched country." The terrain was sandy and covered with pine woods, the few inhabitants described as "poor white trash." By day's end, Battery F went into camp four miles east of Morrisville. The next day, the march continued, with the battery moving ten miles to a camp near Ellis Ford on the Rappahannock, followed by a five-mile travel on the nineteenth to a point three miles west of Stafford Court House.[4]

Battery F's shift toward Fredericksburg mirrored the Army of the Potomac's advance to that city. Halleck and Lincoln finally had given Burnside approval to shift his base of operations as he desired, but counseled that the general's plan would only succeed if carried out rapidly so that Lee could not react quickly enough to block the Union advance. The army began moving on November 15; Sumner's advance arrived at Falmouth on the seventeenth. Instead of allowing Sumner permission to cross some troops to drive away light resistance and seize Fredericksburg, Burnside acted cautiously and decided to await the arrival of the army's pontoon train from Washington. Instead of rendezvousing on time, the pontoons finally arrived on November 25. By that time, Longstreet's Corps of some 45,000 troops was deployed behind the city, while Jackson moved to within supporting distance.[5]

Frustrated, Burnside debated while Lincoln and Halleck came to the front to meet with the general. Burnside had the option of doing nothing, but later said that Northern public opinion demanded an advance. Thus, he

---

[3]*Ricketts Diary, November 11-16, 1862.*

[4]*Ibid., November 17-19, 1862;* Nevins, *Diary of Battle, 127-28.*

[5]*Whan,* Fiasco at Fredericksburg, *20-26.*

decided to cross the Rappahannock at Fredericksburg and assail Lee's positions behind the town.⁶

In the meantime, Battery F shifted its camp to Brooks Station on November 23, a distance of six miles. The men remained quietly in camp, waiting for the generals to decide upon a plan of action. On the first day of December, Lieutenant Ricketts received an order to proceed to Washington to superintend the moving of two sections of artillery and ordnance stores from the artillery depot in the capital to First Corps headquarters. Ricketts complained in his diary that the twenty-four hours allotted him to perform this task was far too short a time.⁷

Leaving Lieutenant Greenleaf T. Stevens of the 5th Maine Battery in charge of Battery F, Ricketts left for Washington on December 2, arriving there late at night. On Wednesday the third, Ricketts reported to Brigadier General William F. Barry, commander of the Artillery Camp of Instruction, asking to have his time extended. Although Halleck's adjutant, Colonel John C. Kelton, refused, Ricketts concluded to take it upon himself to take as much time as he needed to transport the guns to Aquia Creek Landing.⁸

Rickets reported to the quartermaster's department and requested river transportation to take the four guns on December 6. The lieutenant was sent back to Barry with a note asking if the guns could move by land instead. Barry assented and dispatched Ricketts down the Mount Vernon Road. The guns got as far as Dumfries, where the roads became impassable because of so much mud. Compelled to go by water, Ricketts was instructed that the requisite transportation would load his guns on Saturday the sixth. Thus moved, Ricketts superintended the unloading on the seventh and was back in Battery F's camp later that day.⁹

On the ninth, Battery F broke camp, together with the rest of the corps, and headed toward Falmouth, their advance delayed by the larger Sixth Corps which preceded them. Lieutenant W. C. Gillespie reported for duty with Battery F this day. Gillespie was an officer in Battery G, but owing to the lack of officers to help Ricketts, Gillespie was transferred on a

---

⁶*Ibid., 29-32.*

⁷*Ricketts Diary, November 23, December 1, 1862.*

⁸*Ibid., December 3, 1862.*

⁹*Ibid., December 3-7, 1862. Throughout these diary passages, Ricketts does not indicate which batteries were to receive the four guns he brought from Washington. Subsequent strength reports in the* Official Records *indicate plainly that Battery F remained at a four-gun strength.*

temporary basis. Ricketts also received an order that evening to report for duty on the evening of the tenth to Captain Gustavus A. De Russy, 4th United States Artillery. General Hunt had decided to deploy an artillery line along the ridges overlooking the Rappahannock to counter any Confederate artillery fire and protect the laying of pontoon bridges across the stream. Hunt used the small Artillery Reserve, then bolstered it by detaching batteries from the infantry corps.[10]

Captain De Russy was placed in charge of what Hunt styled "The Left." De Russy had command of nine batteries, which comprised forty-two cannon (eight 20-pounder Parrott rifles and thirty-four 3-inch rifles). The batteries were placed in a line beginning near Pollock's Mill on the left and extending along the ridge toward the next grouping of guns which overlooked the middle bridges. The batteries were brought forward at night into position. To deceive the enemy, the unfortunate Yankee artillerists were not allowed to start any fires to keep warm.[11]

Before dawn on December 11, engineers from the Army of the Potomac brought their pontoon bridging material to the river and began construction of bridges at three sites. A heavy fog hid the workers from view until more than two-thirds of the way across the river. At that point, Mississippi troops under command of Brigadier General William Barksdale opened fire and drove them back. Hunt's right flank batteries opened a "terrific cannonade" in support, but a crossing was not effected until infantry volunteers crossed in pontoons and secured the first streets of the city.[12]

The bridging of the river on Franklin's front proved much easier. The engineers were able to complete their bridges by 9:00 a.m. without much opposition from the enemy, who had no cover from which to dispute the bridge laying. Even so, Burnside delayed ordering the infantry to cross because of the delays opposite Fredericksburg. Instead, the army crossed only on December 12. Burnside then spent the rest of the day and most of the night observing the enemy positions and deciding on an attack plan.[13]

The battle of December 13 began with Franklin's assault against Stonewall Jackson's troops at Hamilton's Crossing. George Meade's

---

[10]*Ricketts Diary, December 9, 1862; Special Order Number 76, First Army Corps, December 9, 1862, copy in Ricketts Papers; Nevins,* Diary of Battle, *134-35; O.R., volume 21, 181.*

[11]*Ricketts Diary, December 10, 1862; O.R., volume 21, 183.*

[12]*Whan,* Fiasco at Fredericksburg, *38-42.*

[13]Ibid., *38, 51-58.*

Pennsylvania Reserves, supported by Gibbon's troops, broke into the Confederate line but were repulsed. Franklin, following Burnside's orders, failed to send in reinforcements and after repelling a limited Rebel counterattack, affairs quieted down on the Union left. On the right, Sumner and Hooker were supposed to attack Marye's Heights after Franklin was successful on the left. However, Franklin's initial delay pushed Burnside into ordering an attack in contradiction to his original plan. Sixteen separate assaults were bloodily repulsed before the day ended. Casualties totaled 12,527 Yankees and only 4,756 Rebels.

Battery F spent the day of battle firing from its position near the bridges in support of Franklin's troops. Following the end of the fighting, the army remained in position until the evening of the fifteenth. That night, "the pontoon bridges were sprinkled with dirt to deaden sound, the fires were extinguished, voices hushed, and the entire army withdrew to this side of the river," wrote Lieutenant Brockway, recently paroled and returned to duty. Captain De Russy woke a sleeping Ricketts at ten o'clock to inform him that the army was retreatingñ"astonished," penned Ricketts. "Undoubtedly a wise move however." Battery F remained in position until the sixteenth, when it moved to Stafford Heights and went into line to watch the enemy. Ricketts reported that his four guns expended 201 rounds of ammunition during the period from December 11-15, and suffered no casualties.[14]

The battery remained in position until December 21, when it limbered up and returned to camp about three miles east of White Oak Church. By that time, General Gibbon, wounded in the fighting, had gone to Washington on leave; General Taylor commanded the Second Division in his absence. Lieutenant Ricketts commented that the late December weather was, at times, "magnificent," with the air "soft balmy like a May day" on the twenty-fourth. Anticipating another Christmas in camp, Ricketts penned that it was impossible to get bread and vegetables for dinner, so the holiday fare would be hardtack and salt pork. However, his servant Dixie found a chicken to supplement the mess. On the last day of the year, Brigadier General John C. Robinson replaced Taylor as commander of the Second Division.[15]

---

[14]*Ricketts Diary, December 13-15, 1862;* O.R., *volume 21, 217-18 (Ricketts' brief report); Brockway letter in* Columbia Democrat, *December 27, 1862.*

[15]*Ricketts Diary, December 21, 22, 24, 25, 27, 30, 31, 1862. Robinson was promoted from brigade command in the Third Corps. Taylor, apparently embittered by being superseded, submitted his resignation, which was accepted by the War Department on January 19, 1863. (Warner,* Generals in Blue, *496). Robinson was assigned by General Orders #1, December 31, 1862, First Corps, copy in Ricketts Papers.*

The start of the new year was a busy time for Lieutenant Ricketts. Unable to locate any whiskey to celebrate 1863, a dejected Ricketts turned to the paperwork so prevalent in the army. The army was mustered for pay on December 31, so each unit commander had to submit complete rolls that detailed the whereabouts of each man in his unit. Ricketts also updated ordnance returns and sent the required forms to Washington.[16]

Then, on the sixth, came Special Orders Number 5, First Corps. Battery F was transferred from the Second to the Third Division–the Pennsylvania Reserves—while Battery C, 5th United States Artillery, moved from the Third Division to the Second. Ricketts wrote that "officers in the division very indignant at our being transferred," but nothing was done to protest the transfer. The next day, Ricketts reported to Major James Brady, who went with the lieutenant to select a new campsite for the battery. Battery F broke camp on the eighth and moved to join the artillery of the Third Division, which included Batteries A, B, and G of the 1st Pennsylvania Light Artillery.[17]

Major Brady immediately published a comprehensive order detailing daily calls that each battery was to observe:

Reveille	Sunrise
Stable Call	Immediately after Reveille
Recall from Stables	1 hour after Stable Call
Breakfast Call	8:30 a.m.
Sick Call	Immediately after Breakfast Call
Water Call	9:00 a.m.
Drillñschool of the Piece	10:00 a.m.
Recall from Drill	11:00 a.m.
Dinner Call	12:30 p.m.
Drill to Harness	1:30 p.m.
Recall from Drill	2:30 p.m.
Water Call	Immediately after Recall from Drill
Stable Call	3:30 p.m.
Recall from Stables	4:30 p.m.
Retreat	Sunset
Guard Mount	Immediately after Retreat
Supper	Immediately after Guard Mount
Tattoo	8:00 p.m.
Taps	8:30 p.m.

---

[16]*Ricketts Diary, January 1-3, 1863.*

[17]*Special Orders #5, First Corps, January 6, 1863, copy in Ricketts Papers; Ricketts Diary, January 6-8, 1863; William H. Patterson Diary, January 8, 1863.*

Major Brady further stipulated that Saturdays would be reserved for washing, policing, and for cleaning harness and carriages. Sundays would be observed as usual as far as the exigencies of the service would permit. Officers were held responsible for maintaining clean camps.[18]

The officers and men of Battery F settled into their new camp and drilled daily, waiting for the next movement of the army. Lieutenant Case was still absent home, so on January 9, Ricketts sent in an application to the adjutant general's office asking for Case to be mustered out of service so that another could be appointed in his place. On the sixteenth, Colonel Horatio G. Sickel, then in temporary command of the Pennsylvania Reserves, ordered twelve men of Company F, 2nd Pennsylvania Reserves, to report to Lieutenant Ricketts for duty with Battery F. The lieutenant evidently failed to procure the proper paperwork and forms for these new men; on January 18, Major Brady reprimanded Ricketts, ordering him to make sure their names were entered in the battery records and that the proper descriptive lists were furnished to Battery F. Brady also reminded Ricketts that a note should be made in the battery book of the order assigning these men to the unit. No small wonder that Ricketts took a prominent part in a move to oust Brady from his position as artillery commander of the Third Division.[19]

On January 17, Battery F received orders to prepare for a general movement of the army against the enemy. Burnside, still wishing to engage the enemy on more equal terms, decided to move the Army of the Potomac westward from Falmouth, cross the Rappahannock and Rapidan Rivers as quickly as possible, and attempt to outflank Lee's positions behind Fredericksburg. Troops began moving on January 20. Franklin's Left Grand Division sidled into positions vacated by Sumner's divisions as the army began moving into position for a river crossing. William P. Patterson recorded in his diary that the battery marched to within a mile of Falmouth before going into camp at eight that night.[20]

As if to intervene, the sky clouded up during the day. Only an hour after Battery F went into camp, a cold rain began to fall. Men tried to keep

---

[18]*List of Calls, January 8, 1863*, copy in Ricketts Papers.

[19]*Special Order Number 16, Third Division, January 16, 1863*, copy in Ricketts Papers; *Brady to Ricketts, January 18, 1863*, Ricketts Papers; *Ricketts Diary, January 8, 1863*. Ricketts used his diary to denigrate Brady in a general way. His entries of January 8, 12, 13, 24, 25, 26, all mention Brady and the movement to get him away from the division.

[20]*Ricketts Diary, January 20, 1863; Patterson Diary, January 20, 1863.*

dry as the water descended in torrents; horses shivered and sank into the bottomless Virginia mud as they struggled to keep afloat. The rain continued on the twenty-first–in fact, the downfall continued for thirty hours before it petered out. The army's pontoon train, part of which had reached Banks' Ford, could not be brought forward. Troops straggled badly and both artillery batteries and supply wagons became hopelessly stuck in the mud.

Lieutenant Brockway wrote that cannon, even with twenty horses per piece, could barely be dragged forward. "It is impossible to give you a true idea of Virginia mud," penned the young artillerist. "It is not mud, but more a combination of mire and quick sand. When the horses got in too deep, they were shot to end their misery." "Horses pulled to death by the dozens," wrote Lieutenant Ricketts. Colonel Wainwright at least succeeded in locating a tent and erecting it. "All the afternoon we lay in our tent," wrote the colonel, "as uncomfortable as it was possible to be." "Everything was wet and nasty," complained Wainwright. The ground was too muddy to unpack the wagons, so he and his staff played cards and munched on hardtack, sardines, and coffee, all that could be eaten under such adverse weather conditions.[21]

Thursday, January 22, saw Battery F bogged down in the mud and in temporary camp, unable to move, a situation now spread throughout the army. Rebel pickets across the Rappahannock now were alert to the Yankees and began taunting the dispirited men in blue. Brockway spied a canvas painted with "Burnside's stuck in the mud" across the river, and heard pickets ask "Why don't you lay your pontoons! Shall we send a detail and assist you!" "You can't imagine the effect on us," penned disgruntled Brockway.[22]

January 23 saw orders issued from army headquarters calling off the movement and directing all units to return to their former camps. Lieutenant Ricketts reported that the battery had a "terrible time" slogging through the mud. Although only one horse was lost, Ricketts wrote that all the rest were "played out." By 3:00 p.m. that afternoon, Battery F had trekked through Falmouth and returned to its old camp. The battery wagons were sunk so far in the mud that they were left behind. Ricketts sent men and horses to extricate the wagons on the twenty-fourth, to no avail.[23]

---

[21]*Brockway letter of January 23, 1863, in the* Columbia Democrat, *February 7, 1863; Ricketts Diary, January 21, 1863; Nevins,* Diary of Battle, *159-60.*

[22]*Brockway letter of January 23; Ricketts Diary, January 23, 1863.*

[23]*Ricketts Diary, January 23-24, 1863; Patterson Diary, January 23, 1863.*

Musician William Morrison was a 17-year-old farmer from Montour County.
(SUE BOARDMAN COLLECTION, USAMHI)

While the rank and file fought the elements, the high command saw changes. Burnside, angered over some of his subordinates open dislike of him and over what he suspected was their attempts to backstab him, traveled to Washington and presented Lincoln and Halleck with General Orders Number 8, dated January 23. Burnside relieved several officers from duty with the army, including Hooker, Franklin, William F. Smith, and William T. H. Brooks, for a number of infractions of proper military protocol. Burnside informed the president that if he did not approve of this order, then he wished to be relieved from army command. Lincoln did indeed disapprove of the order and relieved Burnside, as well as Franklin and Edwin V. Sumner, the latter at his own request. Hooker superseded Burnside as commander of the Army of the Potomac, effective on January 26.[24]

After returning to camp, the men of Battery F proceeded to fix up their huts as best they could. On the twenty-seventh, details were formed to begin construction of stables for the battery horses. Snow fell on the twenty-eighth as the men worked on the stables. On the first day of February, an army paymaster appeared in camp and paid the battery for the period from July through October 1862. By this time, rumors floated through camp that the Pennsylvania Reserves would be detached from the army and sent to the Washington defenses to rest and recruit up to strength. Ricketts and his men believed that the artillery would accompany the division to Washington, a welcome respite from the drudgery of winter camp in the mud and snow of the Falmouth area.[25]

Some changes in battery personnel took place during the winter camp near Belle Plain. On February 4, Lieutenant Case was discharged from the service, clearing the way for Ricketts to recommend a replacement for the second lieutenant's slot. Ricketts recommended that Sergeant Brockway be promoted to replace Case. The letter was sent to Harrisburg and after some weeks, Brockway was promoted to second lieutenant to date from February 28.[26]

A more important change took place at regimental headquarters. Ever since Battery F's transfer to the Third Division, Ricketts and others complained about Major Brady and his overbearing behavior toward his

---

[24]These orders can be found in O.R., volume 21, 998-999, 1004-5.

[25]Ricketts Diary, January 28, 30, February 1, 1863; Patterson Diary, January 28, 30, February 1, 1863.

[26]Case was mustered out of service as a supernumerary officer, according to his service file in the National Archives.

subordinates. On February 22, Ricketts led a movement to have Captain Matthews, still at home on leave because of his wound, promoted to major in place of Brady. The other battery commanders in the division endorsed the request and Ricketts sent it on to Governor Curtin. On March 16, Matthews was promoted to major and ordered to report to the First Corps for duty. Brady left for recruiting service and would eventually be promoted to lieutenant colonel of the 1st Pennsylvania Artillery.[27]

The Pennsylvania Reserves began embarking ships for Washington on February 5 and had left the army by the twelfth. Battery A was ordered to report to the commander of the Ninth Corps for duty, leaving only Batteries B, F, and G in the field. Shortly after the Reserves departed, Abner Doubleday was promoted to major general and given command of a new Third Division, which now consisted of two Pennsylvania regiments (121st and 142nd) that had been temporarily attached to the Reserves and five untried Keystone State units that were sent from Washington to replace the Reserves. Major Matthews replaced Brady as artillery commander of Doubleday's division.[28]

Meanwhile, the officers and men of Battery F remained in camp and suffered through the month of February as the weather alternated between rain and snow. Corporal Patterson recorded on the third that the weather was "very cool and disagreeable." It snowed on the fifth, but by February 8 Patterson noted that the day was more like May than February. It rained on the eleventh and fifteenth, then snowed eight inches on the seventeenth. The snow disappeared the next day as rain set in and made the roads all but impassable. Temperatures fell again and another eight-inch snowstorm blanketed the area on the twenty-second. Still, the artillery in the different divisions managed to fire off a salute in honor of George Washington's birthday. Rain again fell on the twenty-sixth, obliging Patterson "to keep in our tent." Ricketts penned in his diary on the twenty-sixth that the roads were "horrible, impassable."[29]

---

[27]*Complaints about Brady can be found in Ricketts' Diary entries of January 8, 12, 13, 24, 25, 26, 29, February 4, 12, 13, 1863. Matthews was promoted to major on March 16, according to his file in the Pennsylvania Commandery of the Military Order of the Loyal Legion of the United States. His official date of promotion was April 11. Brady was sent on recruiting service under Special Orders #5, March 26, 1863.*

[28]*Doubleday's Third Division was organized as follows:*
    First Brigade, Brig. Gen. Thomas A. Rowley: 121st, 135th, 142nd,151st PA
    Second Brigade, Col. Roy Stone: 143rd, 149th, 150th PA
    Artillery, Maj. Ezra A. Matthews: Btys B, F, G, 1st PA

[29]*Patterson Diary, dates as noted; Ricketts Diary, February 26, 1863.*

Ricketts spent a good deal of time throughout the month completing monthly and quarterly returns that needed to be sent in to both division headquarters and regimental headquarters, still located at Fort Monroe with Colonel Robert M. West. On February 24, thirty-three infantrymen from Keystone State regiments in the division reported to Ricketts for duty with Battery F, to help fill up the battery strength. On the 27th, Ricketts was quite pleased to receive the following circular from General Hunt, commander of the army's artillery force:

Circular

Headquarters of Artillery, First Corps, Feb. 25, 1863.

The Colonel commanding the artillery of this corps has the great pleasure of publishing to the batteries under his command the following letter, received by him, viz:

Headquarters of Artillery, Army of the Potomac, Feb. 23, 1863.

Colonel: The reports of the late inspections show that none of your batteries are in bad order–the only corps so reported. The batteries reported in the best order are: Reynolds' L, 1st New York, Matthews' F, 1st Pennsylvania, and Leppien's 5th Maine.

Henry J. Hunt,

Brig. Gen. and Chief of Artillery.[30]

March 1863 passed much like February. The weather continued to display a mix of snow and rain, depending on the differing temperatures. The changeable weather meant that the roads remained muddy, hampering any chance of an early spring campaign. Throughout the winter and on into the spring, General Hooker worked to improve the army's morale. He issued an amnesty policy for all deserters and soldiers otherwise absent without leave. He also began a standardized procedure of allowing furloughs for each company during permanent camp times to allow soldiers who had not been home in more than a year to do so. In mid-

---

[30]*Ricketts Diary, February 5, 9, 11, 17, 18, 1863 (for reports). Colonel West sent a Circular Letter to all 1st Pennsylvania battery commanders decrying the lack of adequate regimental records and advising each officer on how to upgrade existing records. See his Circular Letter of February 1, 1863, copy in Ricketts Papers. Special Orders #1 of February 23, 1863, detached men from infantry regiments to Battery F, copy of this order in Ricketts Papers. Ricketts recorded the order in his diary entry of February 24, 1863. Hunt's February 23 letter is printed in Bates,* Pennsylvania Volunteers, *1:961-62, and noted in Brockway's letter published in the* Columbia Democrat, *March 14, 1863. Colonel Wainwright noted the improvement of Battery F in his diary of February 12; however, he considered Hunt's note a "left-handed compliment" when the general wrote that none of his batteries were in "bad" condition. Still, Wainwright was pleased enough to publish Hunt's letter to all First Corps batteries. See Nevins,* Diary of Battle, *165, 168.*

March, Hooker ordered each corps to adopt a distinctive badge that would identify its wearer more readily. The First Corps was authorized to use a sphere. Troops of the First Division would wear a red sphere on their caps, those in the Second Division would wear a white sphere, with a light blue badge adorning caps of soldiers in the Third Division.[31]

Lieutenant Ricketts applied for a leave of absence on March 12 and had it granted the next day. While making his way to Aquia Creek to board a vessel for Washington, the lieutenant's horse slipped in the mud and fell on him, spraining his knee. "I suffered so much that I had to [go] into the hospital at Aquia Creek," penned Ricketts. On March 14, able to walk with the aid of a cane, Ricketts left the hospital and reached Washington. He arrived in Bloomsburg on the eighteenth and remained on furlough until March 30, when he started back for camp, arriving on April 3.[32]

The month of April saw increased drilling, inspections, and reviews as Hooker readied the army for a spring offensive. Occasional days of rain continued to turn the ground into mud, effectively curtailing any important movement. On the second, Hooker reviewed Doubleday's division; a week later, President and Mrs. Lincoln accompanied Hooker to a review of the entire First Corps. Major Matthews returned to camp on the fourth, prompting Corporal Patterson to record in his diary that there was a "great joy of all the members of the battery."[33]

Hooker now readied the Army of the Potomac for an offensive designed to oust Lee from his fortifications behind Fredericksburg. The cavalry, now grouped into a corps led by George Stoneman, would raid behind Lee's army, drawing the Confederate horsemen after them. With the gray cavalry chasing Stoneman, Lee would be unable to closely monitor the Army of the Potomac's infantry. Hooker then would send three corps–the Fifth, Eleventh, and Twelfth–on a march up the Rappahannock. This force would cross the Rappahannock, then swing quickly south to cross the smaller Rapidan River and move into Lee's rear. At the same time, the First, Third, and Sixth Corps would occupy Lee's attention at Fredericksburg, pinning his troops in their entrenchments. Darius Couch's Second Corps would threaten Lee's left flank north of the Falmouth area. Hooker reasoned that Lee, finding a sizeable force in his rear, would either have to come out

---

[31]*The system of corps badges was announced in a general circular of March 26, 1863, copy in Ricketts Papers. Inspecting officers were admonished to ensure compliance with this circular.*

[32]*Ricketts Diary, entries for March 12-April 3, 1863.*

[33]*Patterson Diary, April 2, 4, 9, 1863.*

in the open to fight or withdraw toward Richmond to avoid being trapped. Either way, the advantage would be with Hooker's 120,000, which outnumbered Lee two to one.

Stoneman's troopers left their camps on April 13, but a series of rainy days delayed the move when the rivers rose and prevented easy movements. Lieutenant Ricketts wrote that on April 16, even as it rained, the battery received orders to carry eight days of rations, five in the knapsack and three in each man's haversack. On the nineteenth, Colonel Wainwright inspected the battery to ensure compliance with the previous order, as well as to see that the horses were provided with five days' forage.[34]

The three-corps flanking column left its camps on April 27 and headed northwest along the Rappahannock. That day, Ricketts' battery received orders to march the next day with five days' rations in knapsacks and three in haversacks; off horses would carry three days of forage, with another five days in rations and four of forage in supply wagons.

Reynolds' First Corps left its bivouacs near Belle Plain at noon on the twenty-eighth and headed toward the Rappahannock south of Fredericksburg. After an abbreviated night of restless camping, Battery F was on the move at two o'clock in the morning of the twenty-ninth. General Hunt, in charge of the army's artillery, had already assigned batteries to cover the crossing sites. A Sixth Corps division would cross at Franklin's Crossing, while Brigadier General James Wadsworth's First Division of the First Corps was given the task of seizing a bridgehead at Fitzhugh's Landing. To cover the bridge, Colonel Wainwright drew up forty pieces of artillery, stretched in a line on both sides of Pollock's Mill. Battery F's four 3-inch rifles joined the 1st New Hampshire Battery (six 3-inch rifles), Thompson's Independent Battery C, Pennsylvania Light Artillery (four 3-inch rifles) below the mill. Ricketts unlimbered Battery F in the middle of a corn field near the Fitzhugh House.[35]

Daybreak began with a blanket of fog that drastically reduced visibility and provided the Union engineers with the cover needed to erect a pontoon bridge before they would be discovered by Rebel pickets on the opposite bank. Unfortunately, Brigadier General Henry W. Benham, in charge of the Engineer Brigade, was drunk and failed to supervise his men. As the fog lifted, Rebel pickets, supported by a regiment lining rifle pits dug along the river, opened fire. Wadsworth sent two regiments across in

---

[34]*Ricketts Diary, April 16, 19, 1863.*

[35]*O.R., volume 25, part 1, 246-47, 303; Ricketts Diary, April 28-29, 1863; William Patterson Diary, April 28-29, 1863.*

pontoon boats. These units flushed out the enemy and allowed the engineers time to build a bridge. Throughout the rest of the day, Wadsworth sent over all four of his brigades and took a defensive position covering the bridge. Ricketts' guns did not open fire this day. [36]

April 30th saw rain before noon as the Union troops continued to occupy the enemy's attention. Heavy fog and mist obscured any long-range viewing, so it was afternoon before the weather cleared enough for observers on both sides to take stock of the situation. Colonel Wainwright recorded that the rain of the night before and early morning had softened the roads enough to make movement of wheeled vehicles difficult.[37]

At 5:00 p.m. a Confederate battery of 20-pounder Parrott rifles opened on the Union infantry lying in mass just north of the bridge, forcing their withdrawal behind some low-lying ridges. The Southern artillerists then turned their attention to the line of batteries in front of the Fitzhugh House. Lieutenant Ricketts reported that the artillery firing lasted until 7:00 p.m., when darkness called a halt to the desultory firing. During the action, the men of Battery F expended 43 rounds of Hotchkiss and Schenkl ammunition. "The distance being so great, and several batteries firing at the same time, it was impossible to determine with any degree of certainty what execution was done," Ricketts reported. Although enemy shells "struck all around & among us," Battery F suffered no casualties.[38]

May 1 was a quiet day along the lines below Fredericksburg. By this time, General Lee had reacted to the Union threat to his rear and had sent Stonewall Jackson's Second Corps to face Hooker's four corps (Sickles' Third Corps had been dispatched to reinforce the Federal buildup at Chancellorsville). Jubal Early's Division deployed in a thin line along the Fredericksburg defenses to watch Sedgwick's and Reynolds' divisions.

On the morning of May 2, the same enemy battery again opened fire on the Union lines. Ricketts' guns were among those that replied, firing seventy-five rounds. An hour before the firing began, an aide finally transmitted an order for Reynolds to move his corps to Chancellorsville. As the troops moved off, the enemy opened fire. Once the infantry was in column, Wainwright gave instructions for battery commanders to follow. Three batteries accompanied the infantry column; Wainwright formed the other batteries under his immediate command and set off. A halt was called

---

[36]O.R., *volume 25, part 1, 303;* Nevins, Diary of Battle, *186;* Stephen W. Sears, Chancellorsville *(Boston: Houghton Mifflin Company, 1996), 154-59.*

[37]*Nevins,* Diary of Battle, *188.*

[38]O.R., *volume 25, part 1, 303-4; Ricketts Diary, April 30, 1863.*

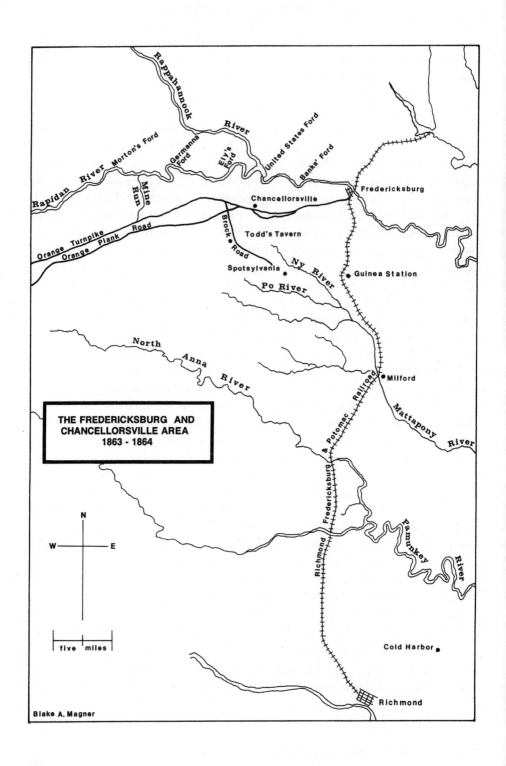

about two miles from Hooker's former headquarters. Here, Wainwright inspected the batteries to see how his orders regarding the packing of the carriages had been carried out. To his dismay, the colonel found that batterymen had loaded down with extra equipment and clothing the men did not wish to carry themselves. Wainwright issued a new order to every battery commander–any item not allowed by orders would be thrown away. "The field where the three Pennsylvania batteries were halted was literally covered with overcoats which the men would not carry," wrote the colonel.[39]

Battery F reached United States Ford early in the morning of May 3, crossing at two o'clock. Reynolds had gone on ahead to find army headquarters and Wainwright was upset at all the constant interruptions when he vainly tried to catch some sleep. "A very fatiguing march," penned Ricketts. "The excitement, loss of sleep &c. has about used me up."[40]

By the time Wainwright arrived, Stonewall Jackson's late afternoon attack on the Union right flank had crumpled up the Eleventh Corps and battered the Union army into a defensive position around the Chancellor House. Fierce fighting continued into darkness. That night, while reconnoitering, Jackson was accidentally shot by his own troops. Lee's tired men resumed the offensive on the morning of May 3, but the Yankees repelled assault after assault as the army slowly withdrew to a V-shaped defensive line covering its bridges. Wainwright had an interview with the badly dazed Hooker, who had been stunned by a falling pillar he was leaning against at the Chancellor House. Unable to locate General Hunt, Hooker placed Wainwright in temporary command of the army's artillery and told him to inspect the line and make sure the several batteries were in position to repel any more attacks.[41]

During the day, Battery F moved toward the front but remained in reserve. Toward evening, Ricketts was instructed to relieve Lieutenant Francis W. Seeley's Battery K, 4th United States, a Third Corps battery then in position on the left of the line held by Meade's Fifth Corps. The battery unlimbered within "short rifle range of the enemy." The battle had wound

---

[39]O.R., *volume 25, part 1, 304;* Nevins, Diary of Battle, *190-91.*

[40]*Ricketts Diary, May 2, 1863;* Nevins, Diary of Battle, *191. Ricketts recorded that the battery crossed United States Ford at 2:00 a.m. on May 3, while William Patterson, in his May 2nd diary entry, wrote that the time was midnight.*

[41]*Nevins,* Diary of Battle, *192-94. It is interesting to note that Wainwright recorded his conversation with Hooker in his diary but not in his official report of the battle (see O.R., volume 25, part 1, 259, for Wainwright's narrative of events on May 3).*

down by the time Ricketts went into battery, but desultory firing meant that the men had little sleep; twice the artillerists were roused and went to their posts, but no attack came. The main problem was enemy sharpshooters ensconced in the woods some 250 yards in front of the battery's position. Ricketts sent his horses to the rear for safety and had the men build earthworks.[42]

The fighting on May 3 was the last heavy engagement on the main front of the army. Sedgwick's corps attacked Marye's Heights early on the morning of the third; after suffering more than a thousand casualties, the Yankees broke through and overwhelmed the defenders. After reforming, Sedgwick started his troops toward Chancellorsville. Lee turned Lafayette McLaws' Division around and repelled Sedgwick's lead division at Salem Church that afternoon. Fearing the worst, Sedgwick drew his corps into a defensive line covering Banks' Ford. On May 4th, while part of his army occupied Hooker's attention, Lee shifted more troops to oppose Sedgwick. After the fighting ended, Sedgwick withdrew across the ford.

Battery F remained in position on May 4 and 5. Corporal Patterson reported picket firing in the morning and a "brisk skirmish" towards evening. On the fifth, there was more firing in the morning, with Lieutenant Ricketts writing that the "enemy made quite a severe attack," but were driven back with canister and grapeshot. Still, the battery suffered no casualties during the battle. That night, Hooker began pulling the army back across the Rappahannock. Rain fell, the roads were muddy, and the going was slow. By May 6, the battery was back in its old camp near Belle Plain. On the seventh, Battery F changed its camp and moved to a site near White Oak Church. The Chancellorsville Campaign was over.[43]

---

[42]*Ricketts Diary, May 4, 1863;* O.R., *volume 25, part 1, 304.*

[43]*Patterson Diary, May 4-8, 1863; Ricketts Diary, May 4-8, 1863.*

Chapter Six

Gettysburg

The month following the Chancellorsville Campaign was a busy one for the officers and men of Battery F. As usual after a period of activity, the army generally went through a period of reporting writing, inspections, and the issuing of replacement clothing and equipment to remedy any losses sustained during the last campaign.

Hooker also worried about the number of regiments that the Army of the Potomac was beginning to lose. Two-year and nine-month regiments were starting to be sent home for disbanding, and the army went through a slow reorganization as the infantry force declined. To compensate, on May 12 General Hooker issued Special Orders Number 129. This order brought to fruition an idea espoused for several months by General Hunt and endorsed by Colonel Wainwright and other top artillery officers. The artillery of each corps was grouped into a single Artillery Brigade. Extra batteries were sent to join the army's Artillery Reserve, commanded by Brigadier General Robert O. Tyler.[1]

Battery F was affected by this reorganization and was dispatched to the Artillery Reserve. Major Matthews was also reassigned and ordered to report to General Tyler. Matthews was placed in command of the Second Brigade of the reserve's Volunteer Division, which was under the command of Major John A. Tompkins. The Second Brigade included Ricketts' Battery F, the 1st New Hampshire Battery, Captain Frank P. Amsden's Battery G, 1st Pennsylvania, Battery C, 1st Rhode Island, and Battery C of the West Virginia Light Artillery. Ricketts, who had finally received his captain's commission on May 8, moved the battery camp on May 15 to a location near Falmouth Station, where the reserve batteries were concentrated.[2]

Lieutenant Brockway felt good about the artillery reorganization, but his May 22 letter to the *Columbia Democrat* echoed hundreds of other

---

[1] O.R., *volume 25, part 2, 471-72.*

[2] O.R., *volume 25, part 2, 586;* Ricketts Diary, May 15, 1863; Patterson Diary, May 15, 1863.

veterans who commented on the late campaign. "We feel quite sore about our late retreat," penned the lieutenant, "and the more so as we feel that the entire strength of the army was not tested." Brockway thought that Hooker seemed to be a fighter, but, when placed in command of an army, was no better than his predecessors–McClellan, Burnside, Pope among them–who then became timid and avoided great risks. "We are no nearer Richmond now than we were a year ago," moaned Brockway. Perhaps it would be good to let the Rebels capture Washington. Then the North would be aroused and send forward enough men to end the conflict.[3]

The remainder of the month of May was spent in camp, attending drill occasionally, mending clothes, and passing the time as best the men could. Corporal Patterson's diary reflects the monotony of camp life at this time:

May 16–Passed the day in camp doing guard duty.
    Weather cool but not unpleasant.
May 17–Attended inspection in the afternoon.
May 18–Passed the day very agreeable.
May 19–Visited M. G. Coughlain of the 143d Pa.
    Had a long walk and the weather very warm.
May 20–Remained in camp. Weather fine.
May 21–Detailed for gard [sic].
May 22–Remained in camp all day. Mended my pants.
May 23–Done my washing. Weather very warm.
May 24–Attended Baty. Inspection fore noon.
    Clothing inspection after noon.
May 25–Weather a little cooler than common.
    Attend stand in gun drill fore noon.
May 26–Moved camp about two miles to a pine grove near White Oak Church.
May 27–Pass the day in camp fixing things convenient around our tents. Signed the pay rolls.
May 28–Relieved from guard at eight o'clock a.m.
    The weather continues very warm and the ground is becoming very dry.
May 29–Remained in camp all day. Mended my pants.
    Received two months pay.
May 30–Done my washing.
    Camp life is becoming very monotonous again.
May 31–The day passed off very quiet.
    Attended battery and clothing inspection.
June 1–Remained in camp. Weather very warm.

---

[3]*Brockway letter of May 22 in the* Columbia Democrat, *June 20, 1863.*

Bust view of 1st Lieutenant Charles B. Brockway.

(USAMHI)

On May 22, Captain Richard Waterman replaced Major Matthews as commander of the Second Brigade. Earlier, on May 17, Matthews had applied for a fifteen-day leave of absence on account of ill health. The attached surgeon's certificate, signed by Surgeon M. F. Price of the 1st Pennsylvania Artillery, attested to the fact that Matthews' leg injury suffered at Antietam was bothering him again, incapacitating him for active service for at least thirty days. The army's medical director ordered Matthews to report to Surgeon R. O. Abbott in Washington.[4]

The Volunteer Division was reorganized and Battery F found itself a part of the Third Brigade, Captain Waterman commanding. The brigade now consisted of Battery F, 1st Pennsylvania, Waterman's Battery C, 1st Rhode Island, Battery C, West Virginia Light Artillery, and the 1st New Hampshire Battery.[5]

A more important change that directly affected the organization of Battery F occurred in early June. Captain Frank Amsden of Battery G had submitted his resignation; it was accepted as effective on May 25. The battery, with four guns, did not have enough men to man the entire outfit. So, General Hooker issued an order dictating that one section of Battery G would turn in its guns to the artillery depot and the remaining two guns would form a section to be temporarily attached to Battery F.[6]

Owing to some misunderstanding in the way the consolidation order was issued, the men of Battery G mutinied. Corporal Abraham Rudisill recorded that many of his comrades thought that the order, which specified that the consolidation would be temporary, was meant to be permanent. Battery G's orderly sergeant, the four acting duty sergeants, and everyone except Corporal Rudisill refused to obey the consolidation order when it was read in front of the assembled company. The evening of June 2, Major Tompkins appeared in front of the battery and directly asked the company, "Is any one present who is willing to obey Gen. Hooker's

---

[4]*Waterman's appointment is contained in Special Order #8, Volunteer Division, Artillery Reserve, May 22, 1863, copy in Ricketts Papers. On Matthews, see his May 17th request letter, Surgeon Price's May 16 letter, and Special Orders #137, Headquarters, Army of the Potomac, May 20, 1863, all contained in Matthews' service record in the National Archives.*

[5]*Special Order #13, Volunteer Division, May 27, 1863, copy in Ricketts Papers.*

[6]*Amsden's resignation was part of Special Orders #142, Army of the Potomac, May 25, 1863, copy in Ricketts Papers. Ricketts mentions the consolidation of Batteries F and G in his June 2, 1863, diary entry. See also James J. Rudisill,* The Days of Our Abraham 1811-1899 *(York, PA: The York Printing Company, 1936), 251,*

orders and go to Battery F and be obedient to Capt. Ricketts, this only 'till the new men come, not more than 60 days?" A neighboring infantry regiment surrounded the battery, the men stolidly gazing at the recalcitrants, bayonets ready to enforce the order.

Corporal Rudisill recalled:

"I at once stepped boldly to the front, at first alone. But the Infantry around us with their glittering bayonets fixed, looked solemn. So one stepped out to my side, then a third. We were ordered some ten paces to the front. Only three of us at first but not long, a fourth, and fifth joined me.

The Sergeants were now repeatedly and individually, by name asked whether they would obey, but persisting to refuse with the remaining part of the company, no one coming to the front. The Infantry guard was now ordered to advance and take charge of the men and officers, non-commissioned officers. This, however, was more than most could endure and immediately crowds came over till the sergeants only were all ordered under guard."

In all, five sergeants and thirteen privates refused to obey and were taken off to military prison. Later that day, the section of Battery G moved its camp adjacent to Battery F. Recently-promoted Lieutenant Belden Spence commanded the section.[7]

The Artillery Reserve remained in its camps around White Oak Church, awaiting the order to move. On June 3, the day when Battery G was attached, Captain Ricketts' command received new shelter tents; the old, worn ones were discarded. The next day, Ricketts received an order to "prepare for action in one hour." However, nothing happened, although the captain noticed some troops and guns moving. The batterymen had packed up camp in anticipation of a move then sadly had to pitch their tents again later in the morning.[8]

The fifth of June saw activity in the Federal front. Hearing rumors of a Confederate movement toward the Shenandoah Valley, General Hooker sent the Sixth Corps to the Rappahannock below Fredericksburg to see if any defenders were still in place. Brigadier General Albion P. Howe's Second Division laid pontoon bridges at Franklin's Crossing and crossed the river, drawing enemy fire. Battery F moved to the front on the seventh, remained in readiness if needed, but saw no action. Sixth Corps infantry

---

[7]Rudisill, Days of Our Abraham, *251-52;* Ricketts Diary, June 2, 1863; Bates, Pennsylvania Volunteers, *1:969.*

[8]Rudisill, Days of Our Abraham, *253;* Patterson Diary, June 3-4, 1863; Ricketts Diary, June 3-4, 1863.

stayed on the south side of the Rappahannock until June 13.[9]

On June 9, Lieutenant Brockway penned a letter to the *Columbia Democrat*. "This inaction is terrible," wrote the lieutenant. "The roads are good, the weather is fine, and the troops are in splendid condition, and notwithstanding their frequent reverses are anxious to advance." Grant was at Vicksburg, "yet this splendid body of men is inactive."[10]

Little did Brockway know that even as he wrote, the cavalry of both armies swirled in combat at Brandy Station. Hooker had heard rumors of Confederate troops heading toward the Valley, and even though the mounted action failed to reveal this, Union intelligence soon pieced together a rough sketch of Lee's movements, which galvanized Hooker into action.[11]

The Army of the Potomac began moving north on June 13. The men of Battery F suspected that something was up; the day before a long train of northward-bound supply wagons passed the camp. When the roads finally cleared on the thirteenth, Battery F moved out at 5:00 p.m., heading north. "The country was hilly, desolate; few houses and far between," recorded Corporal Rudisill. The bad condition of the road resulted in at least one accident. A baggage wagon turned over and fell against one of the pieces, injuring a driver. Rudisill saw more than a dozen wagons upset along the road. Battery F continued to roll forward, passing through Stafford Court House about midnight. A halt finally came at two o'clock in the morning of the fourteenth.[12]

After a rest of only three or four hours, the artillery broke camp and continued north, passing through the small village of Dumfries at 11:00 a.m. Here, the battery left the road to Alexandria and angled off on a road leading northwest. "Still very few houses," wrote Corporal Rudisill, "very extensive and gloomy forrest, dense with under brush. . . . The roads were mostly good; yet some places dusty, while other places were muddy; the road passing through swamps. The timber was mostly oak; passing over many miles without meeting a spring or rivulet. . . . The few houses we met were constructed poorly.[13]

---

[9]*O.R., volume 27, part 1, 140-41.*

[10]*Brockway letter of June 9 in the* Columbia Democrat, *June 20, 1863.*

[11]*Edwin C. Fishel,* The Secret War for the Union *(Boston: Houghton Mifflin Company, 1996), 428-43.*

[12]*Patterson Diary, June 12-14, 1863; Rudisill,* Days of Our Abraham, *263; Ricketts Diary, June 13, 1863.*

[13]*Rudisill,* Days of Our Abraham, *263; Patterson Diary, June 14, 1863.*

The men were treated to occasional views of the mighty Potomac River off in the distance to their right, whenever they crested a hill. At sunset, the battery halted near a creek, beyond which was a high hill. Finally, the battery rolled through the creek and up the muddy road in the darkness. The men expected a halt, but the brigade continued on. The artillerists became fatigued; Corporal Rudisill fell down a number of times and barely escaped being run over. The battery forded the Occoquan River just before daybreak, then halted at four o'clock in the morning of the fifteenth, having marched for twenty-three hours.[14]

After a four-hour halt, the battery again moved on. This time the march was brief; three hours brought Battery F to Fairfax Court House. Captain Ricketts moved his men and guns to a "large beautiful orchard" half a mile from the village. Here the battery would remain for ten days while the cavalry of both armies jockeyed for position and fought each other to the west, struggling for control of the passes through the Bull Run Mountains. Changes to the Third Volunteer Brigade also took place during this time. At some unspecified date, Captain Waterman had been succeeded in brigade command by Captain Frederick M. Edgell of the 1st New Hampshire Battery. While encamped at Fairfax, Waterman's battery was transferred to the Artillery Brigade of the Sixth Corps. Battery H, 1st Ohio, was sent from the First Volunteer Brigade to the Third. By seniority, Captain James F. Huntington of Battery H assumed brigade command.[15]

While Battery F remained in camp at Fairfax, Captain Ricketts spent part of the time as a member of a general court martial. A heavy afternoon thunder shower on June 18 was noteworthy–it was the first substantial rain the battery had experienced in a month. The men could hear cannonading to the west as the cavalry battles of Aldie, Middleburg, and Upperville took place. Some strolled through the village to while away spare time, while most soldiers took joy in obtaining mail from home. Still others foraged in the vicinity.[16]

---

[14]Rudisill, Days of Our Abraham, 263-64; Patterson Diary, June 14-15, 1863; Ricketts Diary, June 14-15, 1863.

[15]Rudisill. Days of Our Abraham, 264; Patterson Diary, June 15, 1863; Ricketts Diary, June 15, 1863. For the transfer of Waterman's battery, see Orders #101, Artillery Reserve, June 18, 1863. Edgell was brigade commander at this time, having replaced Waterman at some previous date. Huntington was brigade commander at Gettysburg, and it is assumed that he replaced Edgell when his battery was transferred to the Third Brigade. The brigade then consisted of the 1st New Hampshire Battery, Battery H, 1st Ohio, Batteries F&G, 1st Pennsylvania, and Battery C, West Virginia Light Artillery.

[16]Ricketts Diary, June 16-24, 1862; Patterson Diary, June 16-24, 1863; Rudisill, Days of Our Abraham, 264-69.

Rumors that Lee's army was in Pennsylvania also floated through the ranks, causing much anxiety to Keystone State men in blue. Scores of prisoners captured in the cavalry fighting passed by on their way to prison camps. Corporal Rudisill remarked that they were a "hard looking crowd, looking like a set of real desperadoes; no soldier's dress about them; clothed in a kind of gray and red, dirty looking Kentucky jean; broad brim hats of all kinds and colors. They looked like a mean, wicked set of rascals. Perhaps more so than any I ever saw before."[17]

The bulk of the Army of the Potomac began moving on Thursday, June 26. The Artillery Reserve followed long lines of infantry away from the vicinity of Fairfax Court House, heading toward the Potomac River. Moving via Dranesville, the artillery reached Edwards Ferry, only to have to wait while the Second, Fifth, and Twelfth Corps all crossed the river. By sunset, rain had set in and continued hard most of the next day (June 27), when Battery F crossed the river and managed to reach Frederick, thirty miles away, at nine that evening.[18]

Sunday, June 28 was a day of rest for Battery F. Most of the army was in the Frederick area while the cavalry ranged ahead, searching for Lee's Confederates. Some of the artillerists received passes to visit the city, while Captain Ricketts, accompanied by Freeman McGilvery (commander of the First Volunteer Brigade) went into the city and dined at the Dill House. The day was also the first for General Meade, who replaced Hooker as army commander by order of the War Department. Hooker had complained about lack of support and offered his resignation, which the administration accepted. Before leaving the army, Hooker briefed his replacement on the state of affairs as he then understood them.[19]

Meade immediately set the army in motion to check the Confederate advance. June twenty-ninth saw the Artillery Reserve moved from Frederick, via Walkerville and Woodborough to Bruceville, a distance of about twenty miles. On the last day of the month, the artillery moved north to Taneytown, site of Meade's headquarters, a short ten mile march. Here, after going into camp, the batteries were mustered for pay. Ricketts' battery count totaled three officers and 162 men.[20]

---

[17]Rudisill, Days of Our Abraham, 265-67.

[18]Ricketts Diary, June 26-27, 1963; Patterson Diary, June 26-27, 1863.

[19]Ricketts Diary, June 28, 1863; Patterson Diary, June 28, 1863.

[20]Ricketts Diary, June 29-30, 1863; Patterson Diary, June 29-30, 1863; John W. Busey and David W. Martin, Regimental Strengths and Losses at Gettysburg (Hightstown, NJ: Longstreet House, 1986), 116.

July 1 found Batteries F&G at Taneytown, awaiting developments. General Meade, thinking that his rapid advance to the Pennsylvania border had deterred Lee from moving father into Pennsylvania, wanted to fight a defensive battle behind Pipe Creek, a tributary of the Monocacy River. His engineer officers had surveyed the proposed line and decided that a Confederate attack could easily be repelled; the line also covered Washington and Baltimore.

But as the day wore on, reports began to come in to army headquarters with information about fighting near Gettysburg. Brigadier General John Buford's First Cavalry Division had occupied the town and then, on the morning of July 1, began fighting with infantry from Henry Heth's Division of A. P. Hill's Third Corps, Army of Northern Virginia. General Reynolds hurried the First Corps to Gettysburg, followed by Howard's Eleventh. Reynolds was killed early in the action and Doubleday succeeded him in corps command. By late afternoon, troops from two Confederate corps arrived on the field and drove the outnumbered Yankees onto the heights south of Gettysburg. Meade sent Major General Winfield S. Hancock, commanding the Second Corps, to the battlefield as his representative. Based on Hancock's analysis of the situation and favorable terrain report, Meade decided to concentrate the Army of the Potomac at Gettysburg and fight there.

General Tyler received orders late in the day to take two brigades of the Artillery Reserve and report to Hancock. On the morning of July 2, Lieutenant Colonel Freeman McGilvery, commanding the First Volunteer Brigade, led the remaining units of the reserve to the battlefield. Captain Huntington's Third Brigade arrived shortly before noon and joined the remainder of the reserve, parked in several fields east of the Taneytown Road.[21]

While the artillery waited for the action to open, the rest of the Army of the Potomac assembled on the field. The Twelfth Corps was positioned on Culp's Hill, anchoring the army's right flank. The Eleventh Corps was concentrated on Cemetery Hill, with the First Corps divided–Wadsworth's remnants occupied the left of the line on Culp's Hill, Doubleday's and Robinson's divisions were held in reserve behind Cemetery Hill. Hancock's Second Corps extended the line southward from Cemetery Hill along the ridge of the same name, with Major General Daniel E. Sickles' Third Corps on Hancock's left. The Fifth Corps, now led by Major General George Sykes, was held in reserve, and Sedgwick's Sixth Corps was en route to the field from Manchester, Maryland, more than thirty miles away.

---

[21]*O.R., volume 27, part 1, 872, 894.*

General Lee's battle plan called for Longstreet's First Corps to assail the Union left while Richard Ewell would use his Second Corps to attack Meade's right and pin down the troops there. Hill, in the center, would assist Longstreet and attack the center if the opportunity arose. Longstreet finally managed to place his two available divisions in position and the attack started at 4:00 p.m.

When Ewell heard Longstreet's cannon on the far left, he sent Major Joseph W. Latimer's battalion of artillery into position on Benner's Hill. Latimer's eighteen guns opened fire on Union positions on Culp's and Cemetery hills. Union batteries on Cemetery Hill returned fire. These batteries were from both the First and Eleventh Corps, and those that replied to Latimer were generally under the supervision of Colonel Wainwright, and included Captain Cooper's Battery B, 1st Pennsylvania, Captain Michael Wiedrich's Battery I, 1st New York, Lieutenant George Breck's Battery L, 1st New York, and Lieutenant Edward Whittier's 5th Maine Battery, the latter positioned on Stevens' Knoll midway between Cemetery and Culp's Hills. The weight of the thirteen Federal 3-inch ordnance rifles finally overwhelmed Latimer and his battered guns were withdrawn after suffering severe losses, including the mortal wounding of Major Latimer.[22]

About 4:00 p.m., during the height of the artillery duel, Captain Huntington received an order to send a battery to Wainwright in case it was needed. Huntington instructed Captain Ricketts to move his battery toward Cemetery Hill. Batteries F&G moved forward in splendid order, so much so that Brigadier General Adelbert Ames, commanding the First Division of the Eleventh Corps, asked Colonel Wainwright what Regular Army battery it was, "which tickled Ricketts greatly." The Pennsylvanians halted on the reverse slope of the hill to await further orders. While here, Captain Ricketts recognized the wounded Lieutenant Chandler P. Eakin (Battery H, 1st United States) being brought back from the front. Ricketts was assisting the wounded officer into an ambulance when the order came to move forward.[23]

---

[22]Harry W. Pfanz, Gettysburg–Culp's Hill & Cemetery Hill *(Chapel Hill: University of North Carolina Press, 1993), 168-89.*

[23]*Nevins,* Diary of Battle, *245. Colonel Wainwright wrote that "Ricketts had everything in very beautiful order, and came up the road as if moving onto a parade ground." Ricketts mentioned helping Lieutenant Eakin in his letter of December 3, 1883, to John B. Bachelder, in David & Audrey Ladd (editors),* The Bachelder Papers, *3 volumes (Dayton: Morningside House, 1994-1995), 2:80-81.*

Edwin Forbes Sketch.
Federal Battery Teams in Evergreen Cemetery. Ricketts' battery position's in front of The Cemetery Gatehouse. A sign posted in front of Gatehouse reads: No guns allowed in Cemetery.

(GETTYSBURG NATIONAL MILITARY PARK, GETTYSBURG, PA)

Sketch of Evergreen Cemetery Gatehouse and batteries posted near and around East Cemetery Hill. Ricketts' position is in front of The Gatehouse.

(GETTYSBURG NATIONAL MILITARY PARK, GETTYSBURG, PA)

Ricketts was ordered to report to Colonel Wainwright for duty. Wainwright sent Ricketts into position across the Baltimore Pike, several rods in front of the gate house. Captain Cooper's Battery B, 1st Pennsylvania, had occupied this position during the previous evening and throughout the day, taking part in the artillery fight with Latimer's Battalion. One of Cooper's guns had been disabled, and, together with the losses sustained on July 1 and heavy expenditure of ammunition on the second, meant that the battery was ready to go to the rear for resupplying.[24]

Ricketts noticed that Cooper's men had thrown up some shallow lunettes to protect the artillery crews, "but as the muzzles of the guns had full play over them, the protection they afforded was of course small." Since Ricketts brought six guns onto the hill, two of his guns were left without any cover at all; Ricketts later wrote that his men did "no digging, nor entrenching of any kind." To Battery F's left was Wiedrich's Battery I, 1st New York, separated from the Pennsylvanians by a low stone wall. Battery L, 1st New York, Lieutenant Breck commanding, was in line to Ricketts' right, farther down the hill.[25]

Captain Ricketts was aware that his battery was placed in an important position. To his front, deployed along a stone wall, was a line of infantry regiments from Ames' division of the Eleventh Corps; more Eleventh Corps units were in position to Ricketts' left and rear, protecting the vital crest of Cemetery Hill. More artillery batteries were in line in front of the Evergreen Cemetery, facing both Gettysburg and the Confederate line on Seminary Ridge. Shortly after Batteries F&G went into position, Colonel Wainwright rode up and said to the captain, "If a charge is made on this point you will not limber up and leave under any circumstances, but fight your battery as long as you can." Ricketts quickly repeated this order to his section officers–Lieutenants Brockway and Spence, and Sergeant Snider–who in turn echoed Wainwright's sentiments to their section members.[26]

About an hour after taking position, Ricketts saw a Confederate line of battle form on Benner's Hill and move forward. This was Major General

---

[24]*Ricketts to Bachelder, March 2, 1866, in Ladd, Bachelder Papers, 1:235.*

[25]*Ricketts to Winfield S. Hancock, December 28, 1885, in Ladd,* Bachelder Papers, *2:1172-73.*

[26]*John P. Nicholson (editor),* Pennsylvania at Gettysburg: Ceremonies at the Dedication of the Monuments Erected by the Commonwealth of Pennsylvania to Mark the Positions of the Pennsylvania Commands Engaged in the Battle, *2 volumes (Harrisburg: E. K. Meyers, State Printer, 1893), 2:898.*

Edward Johnson's Division of Ewell's Corps, moving to attack Culp's Hill. "We opened on them as soon as they appeared on the hill and continued to fire as they advanced down the hill to Rock Creek and into the woods at the foot of Culp's Hill. When they got into the woods . . . our fire was guided by the smoke of the musketry fire rising above the trees." Brockway thought that the battery's accurate fire broke up Johnson's formation, compelling some of the enemy infantry to make a longer circuit to the left to avoid the Yankee artillery fire.[27]

While firing on Johnson's attack, some of the Union gunners noticed movement to their front. This movement was made by two brigades of Jubal Early's Division, which now launched an assault on Cemetery Hill. The two brigades–Brigadier General Harry T. Hays' five Louisiana regiments and Colonel Isaac E. Avery's three regiments of North Carolinians—had been positioned in the low ravine through which Winebrenner's Run flowed, just to the southeast of town. Ewell's Second Corps was to support Longstreet's attack on the Federal left by demonstrating against Meade's right to prevent reinforcements from helping the left. Johnson was to attack first. When noise of the battle on Culp's Hill reached Early's ears, he was to send his division against Cemetery Hill, followed by Robert Rodes' Division on his right. Unfortunately, Early had only half of his division immediately available for the attack. Brigadier General William Smith's Virginians were guarding the York Road to prevent any attack on the army's left rear, while John B. Gordon's Georgia brigade moved up to support Hays and Avery; Gordon went into line over a quarter of a mile to the rear, close enough to support the attack, but also within range to support Smith if that brigade was attacked.[28]

Early's attack began as darkness began to fall. Early himself rode to General Hays, who would command both brigades, and asked him if his troops were ready. After Hays assured Early that his men were ready, Early told his subordinate to advance and "carry the works on the height in their front." Hays' five regiments (5th, 6th, 7th, 8th, and 9th Louisiana) and Avery's three (6th, 21st, 57th North Carolina) together totaled slightly more than two thousand officers and men, were arrayed with Hays on the right and Avery on the left.[29]

---

[27]Ibid., *897; Brockway to David Conaughy, March 5, 1864, in Peter F. Rothermel Papers, Pennsylvania State Archives.*

[28]*Pfanz,* Gettysburg, *235.*

[29]Ibid., *235-37.*

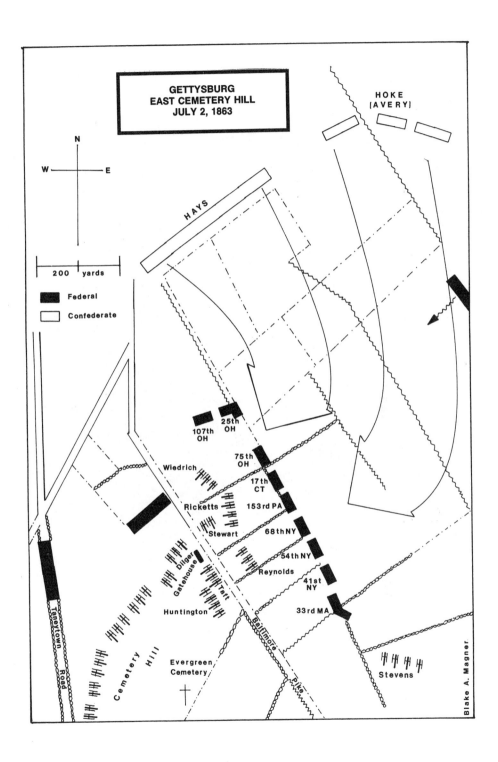

The assult of Hays' brigade on East Cemetery Hill. Sketch by Edwin Forbes.
(GETTYSBURG NATIONAL MILITARY PARK, GETTYSBURG, PA)

To reach the Union line atop the hill, the Confederate line of battle at first moved ahead out of the ravine and marched to the southeast. Hays' right flank, moving along the Brickyard Lane that ran along the base of Cemetery Hill, encountered the refused left flank of the Eleventh Corps infantry deployed along this dirt road. As the left flank of Hays' battle line advanced, it changed direction and curved to the south, heading for the Union infantry and the batteries deployed on the crest of the hill. Avery's three Tarheel regiments had farther to go and moved into the open meadows of the Culp farm before changing direction to strike the batteries atop the hill.[30]

Union skirmishers from several regiments contended with the Rebel advance before retreating to the main line of infantry. The 5th Maine Battery, deployed on a knoll between Cemetery and Culp's Hills, opened a raking fire on the enemy infantry as they moved across the battery's front, heading for Cemetery Hill. Lieutenant Brockway saw the enemy as they approached. The Pennsylvanians at first thought that the attack was aimed at Wadsworth's position on Culp's Hill, but when the enemy (Avery's units) reached a cornfield in front, they changed direction and came straight at Cemetery Hill. Although it was dusk, wrote Brockway, the oncoming enemy could still be seen.[31]

"At their first appearance we threw in their midst shrapnel and solid shot; but when they charged we used single and finally double rounds of canister," recalled Brockway. Isaac Seymour, General Hays' adjutant, recalled that the Union artillery barrage generally went over their heads because the Rebel infantry was moving pretty fast as they charged the hill. R. J. Hancock of the 9th Louisiana thought the brigade would have been annihilated if the attack had started before dark. "As it was, " he wrote, "the enemy's cannon lighted up the heavens but most of the charges they shot over us but even at that we suffered terribly."[32]

As the Rebels came on up the hill, they crashed into the Union infantry in front of the batteries. Captain Ricketts, after the war, was overly critical of their performance. Their conduct was "cowardly and disgraceful in the extreme," penned Ricketts. "As soon as the charge commenced, they, although they had a stone-wall in their front, commenced running in the

---

[30] Ibid., *250-52.*

[31] Ibid., *253-54; Brockway letter of March 5, 1864.*

[32] *Brockway letter of March 5, 1864; Isaac Seymour Journal, William D. Clements Library, University of Michigan; R. J. Hancock to John Warwick Daniel, January 20, 1904, John W. Daniel Papers, University of Virginia.*

Pencil and wash drawing by Alfred A. Waud showing the 5th Maine Battery in foreground, Batteries F&G in center distance, during Confederate attack on July 2, 1863.

(LIBRARY OF CONGRESS)

Woodcut showing the fighting on East Cemetery Hill.

(CHESTER SIEGEL)

greatest confusion to the rear, hardly a shot was fired, certainly not a volley, and so panic stricken were they that several ran into the canister fire on my guns and were knocked over." Lieutenant Brockway, writing in 1864, also recalled that the infantry left their position at the first volley.[33]

Although it is true that some of the supporting infantry fled, many stayed at their posts and fought the enemy hand-to-hand before falling back to reform at the hill's crest. Hays' Louisianians crashed into the left flank of Colonel Andrew L. Harris' Second Brigade of Ames' First Division. The attack was so spirited that Harris' Ohioans on the left fell back, exposing the flank of Wiedrich's battery. Confederates from both brigades struck Ames' First Brigade, led by Colonel Leopold von Gilsa, head on, forcing back most of the thin line deployed behind the stonewall at the base of the hill. Although the 17th Connecticut and 75th Ohio remained in position, they were isolated by the savage Confederate attack. Avery's men punched through the line and drove back the 153rd Pennsylvania and 54th and 68th New York regiments, and forced the 41st New York to refuse its left flank to prevent being outflanked.[34]

By this time, Avery's brigade had lost all semblance of order. Colonel Avery himself was mortally wounded shortly after he gave orders to the brigade to wheel to the right and charge the hill. The hectic rush forward and clash with Union infantry had disorganized the Tarheel regiments. This, plus the growing darkness, meant that regimental commanders were unable to bring order out of chaos. Union artillery contributed to the chaos, spraying shell and canister over the battlefield. In addition to Wiedrich's and Ricketts' batteries, Breck's and Whittier's also fired on Early's men, slowing down the attack and disordering the oncoming enemy. Colonel Wainwright, watching from the crest of Cemetery Hill, thought that the artillery fire was "one continual shower straight down the hill." Continued Wainwright: "The night was heavy, and the smoke lay so thick that you could not see ten yards ahead; seventeen guns vomiting it as fast as they can will make a good deal of smoke."[35]

When the Ohio regiments at the left end of the line were swamped and retreated, several of Hays' men charged into Wiedrich's battery. The cannoneers met them with handspikes, rammers, pistols, and stones. A particularly nasty fight developed, with the Yankee artillerists aided by

---

[33]*Ricketts to Bachelder, March 2, 1866, in Ladd,* Bachelder Papers, *1:235-36; Brockway letter of March 5, 1864.*

[34]*Pfanz, Gettysburg, 256-62.*

[35]*Nevins,* Diary of Battle, *245; Pfanz,* Gettysburg, *258-60.*

reinforcements from Major General Carl Schurz' Third Division of the Eleventh Corps. Schurz himself directed the reinforcements from his command, and they materially assisted in driving back the Louisianians from the New York battery. The fight among Wiedrich's guns, and the fact that a number of "Tigers" moved to the left to attack Ricketts' left section, led Lieutenant Brockway to believe that Wiedrich's guns had been withdrawn, leaving the left flank of Batteries F&G exposed to attack.[36]

Lieutenant Brockway, commanding the center section, wrote that the enemy charged the left section of Batteries F&G, spiking the left gun after rendering hors de combat its entire crew. "Some of the drivers were bayonetted on their horses. Still our men stood at their posts, the officers and drivers supplying the places of those who had fallen," wrote Brockway. "Our canister failing, 'rotten shot' was used, that is shrapnell without fuse, the shell bursting at the muzzle of the gun." Oney F. Sweet, a crew member of the left gun, could see the enemy infantry approaching in the darkness only by the flashes of their muskets as they opened fire on the battery.[37] It was at this moment in the battle that the very well liked Sergeant Myron French fell mortally wounded while he was in the act of reloading his gun.

Continued Brockway:

A Rebel First Lieutenant attempted to seize our battery guidon, which was planted in one of the central earth-works, but while in the act of grasping it, the bearer James H. Riggin, rode up and with his revolver shot the officer through the body. Seizing the colors he wheeled his horse, but at the same moment was shot himself, and died soon after. A serg't of the 'Tigers' got clear back to the limbers, and there caught Riggin's horse, and picked up the fallen colors. While leading back the horse he was encountered by Serg't. [Richard S.] Stratford, who, unable to recognize him in the dark, demanded to know 'where he was going with that horse.' The rebel brought his musket to his shoulder and demanded Stratford's surrender. At this moment I walked up, and a glance showed me the true state of affairs. Having no side arms by me, I picked up a stone, and in a most unmilitary manner broke the

---

[36] *Brockway letter of March 5, 1864; Pfanz,* Gettysburg, *263, 269, 272-73.*

[37] *Brockway letter of March 5, 1864; Oney F. Sweet, "Ricketts's Battery,"* National Tribune, *April 29, 1909. All three men taken prisoner were at the left gun. Corporal Thurston, wounded that evening, escaped capture by lying down on the ground between the cannon and the small lunette to its front. See Thurston, "A Ricketts Batteryman Support's Carroll's Brigade Claim,"* National Tribune, *October 13, 1892. R. M. Stocker,* Centennial History of Susquehanna County, Pa., *264.*

Death of James H. Riggin at Gettysburg.

(CHESTER SIEGEL)

fellow's head. He tumbled to the ground, but Stratford, not knowing the cause, seized his musket and shot him in the abdomen. Fearing he had missed him in the darkness, he clubbed the musket, and broke the fellow's arm whereupon he asked for 'quarter,' which was of course given. I don't think he lived long.

The scene was now one of wildest confusion. Friends and foes were indiscriminately mixed, and our brave men, though outnumbered and without arms, by means of hand-spikes, rammers, stones, etc. made a sturdy resistance, animating each other with shouts and cries, 'to conquer on the soil of our native State, or perish.'[38]

Captain Ricketts admired the resistance his men made to the enemy charge. The captain recalled the scene with Stratford, Brockway, and the enemy soldier, and remembered that he grabbed Stratford's gun and prevented the downed Rebel from being clubbed yet again. When Riggin was shot, he fell from his horse, apparently, got up, and saw Captain Ricketts, crying "help me captain" as he staggered against Ricketts. "The sleeve of the right arm of my coat was covered with the brave fellow's blood," said Ricketts. A bullet had cut the guidon staff in two and then hit Riggin in the stomach, the wound proving mortal.[39]

In addition to the flank attack of the Tigers, perhaps 75 Tarheels charged into the battery from the front, fighting hand-to-hand with the cannoneers. The weight of the Rebel attack began to drive the Pennsylvanians from their guns. Lieutenant Brockway admitted that his men were driven back for a moment, but, just then, help arrived.[40]

When the Confederate attack began, General Howard, watching from his headquarters post on Cemetery Hill, realized that his corps would need assistance. The general immediately dispatched an aide to locate General Hancock and request help. Hancock, already hearing the noise from the attack, ordered Brigadier General John Gibbon, now commanding the Second Corps, to send a brigade to Howard. Gibbon, or Hancock himself, depending on the source, recommended Colonel Samuel S. Carroll's brigade be sent.[41]

---

[38]*Brockway letter of March 5, 1864.*

[39]*Nicholson,* Pennsylvania at Gettysburg, *2: 898; Ricketts to Bachelder, March 2, 1866, in Ladd,* Bachelder Papers, *1:238.*

[40]*Brockway letter of March 5, 1864.*

[41]*See O.R., volume 27, part 1, 372, 707, for Hancock's and Howard's reports of the battle and the dispatch of Carroll's brigade.*

Colonel Carroll was in charge of the First Brigade, Third Division, Second Corps. His four regiments included the 14th Indiana, 4th and 8th Ohio, and 7th West Virginia, all veteran units. The 8th Ohio was deployed as skirmishers facing the Bliss farm area between Cemetery and Seminary ridges, leaving Carroll with three regiments. As soon as he received his orders, Carroll directed his veterans toward the sounds of the firing on Cemetery Hill. Led by the 14th Indiana, the Federals arrived just as Rebel infantry swarmed into Ricketts' battery. "Owing to the artillery fire from our own guns, it was impossible to advance by a longer front than that of a regiment, and it being perfectly dark, and with no guide, I had to find the enemy's line entirely by their fire." wrote Carroll.[42]

Brockway recalled that Carroll's brigade passed by the battery's right flank "and poured such a murderous fire in the enemy's flank that they fled precipitately." The men returned to their guns and gave the fleeing enemy a round of double-shotted canister. Lieutenant Colonel E. H. C. Caines of the 14th Indiana, leading the brigade, heard one of Ricketts' men ask what regiment it was. When the answer was the 14th Indiana, the Pennsylvanian exclaimed, "Glory to God. We are saved." The Hoosiers crossed the Baltimore Pike just south of the gate house, and could see the fighting in Ricketts' battery. The 14th charged into the battery and fired at least two volleys before the Rebels fell back down the hill. The 14th's color bearer was killed and the regiment suffered other casualties as it drove forward into the retreating enemy.[43]

As the 14th Indiana cleared the enemy from the area around Ricketts' battery, the 4th Ohio angled down the hill, sweeping the retreating Tarheels in front of them, capturing the colonel, major, and colors of the 21st North Carolina. Meanwhile the 7th West Virginia faced to the north and drove a few of the enemy soldiers from behind the stonewall near Wiedrich's battery. Colonel Wainwright passed an order along the line for the artillery to cease firing, partly to allow the heavy, acrid smoke to clear, and partly

---

[42]O.R., *volume 27, part 1, 457;* Pfanz, *Gettysburg, 263-68*

[43]*Brockway letter of March 5, 1864;* E. H. C. Caines, *"A Gettysburg Diary. Carroll's Brigade and the Part It Played in Repulsing the 'Tigers',"* National Tribune, *December 23, 1909;* Gary G. Lash, The Gibraltar Brigade on East Cemetery Hill *(Baltimore: Butternut & Blue, 1995), 83-87.*

Captain David E. Beem remembered the arrival of the 14th Indiana somewhat differently. He said that one of the artillerymen called out to ask the regiment's identity. Upon hearing the reply, the artillerist cried, "God bless the 14th Indiana." Beem manuscript entitled "The Battle of Gettysburg," a speech given in ca. 1897, Beem Papers, Indiana Historical Library.

Sergeant Myron French, killed at Gettysburg.

(SUSQUEHANNA COUNTY HISTORICAL SOCIETY)

on request of one of Carroll's officers, who informed the colonel that the brigade was moving forward down the hill in front of the cannon. Indeed, Carroll's regiments moved down the hill and stopped at the stonewall, capturing perhaps a hundred prisoners and trading shots with the retreating Southerners. Hays' men had also been driven from Wiedrich's guns by Eleventh Corps regiments, and the fighting was now generally over on Cemetery Hill.[44]

That night, Ricketts opened his pocket diary and penned the day's action:

Marched to Gettysburg–distance 13 miles. Ordered into position at 4 P.M. on Cemetery Hill under heavy art[illery] fire. Heavy art[illery] fighting until dusk. My bat[tery] charged by Gen. Early's Div. just at dusk punishing them terribly with our cannister. They took my left gun, spiked it. Killed 6 men, wounded 11, & took 3 prisoners. The boys fought them hand to hand with pistols, handspikes & rammers.[45]

Carroll's three regiments remained in position on Cemetery Hill throughout the rest of the battle. That night, Batteries F&G also stayed atop the hill, the men resting after resupplying the battery's depleted stock of ammunition. Ricketts wrote later in his report that the battery's six cannon had expended every round of canister available; the gunners then fired case shot without fuses, so that the shells burst the moment they emerged from the barrels. Over the next couple of days, officers of Carroll's brigade told Ricketts of the havoc his battery had caused to their attackers. Colonel John Coons of the 14th Indiana told the captain that one canister discharge killed fifteen men, including a lieutenant colonel, a major, and two lieutenants. Six captains also lay dead in one line farther down the hill. The colonel also took the occasion to present Ricketts with a sword captured from a major wounded by the battery's canister fire.[46]

---

[44]*Lash*, Gibraltar Brigade, *87-94;* Nevins, Diary of Battle, *246.* Lash's book examines the post-battle controversy that erupted between members of Carroll's brigade and the Eleventh Corps. Arguments centered on how much fighting Carroll's men did and whether or not they were instrumental in driving the enemy from Cemetery Hill. Eleventh Corps veterans believed that Carroll's men claimed too much credit and belittled Howard's contributions, while Carroll's veterans claimed that their attack was key to holding the hill.

[45]*Ricketts Diary, July 2, 1863.* The prisoners–Francis Neid, Oscar G. Larrabee, and John M. Given–were all captured at the left gun. See Nicholson, Pennsylvania at Gettysburg, *2:898,* for the names of the captured men. Nicholson used Lanabee rather than Larrabee, and spelled "Neid" rather than "Need" as listed on the battery roster.

[46]*Ricketts Diary, July 4-5, 1863;* O.R., *volume 27, part 1, 894.*

The men of Batteries F&G, or at least those who were sleeping, were suddenly awakened about 4:00 a.m. on July 3 when massed Union artillery deployed along the Baltimore Pike opened a heavy fire on the Confederate brigades on the east slope of Culp's Hill. General Slocum had been reinforced during the night by some Sixth Corps units and the return of Geary's division. After a brief bombardment, Johnson's Confederates began a series of attacks on the Federals, only to be repelled each time. By eight o'clock, the Federals had regained their line of breastworks and Johnson's men had begun to retreat out of rifle range, ending the contest for Culp's Hill. Colonel Wainwright could scarcely believe that such a roar could continue. Lieutenant Brockway wrote that "it was a sullen, deadly roar, without a stop or break." Captain Huntington, commanding the artillery brigade, claimed that the noise was enough to waken the "seven sleepers."[47]

Awakened, Huntington surveyed his batteries. He suggested to Ricketts that Batteries F&G be withdrawn because of the severe loss incurred last evening. "But Ricketts, who was a plucky fellow, preferred to see the thing out and at his urgent request I consented that he should remain on the front line."[48]

Then, at one o'clock, Confederate artillery opened fire in the massed bombardment preceding the Pickett-Pettigrew assault on the Federal center. Brockway recalled that Batteries F&G were in an "unfortunate position," being completely enfiladed by some of the opposing batteries. Brockway's section, acting on Colonel Wainwright's orders, was pulled out of line and repositioned behind the stonewall to the left in an effort to reply to the guns on Seminary Ridge. The remaining four guns opened fire on Rebel guns across Rock Creek. "The rapid diminution of our ammunition however soon caused us to cease firing, while we were directed to watch the town closely from which we expected an attack," recalled Brockway. Sharpshooters occasionally annoyed the artillerists. Finally, the artillerists turned one of the guns and fired several shots at a house in town, and succeeded in dislodging the enemy.[49]

---

[47]*Nevins, Diary of Battle, 248;* Brockway letter of March 5, 1864; James F. Huntington, "Notes of Service with a Light Artillery at Chancellorsville and Gettysburg," James Barnett Papers, Western Reserve Historical Society.

[48]Huntington, "Notes of Service."

[49]*Nevins, Diary of Battle, 249;* Brockway letter of March 5, 1864. Corporal L. Eugene C. Moore recalled that Sergeant Frank Brockway fired the gun that silenced the enemy sharpshooter. See Moore's article in the *National Tribune, August 5, 1909.*

Pencil and wash drawing by Alfred A. Waud showing the fighting at Batteries F&G on East Cemetery Hill.

(LIBRARY OF CONGRESS)

Later in the day the men received word of the repulse of Pickett's Charge, many feeling that this was the enemy's last effort on the battlefield. Saturday, July 4, brought gloom and then heavy rain. Both armies remained in position during the day, tired and worn out from three days of fighting. Ricketts tallied his battery's loss as six killed, fourteen wounded, and three captured. Twenty horses had been killed, and the battery expended twelve hundred rounds of ammunition. The gun that had been spiked on July 2 was repaired and ready for service the next day.[50]

That evening, Lee's army began to retreat through the South Mountain passes, heading for Williamsport and the Potomac River crossings there. Union pickets had already occupied the town of Gettysburg when the Rebels withdrew to Seminary Ridge on the fourth, and then, early on the morning of the fifth, advanced to report that the enemy had disappeared from their front. The battle was over and Meade's Army of the Potomac, though battered with twenty-three thousand casualties, had fended off Lee's army and forced the great Southern captain to withdraw.

Batteries F&G were relieved from the position on Cemetery Hill sometime around 4:00 p.m. on July 5. The Artillery Reserve was concentrated behind the lines and began moving south to Littlestown, about ten miles from Gettysburg. Here, the batteries went into camp about ten o'clock that night, then remained encamped throughout the sixth. Captain Ricketts recorded in his diary that the battery horses were now completely "used up." They had not been unharnessed since the morning of July 2 and had gone most of that time without proper food and water. Thus, July 6 was a day of rest and refurbishing, especially for the surviving horses, in spite of an all night rain on the 5th and showers throughout the day on July 6.[51]

On July 7, the Artillery Reserve moved twenty-five miles to Woodborough, Maryland. Corporal Rudisill wrote that the battery was up at three in the morning and then endured a hard day's march through rain and mud. The rain continued "very hard" in the morning of July 8 as the battery trudged along for ten miles to encamp a mile from Frederick in mid-afternoon. On the ninth, Batteries F&G moved west, crossing South Mountain to Boonsboro, an eighteen mile trek. The next day, Batteries F&G moved through the small village and went into camp on the opposite side of Boonsboro. The weather was now warm, but military operations

---

[50]*Ricketts Diary, July 4, 1863;* O.R., *volume 27, part 1, 895; Brockway letter of March 5, 1864. Brockway recorded the battery loss as nine killed, fourteen wounded, and three missing, with forty horses slain.*

[51]*Ricketts Diary, July 5-6, 1863; Patterson Diary, July 5-6, 1863.*

continued as Lee entrenched his army to cover Williamsport while waiting for the rain-swollen Potomac River to go down to enable his men to cross. July 11 found Ricketts' command moving three miles to Funkstown.[52]

On July 12, Ricketts received orders that detached his command from the Artillery Reserve and assigned him to the Artillery Brigade of the Second Corps. Ricketts was ordered to report immediately to that corps and Batteries F&G left camp at 3:00 p.m. and moved six miles to the front, taking up a position to cover the Williamsport Road. "Rained furiously during the whole of our march," wrote William Patterson. Monday, July 13, saw the six cannon still in position while the supporting infantry entrenched. "Everybody wonders why Meade does not attack," penned Ricketts in his diary. Indeed, Meade wished to attack, but his corps commanders, sensing the strength of the enemy entrenchments, hesitated. A council of war on the night of July 12 decided not to attack. On the thirteenth, Meade's troops reconnoitered and the general overruled his subordinates and scheduled an attack for July 14. However, when Meade's skirmishers went forward, they found the strong entrenchments empty. That night, Lee had gotten pontoon bridges in position and crossed the army back to Virginia. Union cavalry attacked and bloodied Heth's Division, the rearguard, but the pursuit ended on the banks of the Potomac.[53]

Disappointed, Meade nevertheless moved the Army of the Potomac forward after Lee. Ricketts' battery broke camp at 5:00 a.m. on July 15 and moved twenty-seven miles to near Harper's Ferry before going into camp at eight that evening, having passed through Sharpsburg en route. On the 16, the battery moved only seven miles, encamping near Sandy Hook, on the north bank of the river east of Harper's Ferry. Friday, July 17 saw a day of rain while the battery remained in camp. Ricketts had the battery in motion by seven o'clock the next morning, crossing the Potomac at Harper's Ferry.[54]

Lee's army was near Bunker Hill as the Army of the Potomac crossed its namesake river. Meade moved the army southeast, into the Loudoun Valley, keeping between Lee and Washington. Lee had intended to occupy this same valley, but the flooded Shenandoah River prevented him from doing so before Meade took the initiative and brought his troops into the valley. Lee thereupon decided to retreat and sent his advance corps under

---

[52]*Ricketts Diary, July 7-14, 1863; Patterson diary, July 7-11, 1863; Rudisill,* Days of Our Abraham, *275.*

[53]*Ricketts Diary, July 12-14, 1863; Patterson Diary, July 12-14, 1863.*

[54]*Ricketts Diary, July 15-17, 1863; Patterson Diary, July 15-17, 1863.*

Longstreet toward Culpeper, to stay ahead of Meade and keep open his lines of communication with Richmond. Ewell's corps had moved west in an attempt to destroy Federal troops protecting the Baltimore & Ohio Railroad west of Martinsburg, but Meade's movement forced Lee to recall Ewell as Longstreet headed toward Culpeper. The Army of Northern Virginia was strung out and in danger of being cut in two.[55]

Indeed, Meade sent the Third Corps, now under William H. French, toward Manassas and Chester gaps. French's troops struck one of Hill's brigades, later supported by some of Ewell's troops, at Chester's Gap, on July 23. In a skirmish known as Wapping Heights, French's troops pushed Hill's brigade out of Chester Gap and threatened Ewell. Behind French came the Second and Fifth Corps, but French failed to aggressively attack and Ewell fell back behind the Shenandoah River. His corps moved up along the South Fork of the Shenandoah to Luray and crossed the mountains at Thornton's Gap.[56]

Batteries F&G . . . Markham Station. Sometime after the battery halted at the station that afternoon, Brigadier General William Hays, the new temporary commander of the Second Corps, saw Sergeant Francis Snider riding near a battery cart. The general called out to his staff loud enough for Snider to hear, "There are some more of those damned wagons and carts interfering with the trains." Hays rode over to Snider, swearing and loudly proclaiming that here was another stolen battery cart with fresh beef piled on it. The sergeant had just returned from drawing rations for the battery, and was preparing to distribute the fresh meat to the battery. Hays, seeing a second cart behind Snider also piled with beef, ordered that both carts be confiscated and taken from the column. As he prepared to ride away, General Hays pointed to a cart and asked, "What cart was that?" Snider saluted the general and replied, "That is government property drawn with the battery at Washington and belonging to it."

Hays suddenly turned in his saddle, looked at Snider, and struck him across the left side of his face. "You damned son of a bitch," roared the general. "How dare you interfere with me when I give an order."

"General, have you a right to strike me," questioned the sergeant.

Hays answered, "Yes sir, I have when you dispute my orders."

Retorted Snider: "I have not done so, sir. You asked me a question and I answered it in a respectful manner. I shall test the matter as to whether you have the right to strike me."

---

[55]Andrew A. Humphreys, From Gettysburg to the Rapidan: The Army of the Potomac July, 1863, to April, 1864 *(New York: Charles Scribner's Sons, 1883), 8-9.*

[56]Ibid., *9-10.*

At this point, one of Hays' staff officers nudged Snider lightly with his whip and said, "For God's sake, say no more now. It will be the best thing for you."

Hays angrily rode off. Snider in turn reported to Captain Ricketts what had just happened. The captain ordered Snider to write down his account of the incident.

By July 25, Ricketts . . . over.[57]

---

[57]*Ricketts Diary, July 18-30, 1863; Patterson Diary, July 18-August 1, 1863.*

Chapter Seven

Autumn 1863

The beginning of August 1863 found Ricketts' battery in camp near the village of Morrisville, southeast of Warrenton, about halfway between the line of the Orange & Alexandria Railroad and Stafford Court House and Captain Ricketts busy writing up a complaint to Headquarters of the Army of the Potomac against General Hays. Here the Second Corps rested throughout the month. Meade's cavalry crossed the Rappahannock on August 1, with Buford fighting Stuart's grayclad horsemen in a second battle of Brandy Station that day, until forced back by the arrival of Southern infantry from Hill's corps. Union infantry from the First Corps remained south of the Rappahannock until August 9, when Meade pulled his troops back and ordered them into camps scattered behind the river.[1]

Lee's troops remained behind . . . Fredericksburg to Gettysburg and back again. Thus, the remainder of August, at least for the Second Corps, was a time of rest and resupply. Corporal Petterson'a diary provides a glimpse at the daily log of Batteries F&G during this quiet period. "Weather extremely warm," he penned on August 3. As a result of the summer heat, Ricketts ordered a change of camp into a nearby grove of trees, which took place on August 4-5.[2]

Two days later, Ricketts' complaint that he filed with headquarters against General Hays reached the general. Hays, incensed by it, immediately placed Ricketts under arrest for disobedience of orders with regard to the battery carts. The captain felt Hays' action was only a bluff to detract him from settling his dispute with Snider. Several batterymen and various other friends visited Ricketts and sympathized with his plight. The

---

[1]*William D. Henderson,* The Road to Bristoe Station *(Lynchburg, VA: H. E. Howard, 1987), 16-25. Ricketts Diary, August 7, 1863.*

[2]*Patterson Diary, various August 1863 entries.*

2nd Lieutenant Francis H. Snider served his three-year term and went home in October 1864.

(GARRY LEISTER COLLECTION, USAMHI)

captain was not only well-liked, it seems, by his own men, but was highly regarded by other officers as well. Many of them sent messages to Hays, advising him to back down from his stand against Ricketts. Hays stood his ground until August 15, when he released the captain from arrest and decided not to press ahead after receiving assurances from Ricketts that he would not continue to press charges against the general for striking Sergeant Snyder. Thus ended the feud.[3]

By the time Hays was finished with Ricketts, he had been replaced as commander of the Second Corps. Gouverneur K. Warren, recently promoted to major general as a reward for his services at Gettysburg, replaced Hays as corps commander on August 12. Warren received command of the Second Corps until such time as Hancock, at home recovering from wounds, would be able to resume his duty as the permanent corps commander.[4]

The month's other highlight was the arrival of a government paymaster, who dispersed two months' pay to the battery on the ninth. For Patterson, the month consisted of occasional guard duty, fixing his clothes, taking care of horse teams, and avoiding the brief periods of rain. Company inspections, mandated by regulations to occur on Sundays, began again on the sixteenth and continued each Sunday thereafter. On the twenty-first, General Warren reviewed the corps; Captain John G. Hazard then inspected the batteries comprising the Artillery Brigade.

Patterson also recorded the executions of three deserters from the corps. A single execution took place on the twenty-first, while two men—William F. Hill (20th Massachusetts) and John Smith (15th Massachusetts)—were executed on the twenty-eighth. These men had all been apprehended for deserting earlier in the war and were made examples to discourage others from following in their footsteps. The oftimes shocking sites of military executions would become far too common soon, as the drafted men and substitutes brought into the military as a result of the recent draft included many scores of undesirables in their ranks.

Near the end of the month, Batteries F&G made a slight movement in support of a Union cavalry raid. On August 23, Confederate naval Commander John T. Wood and his men captured two Federal

---

[3]*Ricketts Diary, August 7-15.*

[4]*Francis A. Walker,* History of the Second Army Corps in the Army of the Potomac *(New York: Charles Scribner's Sons, 1886), 310-11.*

gunboats–*Satellite* and *Reliance*–near Urbana on the Rappahannock River. Meade sent Judson Kilpatrick's Third Division of the Cavalry Corps to recapture the boats, which had moved upriver to near Port Conway, just below Fredericksburg. Kilpatrick's blueclad horsemen found the vessels and drove them across the wide river. He unlimbered his cannon and shelled the two ships, setting them afire and destroying them.[5]

Warren's Second Corps moved downriver to Banks' Ford, prepared to move to Kilpatrick's assistance if needed. Ricketts moved his command eighteen miles from Morrisville to the ford on August 31, accompanying the Second Division, Brigadier General Alexander S. Webb commanding. After the battery pitched camp sometime after 5:00 p.m., one section remained hitched at all times, ready to move if needed. The battery remained in position until 5:00 p.m. on September 3, when word was received of Kilpatrick's success. Warren then withdrew the Second Corps. Batteries F&G rolled along until 2:00 a.m. on the fourth, when it reached its old camp, finding "our tents and other things as we left them."[6]

The Second Corps again supported cavalry in mid-September. Earlier, on September 7-8, General James Longstreet's First Corps of the Army of Northern Virginia boarded trains and headed off to join Braxton Bragg and the Army of Tennessee. Bragg's outnumbered troops had been driven out of Tennessee by Major General William S. Rosecrans and the Federal Army of the Cumberland, which occupied Chattanooga on the ninth. Longstreet's regiments had to go south along the coast before steaming into Atlanta because troops from Ambrose Burnside's Department of the Ohio had occupied Knoxville on the second, cutting the direct rail connection with Chattanooga. More Southern troops rushed to join Bragg. The resulting two-day battle of Chickamauga (September 19-20) was a hard-fought Confederate victory. Rosecrans withdrew to Chattanooga; Bragg followed and placed the city under siege.

Within a week of Longstreet's departure from Virginia, Meade had heard rumors of the troop movement. Accordingly, his cavalry crossed the Rappahannock on September 13, skirmished with Stuart's horsemen throughout the day, and occupied Culpeper, forcing Stuart to withdraw across the Rapidan. Warren followed the cavalry with the Second Corps, trying to keep out of sight of Confederate signal stations atop Pony Mountain. Later in the day, as the cavalry advanced beyond Culpeper, Warren sent a brigade to occupy the town, bivouacking the rest of the

---

[5]O.R., volume 29, part 1, 76-77, 96-99.

[6]Patterson Diary, August 31-September 4, 1863; Ricketts Diary, August 31-September 3, 1863.

corps in the Brandy Station area. Ricketts' battery crossed the Rappahannock that morning via a pontoon bridge thrown across the stream near Rappahannock Station. The cannoneers could hear the sound of artillery firing as the cavalry battled each other, but they saw no action.[7]

Batteries F&G remained in camp on September 14, then took up the line of march at 3:00 p.m., passed through Culpeper, and went into position a mile south of town, supporting Brigadier General John C. Caldwell's First Division. On the seventeenth, the battery limbered and rolled south, passing the old Cedar Mountain battlefield before going into camp at the foot of the mountain. An all-night rain set in at sundown, not stopping until mid-afternoon on the eighteenth. The next day, the battery moved its camp about a mile. Since Cedar Mountain was the highest elevation in the area, its peak attracted lots of curious Yankees, hoping to catch a glimpse of "rebeldom" to the south.[8]

With Meade's army in control of the Culpeper area, the Second Corps remained bivouacked around Cedar Mountain as the cavalry ranged across the river, competing with Stuart's horsemen in a series of skirmishes for the next several weeks. Meade had contemplated another offensive, but the Union defeat at Chickamauga altered the strategic situation. Worried about Rosecrans' ability to hold Chattanooga, the War Department began rounding up troops from around the country to reinforce the Army of the Cumberland. General Grant, at Vicksburg, began moving the Army of the Tennessee toward Rosecrans. Lincoln, Halleck, and Stanton decided, after discussions with Meade, to detach part of the Army of the Potomac and send it to Tennessee. Accordingly, Meade was instructed to concentrate both the Eleventh and Twelfth Corps for transport to the west. The first elements of Slocum's corps boarded trains on September 25. General Hooker was assigned to command the two corps and lead them to Chattanooga.[9]

General Lee soon learned of the departure of some of Meade's troops, but Stuart's original estimates of the numbers detached from the Army of the Potomac doubled the actual troops involved in the operation. Lee decided to launch an offensive that would essentially repeat the movements of the Second Manassas Campaign. Leaving a division of cavalry supported by some infantry in Meade's front, Lee would take both

---

[7]Henderson, Bristoe Station, *31-41*; Patterson Diary, September 12-13, 1863; Ricketts Diary, September 12-13, 1863.

[8]Ricketts Diary, September 14-20, 1863; Patterson Diary, September 14-20, 1863.

[9]Henderson, Bristoe Station, *50-69*.

Ewell's and Hill's corps on a circuitous march around Meade's right flank, hoping either to force Meade to retreat or bait him into attacking the Rebels on ground of their own choosing.[10]

While all this was happening, the officers and men of Batteries F&G remained in camp near Cedar Mountain. Corporal Patterson's daily entries in his diary provide the best glimpse into the camp routine of the artillery unit during the last days of September and beginning of October. The men could hear the occasional cannonade as the cavalry dueled with each other, and several took the opportunity to forage a bit in the surrounding countryside. On the twenty-fourth, a government paymaster appeared in camp and disbursed two months' pay to the battery. The first frost of the season appeared on September 23, with the nights then becoming cooler, adding to the discomfort of the troops. Soldiers wrote and received letters, lounged in camp, and spent some time on guard duty. Battery inspections took place on Sundays, as per regulations. Another deserter was shot on October 2.[11]

By the end of the first week in October, Lee had decided on his offensive and had begun to shift his army westward, behind the Rapidan, toward Meade's right flank, in preparation for a move around the enemy flank. Union signal stations on top of the higher mountains detected some of these movements and duly notified headquarters. On the sixth, the same day that most Confederate infantrymen began to break up their camps and prepare to march, Meade shifted the Second Corps into reserve by moving the corps west of Culpeper, strengthening his right flank. That morning, Ricketts' men were awakened at four o'clock and on the march two hours later. The column went through Culpeper and halted a mile west of town, on the Culpeper-Sperryville Turnpike.[12]

Ricketts' battery rested in its camp, awaiting events. The Bristoe Station Campaign opened on October 10, as Stuart's horsemen engaged Kilpatrick's cavalry along the Robertson River fords, masking the advance of the Confederate infantry. Soft roads caused by recent rains slowed the Rebel advance, which bivouacked for the evening between Madison Court House and Griffinsburg, a small village on the Culpeper-Sperryville Turnpike. Meade reacted slowly to the Rebel advance. His chief of cavalry,

---

[10]Ibid., *69-72.*

[11]*Patterson Diary, September 21-October 5, 1863.* Actually, two deserters were executed on October 2nd–a soldier from the 66th New York in the Second Corps, and a man from the 90th Pennsylvania, a First Corps regiment. See Alotta, Civil War Justice, *84.*

[12]Henderson, Bristoe Station, *71-72; Patterson Diary, October 6, 1863.*

Alfred Pleasonton, believed that the Confederates might abandon Virginia and concentrate their forces in Tennessee; hence Lee was merely covering up such a move. To check Pleasonton's theory, Meade sent Buford's cavalry across the Rapidan with orders to reconnoiter the area south of the river fords. If Lee was retreating, Union infantry would follow. In case the enemy was advancing toward his right, Meade had Warren shift the Second Corps to the army's right, connecting with the Third Corps northwest of Culpeper. On the tenth, Ricketts moved his battery two miles as the corps moved to its new position.[13]

Later in the day, however, Meade decided to withdraw and play it safe. He began to suspect that Lee was not feinting and was instead attempting to turn his right flank. Orders were issued for a three o'clock a.m. withdrawal across the Rappahannock. The Army of the Potomac would occupy a line behind the river, stretching from Kelly's Ford on the left to Fauquier White Sulphur Springs on the right. At 1:00 a.m. on October 11, Batteries F&G broke camp and moved at three o'clock. By nine, the battery was crossing at Rappahannock Station. Warren continued to move to the rear and went into reserve around Bealton Station, with Ricketts halting sometime around two o'clock that afternoon.[14]

The next morning, after talking with his subordinates, Meade issued an order for a reconnaissance in force across the Rappahannock. Some of his officers conjectured that Lee was sending more reinforcements to Tennessee and was merely bluffing to prevent the Army of the Potomac from attacking. Although Meade did not believe these arguments, he decided to see where Lee's infantry was. Accordingly, General Sedgwick took the Fifth and Sixth Corps, led by Buford's cavalry, back across the river. If Brandy Station was unoccupied, Sedgwick was to halt here and send the cavalry on ahead to reconnoiter Culpeper. If Lee attacked, Sedgwick would halt and give battle as Meade rushed the rest of the army forward. If the enemy was at Brandy Station, Sedgwick would halt and await further orders.[15]

And so, shortly after noon, Sedgwick's command splashed across the river and rolled forward. At the last moment, Meade ordered Warren and the Second Corps across the river as a support. Captain Ricketts' battery left Bealton Station at one o'clock and crossed the river an hour later. The

---

[13]Henderson, Bristoe Station, *75-85;* Patterson Diary, October 10, 1863.

[14]Henderson, Bristoe Station, *87-105;* Patterson Diary, October 11, 1863.

[15]Henderson, Bristoe Station, *122-24.*

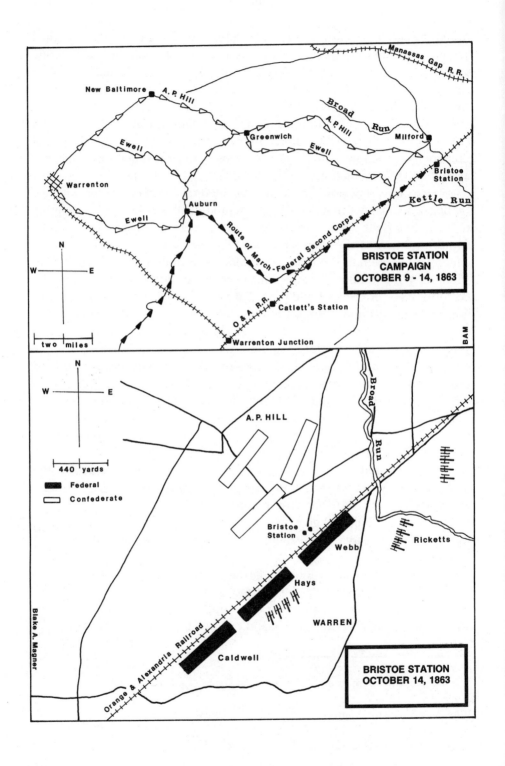

battery halted two miles from the stream, bivouacking along the road leading to Culpeper.[16]

Meanwhile, Lee's infantry continued its march toward the Union right flank as cavalry engaged Buford's advance toward Culpeper. David Gregg's Second Division of the Cavalry Corps slowed the Rebel advance, but by nightfall, elements of Ewell's corps had crossed the Rappahannock and were ready to move at first light. Upon hearing of Gregg's fighting, Meade realized that Sedgwick must withdraw before Lee was in the army's rear. Late that evening, Meade ordered Sedgwick to pull his troops back across the Rappahannock. It was midnight before most of the troops had recrossed, with the Second Corps using the Rappahannock Station ford.[17]

Batteries F&G, according to Corporal Patterson, crossed the stream at one o'clock in the morning of the thirteenth and kept going, as Meade, now aware the Lee was definitely trying to march around his right flank, ordered a withdrawal to Centreville. The main force of the Army of the Potomac used the line of the Orange & Alexandria Railroad, while the Second and Third Corps moved on a parallel course, with Gregg's Second Cavalry Division protecting the flank and rear. Warren's men reached Bealton Station at daybreak and kept going, weary though they were. The corps went into line of battle astride the Warrenton Road in the vicinity of Fayetteville, then waited for the Third Corps to catch up.[18]

Many tired Second Corps soldiers managed to sleep at least an hour; others cooked food while waiting for Major General William H. French and the Third Corps. French was dilatory on the thirteenth, and his divisions were widely separated as they moved up past the rear of Warren's battle line, heading toward Greenwich. Warren's corps did not begin to march until later in the afternoon and was delayed by French's columns. Kilpatrick's Third Division of the Cavalry Corps moved along the flank, while Gregg brought up the rear. French's men reached the small village of Auburn–described as a "little hamlet" which consisted of a dwelling house, post office, and a blacksmith's shop–in late afternoon, crossing Cedar Run via a bridge over the stream. French's men ran into Confederate cavalry south of Cedar Run and pushed them out of the way, clearing the road to

---

[16]Ibid., *124;* Patterson Diary, October 12, 1863.

[17]Henderson, Bristoe Station, *125-34.*

[18]Patterson Diary, October 13, 1863; Henderson, Bristoe Station, *137-39;* O.R., *volume 29, part 1, 236 (Warren's report).*

Greenwich. The Third Corps continued on and went into bivouac sometime around eight o'clock that night.[19]

Warren halted his corps about a mile south of Auburn as darkness ended the day. The terrain did not favor a night march, and the general did not want to take the wrong road. His orders stipulated that the Second Corps would cross Cedar Run and turn right, taking the road to Catlett's Station on the Orange & Alexandria Railroad, then proceed to Centreville via the rail line. Although there was a bridge over Cedar Run, its approach road skirted a hill, then sloped down to the bridge. The muddy road was a mess after the Third Corps had passed over it. After crossing the run, the road forked. The left-most road was the direct route to Greenwich, while the right-hand road went south to Catlett's Station. Just beyond the fork in the road was a "bald and tolerably prominent hill" which commanded the surrounding wooded terrain.[20]

Unbeknownst to the Federals, the cavalry that opposed French's troops were two brigades led by Jeb Stuart himself. Unable to halt the Yankees, Stuart moved his units south along the St. Stephens Church Road and hid his men in heavy woods. Cut off from the main army, Stuart could do little else except hide and wait for an opportunity to slip away. He sent six scouts, dressed in captured uniforms, through the columns of marching Yankees, to report his position to General Lee. All six reached Warrenton and informed Lee of his cavalry chief's predicament. Lee issued orders for Ewell to send all three of his divisions to rescue the cavalry. Early's Division, preceded by horsemen, would approach Auburn from the west, south of Cedar Run, while Rodes and Johnson would approach on the Dumfries Road, north of Cedar Run. Lee believed that the Second Corps would thus destroy any Union troops that interposed between Stuart and the approaching infantry.[21]

General Warren did not know any of this, of course, but he did know of the presence of enemy cavalry and its skirmishing with French's corps. The general realized that the Rebel horsemen probably reported to Lee and that Southern infantry would probably show up sometime early the next morning. Accordingly, Warren had his men awake long before dawn. His orders for the day's march on October 14 called for the Second Corps to cross Cedar Run, then turn right, following the St. Stephens Church Road

---

[19]*Henderson,* Bristoe Station, *142-49;* O.R., *volume 29, part 1, 236-37;* Walker, Second Corps, *327-28.*

[20]*Walker,* Second Corps, *324-28;*

[21]*Henderson,* Bristoe Station, *146-50.*

to Catlett's Station. From here the corps would turn left and follow the Orange & Alexandria Railroad to Centreville.[22]

Brigadier General John C. Caldwell's First Division crossed Cedar Run shortly after 6:00 A.M. and continued to the crest of the hill overlooking the road junction on the other side. Colonel John Brooke's Fourth Brigade was given the task of picketing the northern approaches, which were also covered by elements of Gregg's cavalry division. The rest of Caldwell's men went into bivouac on the hill and were allowed to make coffee while waiting for the rest of the corps to pass behind them. Parked with Caldwell were three batteries–Ricketts' Batteries F&G, 1st Pennsylvania; Captain William A. Arnold's Battery A, 1st Rhode Island (six 3-inch rifles), and Captain Nelson Ames' Battery G, 1st New York (six 12-pounder Napoleons). Brigadier General Alexander Hays' Third Division then took the lead in the column of march, while the corps trains and ambulances followed Hays. Brigadier General Alexander S. Webb's Second Division brought up the rear, while Gregg's horsemen also provided more protection to the western flank and rear of the corps.[23]

Soon, the morning's stillness was broken by the sound of distant gunfire, as skirmishers of Ewell's advancing infantry (Rodes' Division) encountered Gregg's cavalry pickets. Farther to the southeast, Stuart could hear the musketry and concluded that Lee was sending troops to rescue him. Determined to have a hand in the engagement, Stuart ordered Major Robert F. Beckham to wheel his seven cannon into position and open fire on Caldwell's troops. The morning had dawned with a heavy fog in the Cedar Run valley, but the infantry on top of the hill were above the fog level, and could be seen cooking breakfast.[24]

Beckham's position was some eight hundred yards from Caldwell's men. The sudden fire from the rear threw the Yankees into confusion. A soldier in the 53rd Pennsylvania remembered the scene. Quite a crowd was watching the distant cavalry skirmish, "congratulating ourselves that minnie balls were harmless when we were out of range; when, quick as gunpowder, the rebels opened on us in our rear with a battery, and they planted their shells right among us. The fact of the matter is, it was decidedly bad."[25]

---

[22]Ibid., *150-52.*

[23]*Walker,* Second Corps, *329-31;* O.R., *volume 29, part 1, 239, 253-54, 305;* Henderson, Bristoe Station, *153-55.*

[24]*Henderson,* Bristoe Station, *155-56.*

[25]*Levi J. Fritz letter of November 15, 1863, in the* Montgomery Ledger, *November 24, 1863.*

As the enemy shells rained down on the hill, thereafter nicknamed "Coffee Hill" by the men in blue, General Caldwell quickly issued orders to his brigade commanders to move their men to the reverse slope of the hill to evade the shelling. He also ordered Captain Ricketts to unlimber and reply to this unexpected enemy battery. "We wheeled into line," penned Lieutenant Brockway, "instead of breakfasting commenced firing, and after using 100 rounds completely silenced and drove off the enemy's artillery."[26]

Captain Arnold brought his Rhode Island battery into line beside Ricketts, and the combined weight of twelve Yankee cannon overmatched Beckham's seven. General Stuart later reported that he was 'compelled most reluctantly to withdraw the artillery." Pressure from Union infantry speeded the Confederate withdrawal. General Hays deployed part of a brigade and sent it forward, supporting it with other regiments from his Third Division. Stuart ordered an attack to delay Union pursuit, during the course of which Brigadier General John B. Gordon was wounded and the colonel of the 1st North Carolina cavalry mortally wounded. Stuart's horsemen moved down the St. Stephen's Church Road a distance, then crossed Cedar Run and eventually rejoined the main army.[27]

Geneal Warren, seeing the peril in which his corps was placed, issued orders for a rapid movement, using Caldwell's division as rearguard. Hays led the column as it moved down the road to Catlett's Station, followed by Webb's troops and the corps trains. Meanwhile, General Rodes deployed his division and pushed Gregg's troopers back toward Coffee Hill. Brockway wrote that his cannoneers had scarcely finished driving off the Rebel artillery when the command "Fire to the rear" was issued. Immediately, the veteran gunners of Batteries F&G executed this maneuver, by which the gunners swung the trails of their pieces to the left until the gun barrel was pointed to face the new threat, while the caissons were driven past the right of each piece and placed in the proper position behind each gun.[28]

"Every one was bewildered," wrote Brockway. "We were fired on from three sides, the only avenue of escape being in the direction of Richmond." However, the Confederate infantry did not attack, but waited for their artillery to get into position to reply to Ricketts and Arnold. As an hour-

---

[26]Ibid., *156; Brockway letter of October 17, 1863, published in the* Columbia Democrat, *October, 31, 1863.*

[27]O.R., *volume 29, part 1, 254, 289, 448; Henderson,* Bristoe Station, *157-59.*

[28]Henderson, Bristoe Station, *160; Brockway letter of October 17, 1863;* Instruction for Field Artillery, *335, and Plate 71, illustrating this maneuver.*

long artillery duel ensued, Warren sent his corps down the St. Stephen's Church Road, heading toward Catlett's Station. Once the corps was some distance ahead, Caldwell, accompanied by Colonel Carroll's brigade of the Third Division, and further reinforced by Gregg's horsemen, began withdrawing under the constant enemy pressure. Fritz wrote that Brooke's brigade, which was the rearguard, faced about six times to drive off enemy skirmishers. Some two miles south of Auburn, Caldwell halted the division and formed a line of battle across the road, unlimbered the artillery, and prepared to resist Rodes' onslaught. However, the Confederate infantry, after chasing the Second Corps south, turned around and continued its march toward Broad Run and Greenwich, following the line of march of French's troops. Warren was free to concentrate his corps at Catlett's Station.[29]

Sometime after noon, as the corps was concentrated at Catlett's, Warren received a noon message from General Meade. The commanding general reported that the line of march along the railroad was open and that General Sykes and the Fifth Corps was at Bristoe Station. When Warren's men reached Bristoe, continued Meade, Sykes would take the Fifth Corps across Broad Run and continue on to Centreville, allowing the oncoming Second Corps to then continue its march.[30]

Led by the 1st Minnesota, the Second Corps then took up the line of march along the Orange & Alexandria Railroad. Webb's division marched to the north of the rail line, while Hays' Third Division trudged along south of the tracks. Caldwell again brought up the rear, while Gregg's cavalry ranged across the rear and flanks, watching for any enemy soldiers. Sometime around 1:00 p.m., General Sykes received an erroneous message that the head of the Second Corps had been sighted, so he gave orders for the Fifth Corps to cross Broad Run and march to Centreville. An hour later, most of the corps had marched a mile north of Bristoe to Milford and crossed the run there, where the stream was narrower and more easily fordable than at Bristoe.[31]

This was the situation at about two o'clock when a Confederate battery from Major William T. Poague's artillery battalion unlimbered and opened fire on the rear elements of the Fifth Corps. General Hill, accompanying his lead division, that of Major General Henry Heth, had

---

[29]*Brockway letter of October 17; Fritz letter of November 15; Walker,* Second Corps, *336-38;* Henderson, Bristoe Station, *160-62;* O.R., *volume 29, part 1, 254-55.*

[30]O.R., *volume 29, part 1, 241.*

[31]*Henderson,* Bristoe Station, *167-68.*

reached the area and saw the Yankees just completing their crossing of Broad Run. Assuming these elements were the rear of French's command, Hill ordered an immediate attack. Poague's guns opened fire, scattering the remaining Yankees and hastening the retiring columns of Fifth Corps soldiers. Heth deployed two brigades–one of his own, led by Brigadier General W. W. Kirkland, and a newly-arrived brigade from North Carolina, consisting of more than twenty-five hundred men led by Brigadier General John R. Cooke, which was temporarily unattached to any division–and sent them forward as the remainder of his division deployed in support. Hill sent orders to Major General Richard H. Anderson to hurry his division to the scene, with a similar message sent to Major General Cadmus M. Wilcox to bring his four brigades to the battlefield.[32]

The artillery firing spurred General Warren forward to the head of the corps. By the time Warren reached the scene, his skirmishers had made contact with the right flank of Heth's battle line, which at the same time spied Webb's division marching along the railroad line. Alarmed by this unexpected appearance of Yankees in his right rear, Heth sent a message to Hill, who replied that Anderson was coming up and would protect his right. Hill apparently believed that the force seen to the right rear was only a small force of skirmishers, not the advance of an entire army corps.[33]

General Webb, upon seeing the advance of Heth's two brigades, ordered his two brigades to quickly move to the right and take position behind the railroad embankment. Lieutenant T. Fred Brown's Battery B, 1st Rhode Island, galloped forward, splashed across Broad Run, and took position on a hill on the other side of the stream. Webb was beginning to move a brigade across in support when Warren arrived and countermanded the order, realizing that Sykes was too far away to provide any support. As Webb took position, Heth turned Kirkland and Cooke to the south and moved toward the railroad, but Webb's men went into position perhaps only five minutes ahead of the oncoming Tarheels. General Alexander Hays moved his two available brigades into position on Webb's left, bringing the Union infantry strength up to perhaps three thousand men.[34]

As the infantry hurried into position along the railroad embankment, Captain Hazard rushed his available batteries into position. Moving with mounted cannoneers, Captain Arnold's Rhode Islanders went into position

---

[32]Ibid., *170-72.*

[33]Ibid., *172.*

[34]Ibid., *173-75.*

Corporal William Umberhower poses for the camera in a studio, hand on chair and the bottom of a posing frame visible just behind his right shoe.
(GARRY LEISTER COLLECTION, USAMHI)

behind the Union infantry, on a small ridge. Hazard ordered Ricketts into line still farther to the right, closer to Broad Run. Lieutenant Brockway wrote that the battery galloped across open fields a quarter of a mile, exposed to enemy fire all the way. Batteries F&G went into line and immediately opened fire on the advancing Southern infantry, using shrapnel and canister "until they broke, when I engaged a battery in my immediate front." "We paid no attention to their artillery," penned Brockway, "though their shell were making wild music in our midst." Without immediate infantry support, Ricketts' gunners fired round after round, compelling the enemy to shift to their right in an effort to avoid the severe fire. As other batteries arrived to add their metal to the storm, "the rebel line gave way, and fled in confusion to the woods."[35]

Warren's infantry gallantly repelled the attack. Both Confederate brigadiers were wounded and officer casualties were high. Ripped apart by the musketry and artillery fire of the Second Corps, Heth's Tarheel brigades went to pieces and had to withdraw. Captain Hazard was generous in his praise. When writing his report, he said the following about Arnold and Ricketts: "The fire of these batteries upon the charging lines of the infantry was most effective and deadly, and assisted greatly in securing their demoralization." Once the infantry attack fell apart, Ricketts and Arnold shifted their attention to a rebel battery supporting their infantry. This artillery consisted of sections of two batteries of Major David G. McIntosh's Battalion. Ricketts and Arnold simply annihilated the battery, their fire producing high casualties among men and horses, which silenced the Rebel cannon. Shortly thereafter, the 19th Massachusetts moved forward and hauled off with ropes five of the rebel guns, the sixth being too disabled to be removed from the field.[36]

The repulse of Heth's two brigades and the capture of the rebel artillery effectively ended the engagement of Bristoe Station. The Confederate loss in this ill-advised attack included 143 killed, 773 wounded, and 445 captured, for a total of 1,361. Warren reported his loss for all of October 14th as 546 (50 killed, 335 wounded, 161 missing). Batteries F&G suffered a loss of seven wounded, with three horses killed and five wounded. The battery's six guns expended 633 rounds during the day.

---

[35]O.R., *volume 29, part 1*, 306-7; Brockway letter of October 17.

[36]Henderson, *Bristoe Station, 176-86;* O.R., *volume 29, part 1*, 306; Brockway letter of October 17th.

Ricketts reported that Lieutenants Brockway, Spence, and C.H. Mitchell "fought their sections with great coolness and gallantry."[37]

Warren withdrew the Second Corps that night, rejoining the army as it dug in on the high ground around Centreville. Heavy rains soaked the ground on October 16 as Lee reconnoitered Meade's strong positions. Lee decided to withdraw, his men destroying the railroad as they marched south, recrossed the Rappahannock and took position between that river and the Rapidan. Meade began an advance on the nineteenth, reaching Gainesville and Bristoe Station. Batteries F&G, on the nineteenth, marched twelve miles from the camp near Centreville to Bristoe, then rolled eighteen miles to Auburn the next day, the men surveying the scene of their recent engagement. After a brief stay at Auburn, on October 23 the battery moved six miles towards Warrenton and went into camp.[38]

The Army of the Potomac went into camp in the vicinity of Warrenton while railroad crews began the laborious job of rebuilding the line and its bridges. By early November, Meade was prepared to advance. He divided the Army of the Potomac into two columns. Major General John Sedgwick led the right, composed of the Fifth and Sixth Corps, and General French the left, which included the First, Second, and Third Corps. Sedgwick was ordered to move to Rappahannock Station and cross the Rappahannock at that point, while French's column would effect a crossing a few miles downstream at Kelly's Ford. On November 7, elements of the Sixth Corps charged and captured the entrenched bridgehead Lee had on the north bank of the river at Rappahannock Station, seizing more than fifteen hundred prisoners in the process. Units of French's Third Corps forced a crossing at Kelly's Ford the same day, whereupon Lee began to retreat, moving to the rear and taking a new position behind the Rapidan River, in effect abandoning the triangle of land between the Rapidan and Rappahannock to Meade, whose army occupied Culpeper and deployed to face Lee.[39]

Ricketts' battery was not actively involved in these operations, marching thirty-three miles between November 7 and 10, before going into camp near a hamlet called Berry Hill, located near Stevensburg, where the

---

[37] O.R., *volume 29, part 1, 250, 307, 428.* One of the wounded was Corporal Patterson, who was hit in the thigh and sent to a Washington hospital, thereby ending his 1863 service with the battery.

[38] O.R. Supplement, *part 2, volume 58, 109;* Walker, Second Corps, *360-64;* Humphreys, Gettysburg to the Rapidan, *30-36.*

[39] *Humphreys,* Gettysburg to the Rapidan, *37-48.*

Second Corps would remain for two weeks. A few changes occurred in the corps Artillery Brigade. Captain Hazard was replaced by Lieutenant Colonel John A. Monroe of the 1st Rhode Island Artillery as brigade commander on October 28. Battery I, 1st United States was transferred to the Cavalry Corps, and two new batteries–Battery C, 5th United States, and Independent Battery C, Pennsylvania Light Artillery–were added to the brigade. Captain Ricketts obtained a leave because of physical disability and left for home on November 21; he would not return to command until the last day of February 1864. In Ricketts' absence, Lieutenant Spence directed Batteries F&G.[40]

In late November, Meade decided on another advance in an effort to outflank Lee and force a battle before going into winter camp. Lee's two corps were entrenched behind the Rapidan River, forming a line some eighteen miles long. Meade proposed to cross the river downstream from Lee's right and attempt to get in behind Lee's troops before his entire army could be concentrated. Meade hoped to push his troops forward as fast as possible to ensure success. Because of the wooded terrain, Meade cautioned his corps commanders to move rapidly, using the Orange Plank Road and Orange Turnpike to move their troops west toward Orange Court House, where Lee's headquarters were located. If all went well, Meade's five corps would crush Ewell's corps before A. P. Hill could bring his troops to reinforce Ewell.[41]

A heavy rain delayed the start of the Mine Run Campaign for a day, and the Army of the Potomac did not begin moving until November 26. Warren's Second Corps was scheduled to cross the Rapidan at Germanna Ford, then move south to the Orange Turnpike before heading west. Warren's lead elements seized the ford and the corps spent the day crossing, with the advance some four miles beyond the river by nightfall. The tardy movement of the Third Corps this day irritated Meade, who had ordered a simultaneous crossing at three fords to dilute enemy opposition. Thus, by the end of the twenty-sixth, the plan was already behind schedule.[42]

---

[40]O.R. Supplement, *part 2, volume 58, 109;* Walker, Second Corps, *365-67.* The Second Corps *Artillery Brigade now included the following batteries: Battery G, 1st New York; Pennsylvania Batteries C and F; Batteries F&G, 1st Pennsylvania; Batteries A and B, 1st Rhode Island; and Battery C, 5th United States. For Ricketts' leave, see his diary entries of November 20-21, 1863.*

[41]*Humphreys,* Gettysburg to the Rapidan, *49-50.*

[42]Ibid., *52-55;* Walker, Second Corps, *368-69.*

On the twenty-seventh, Warren's corps moved on to Robertson's Tavern, situated on the Orange Turnpike. Here, Union cavalrymen encountered Rebel pickets but pushed them back. Two miles beyond the tavern, the cavalry ran into grayclad infantry. Warren eventually deployed his entire corps into line of battle to oppose whatever strength the enemy (Early's and Rodes' divisions) had in front of him. General French was still absent, having been delayed again, and Warren's right flank was unsupported. Thus, rather than attack, Warren remained inactive, Meade all the while raging about French's delays. Lieutenant Brockway recalled that "our artillery was posted as well as the nature of the ground would permit, and the cannoneers immediately threw up earthworks in front of the guns." Skirmishing continued all day, but no serious fighting occurred on the Second Corps front.[43]

Meade ordered an advance the next morning (November 28), but Warren's skirmishers discovered that the enemy had pulled back during the night. The line moved forward to Mine Run, a substantial stream that flowed north into the Rapidan. Here, the Yankees discovered the Rebels, posted behind the stream. Wrote Brockway: "The opposite bank was steep, and on its summit they had erected very formidable earth works, covering guns which commanded every avenue of approach for a mile at least." Rain set in and lasted all day, reducing visibility and chilling the soldiers of both armies. Lee's regiments were still deploying, and at noon, some enemy infantry was seen moving to Warren's left. Arnold's and Ricketts' batteries were ordered into line at a gallop and opened fire, scattering the infantry and silencing a battery that replied to their fire. Later, Brockway wrote, his battery threw some percussion shells into the woods at some parties of Rebels who could be seen working on their entrenchments, forcing them to halt until after dark.[44]

General Meade, frustrated thus far, determined to outflank Lee's strong position. He withdrew the Second Corps from the line after dark and ordered Warren to flank Lee's right. Meade reinforced Warren with a division from the Sixth Corps. Because of the need to move quickly, Warren decided to take only three batteries of artillery–Ricketts', Arnold's, and Thompson's–all rifled guns. Brockway wrote that each battery was ordered "to strip their carriages of rations, forage, baggages, and to dismount one ammunition chest, thereby making themselves as light as flying

---

[43]Humphreys, Gettysburg to the Rapidan, *55-63; Walker,* Second Corps, *369-73;* Brockway letter of December 3, 1863, in the Columbia Democrat, *December 12, 1863.*

[44]Brockway letter of December 3; Humphreys, Gettysburg to the Rapidan, *63; Walker,* Second Corps, *374-76.*

artillery–and to prepare for a rapid flank movement in connection with the infantry of the 2nd Corps."⁴⁵

Warren did not start his flank movement until daylight on November 29, after ensuring that his troops were issued rations and that excess baggage had been sent to the rear. The corps retraced its steps to Robertson's Tavern, then headed south "through woods along bad roads." About three miles beyond Good Hope Church, near the hamlet of Verdiersville, the skirmishers of both armies came into contact with each other. Warren, his main column moving on the Orange Plank Road, pushed the enemy back to a main line, which was entrenched. By the time Warren brought his entire corps forward, darkness was coming and there was no time for an assault. Still, the opposing earthworks did not appear as formidable as those behind Mine Run, and Warren reported to Meade that an attack seemed likely to succeed. Accordingly, Meade sent two divisions from the Third Corps to reinforce Warren, giving him more than twenty-five thousand men. The attack would begin at 8:00 a.m. on November 30; an hour later, Sedgwick and Sykes would strike Lee's left.⁴⁶

But the enemy failed to cooperate with Meade. Lieutenant Brockway recounted the scene at daylight on November 30. "During the night they threw up breastworks of great height and strength and in their front placed an abatis of jagged trees through which it would be difficult to penetrate even when no opposition was made. We could even count their guns and limbers, from which the horses had been unhitched, showing their confidence in their ability to repulse any assault." Warren, surveying the scene, hesitated. Taking it upon his own responsibility, Warren decided not to attack. He rode to army headquarters and reported his actions; Meade came forward and agreed that an attack was likely to fail. The armies remained in place during the day while Meade pondered future action. Rather than move the entire army around to Lee's right and risk jeopardizing his communications, Meade decided to withdraw.⁴⁷

The armies confronted each other on December 1 as well. That night, leaving behind a picket line to tend the campfires, Meade's army silently withdrew and headed back across the Rapidan to its camps near Culpeper. Batteries F&G suffered only one casualty during the campaign; Sergeant

---

⁴⁵*Brockway letter of December 3; Humphreys,* Gettysburg to the Rapidan, *64; Walker,* Second Corps, *376-77.*

⁴⁶O.R., *volume 29, part 1, 696-97; Walker,* Second Corps, *376-81.*

⁴⁷*Brockway letter of December 3; Walker,* Second Corps, *382-88;* O.R., *volume 29, part 1, 698.*

Francis H. Snider was slightly wounded in the thigh on November 27. By December 8, having marched 104 miles since November 7, the battery was in camp near Cole's Hill. The hard campaigning of 1863 was now over and the Army of the Potomac went into winter camp.[48]

---

[48]*Brockway letter of December 3; Walker,* Second Corps, *388-92;* O.R. Supplement, part 2, volume 58, 109

2nd Lieutenant Truman L. Case. He left Battery F in February 1863, mustered out of service as supernumerary.

(RONN PALM COLLECTION, USAMHI)

Private Henry J. Carson transferred from Battery G. He was Battery F's sole member from Allegheny County.

(RONN PALM COLLECTION, USAMHI)

Private James H. Phillips was wounded at Deep Bottom in August 1864 and was still in a hospital when the battery disbanded in June 1865.

(ELAINE KLINE)

Private William G. Pinkerton wore his heavy winter overcoat to have this image taken.

GARRY LIESTER COLLECTION, USAMHI)

Sergeant Charles G. Matthews, at age 31, was one of the battery's older members. His pre-war occupation was an armorer in Philadelphia.

(GARRY LEISTER COLLECTION, USAMHI)

Private George W. Ackerman served with Battery F from February 1864 until June 1865.

(GARRY LEISTER COLLECTION, USAMHI)

Private William Frederick wears a rain cover on his forage cap.
(GARRY LEISTER COLLECTION, USAMHI)

2nd Lieutenant Franklin P. Brockway. Charles Brockway's younger brother ended the war as an officer after enlisting as a corporal in January 1862.

(GARRY LEISTER COLLECTION, USAMHI)

Private John Marquart served for seventeen months at war's end. He was a 17-year-old boatman from Berks County.

(GARRY LEISTER COLLECTION, USAMHI)

Private Albert Herbine, showing his service stripes on both sleeves.
(GARRY LEISTER COLLECTION, USAMHI)

Private Henry J. Carson, transferred from Battery G in 1864. He enlisted in Pittsburgh, age 19, by occupation & laborer.

(GARRY LEISTER COLLECTION, USAMHI)

Captain John F. Campbell in civilian clothes. Campbell enlisted as a private and rose through the ranks to become the last captain of Battery F in 1865.
(Sue Boardman Collection, USAMHI)

Chapter Eight

Veterans

Following the Mine Run Campaign, Meade withdrew the Army of the Potomac back across the Rapidan River and instructed his corps commanders to place their men in winter camps. Brandy Station became the army's principal supply depot, with the army corps spread out in a horseshoe around the station. The First Corps bivouacked in the Culpeper area, with the Third Corps divisions separated, taking camps on each side of the First. Warren's Second Corps went into camp south of Brandy Station, with headquarters at Cole's Hill. Sedgwick's Sixth Corps camped north of Brandy Station, while the Fifth Corps occupied camps east of the Rappahannock. Cavalry pickets covered the camps in a line some sixty miles long. Meade's own headquarters were on a knoll just east of Fleetwood Hill, near Brandy Station.[1]

The individual regiments and batteries then spent time constructing their winter camps. Many soldiers cut trees and fashioned log huts, using their canvas tents as roofs. The time was generally spent resting at first, as the generals allowed much free time so their soldiers could rest and recuperate after a hard year of campaigning. Food became plentiful as train after train came chugging into Brandy Station to unload fresh supplies. Sutlers were allowed to set up their establishments to further tempt the men. Picket duty was the most tiring duty, but because of the enemy, just across the Rapidan, the army's pickets had to remain alert. Fatigue details built miles of corduroy roads to allow wagons to escape the now-famous Virginia mud, distributed supplies, cooked meals, and performed other mundane tasks.[2]

Most of the soldiers in the army had enlisted for three years, and most units then present had been organized in the summer and early fall of 1861,

---

[1]*Clark B. Hall, "Season of Change: The Winter Encampment of the Army of the Potomac, December 1, 1863-May 4, 1864,"* Blue & Gray Magazine *8 #4 (April 1991): 12-16.*

[2]*Ibid., 18-22, 48.*

in the weeks after the defeat at Manassas. The government knew that perhaps fifty thousand soldiers in the Army of the Potomac would be eligible for discharge. To encourage them to remain in the army, the administration offered incentives. If a soldier re-enlisted for another three years, he would receive a four hundred dollar bounty, plus whatever his state and local community might offer. The veterans would also get a special chevron to sew on their sleeves, and allowed a thirty-day furlough. If three-quarters of a unit re-enlisted, it would be classified as a "veteran volunteer" unit, retain its identity, and all re-enlisted men would go home on furlough together.[3]

The government had started issuing instructions for recruiting veteran volunteers earlier in the year, when the Adjutant General's Office issued General Orders Number 191 on June 25. By November, the Adjutant General's Office had begun to specify how the process of creating veteran volunteers was to work. Shortly before the Mine Run Campaign began, the office issued more information on furloughs and other benefits.[4]

Apparently, Lieutenant Brockway was quick to act on the orders relating to the reenlistment of veteran volunteers. On November 25, Brockway penned a brief letter to Captain Ricketts, in which he informed his captain that he had already sworn in twenty-three men in Battery F, including Sergeants Campbell, Thurston, and Wireman. Then, after going home on a brief leave of absence, Brockway returned and was able to report on December 24 that over three-quarters of the battery had reenlisted. The lieutenant even had induced a dozen Battery G soldiers to transfer to Battery F. Lieutenants Spence and Mitchell were angered over Brockway's high-handedness, but Spence went home on a fifteen-day leave, and Mitchell, penned Brockway, "is not in camp an hour during the day."[5]

On January 3, 1864, Lieutenant Brockway applied for the return of Battery F to Pennsylvania on furlough. The next day, Brockway reported to Captain Henry H. Bingham of Second Corps staff that even more men had reenlisted. As it stood on January 4, ninety-eight men had reenlisted and three men had pledged to reenlist as soon as their two-year terms expired. This meant that 101 of 112 officers and men in the battery had reenlisted,

---

[3]Ibid., 52.

[4]O.R., Series III, volume 3, 414-16 (General Orders #191), 997-99 (General Orders #359, November 6, 1863), 1084 (General Orders #376, November 21, 1863).

[5]*Brockway to Ricketts, November 25, December 24, 1863, Brockway Papers. Eventually, 39 veterans from Battery G re-enlisted in Battery F.*

and "could we include recruits who have been in service only six months, the company would be almost unanimous."[6]

The reenlisted veterans of Battery F left their camp on January 10. They went by rail back to Alexandria, ferried up the river to Washington, then took a train for Philadelphia, where they arrived a couple of days later. Captain Ricketts made an appearance and met his command on January 13; the men officially began their thirty-day furlough on the sixteenth. While they were absent from camp, those men remaining behind were under the command of Lieutenant Spence.[7]

Ricketts was still on disability leave. The surgeon who examined Ricketts back in November 1863 recorded that the captain was suffering debility "occasioned by continued derangement of the digestive system" and recommended a thirty-day leave. On December 9, Dr. D. W. Montgomery, of Orangeville, Columbia County, examined Ricketts and wrote that the captain was "laboring under chronic disease of the inferior portion of the lung and also chronic disease of the bowels, with ulceration of the upper portion of the rectum." Dr. Montgomery recommended a further leave of forty or sixty days. Ricketts promptly turned in the doctor's report for official review. After seeing his battery off, the captain went to Washington, then back to Philadelphia. On January 30, Ricketts paid a visit to the Gettysburg battlefield. Deep mud prevented the captain from touring the entire field, but he was able to visit Professor Michael Jacobs of Pennsylvania College that afternoon. Major Matthews and another man accompanied Ricketts.[8]

Thirty days passed all too quickly for the men of Battery F. As their leaves expired, orders were received to report to Chester Hospital, located fourteen miles south of Philadelphia, conveniently placed near the tracks of the Baltimore and Wilmington Railroad. The government had commandeered a local high school and converted it to a hospital, then

---

[6]*Brockway to Bingham, January 4, 1864, Battery F Papers, NA.*

[7]*Lt. Col. John A. Monroe to Captain John N. Craig, January 9, 1864, Battery F Papers, NA. In this letter, Monroe proposed merging the remaining men of Captain Thompson's Independent Battery C, Pennsylvania Light Artillery, with Ricketts' battery while the veterans of both commands were on leave. Even though Second Corps headquarters approved Monroe's idea, it seems not to have been carried out because both batteries took part in the February 1864 fighting at Morton's Ford. For the battery going to Philadelphia, see Ricketts Diary, January 13, 16, 1864.*

[8]*Ricketts Diary, January 17, 18, 28-30, 1864; Surgeon H. B. Buck, November 20, 1863; and Dr. D. W. Montgomery, December 9, 1863, both in Ricketts Service File, NA.*

added more buildings to the site. Captain Ricketts appeared on time on the sixteenth and found that eleven of his men had reported that day. More continued to trickle in over the next few days.[9]

Sergeant Thurston was less than impressed with his new home. Having spent thirty days among family and friends, Thurston was dismayed to find that there were no beds; the men used their bulky winter overcoats to sleep on. Lunch on the eighteenth was two pieces of hardtack and a cup of coffee. This wasn't home, mused Thurston, but "plenty for a hungry soldier." Dinner was better–"a cup of good rice soup boiled with beef." Thurston could not wait to get back to camp, as he wrote to a friend that he was unable to enjoy himself in such surroundings. Yet other men were depressed, regretting their decision to reenlist. "I have kept up the best appearance," wrote Thurston, "but I have done it with much difficulty."[10]

On Friday, February 26, Captain Ricketts received orders to prepare his company to return to camp "without delay." Eighty men of Battery F left Chester Hospital on the 4:00 p.m. train. After passing through Wilmington, the train continued on to Baltimore, arriving there on Sunday morning at two o'clock. Here, wrote Thurston, "our Boys had quite a run. We went to the Union Relief, and ask for assistance which they refused, we broke it open and helped ourselves. They brought a guard to arrest us, but after we ate our fill we opened a back door and escaped."[11]

By noon, Battery F was back on a train heading for Washington. The 90th Pennsylvania Veteran Volunteer Infantry was on the same train, with the batterymen in the front cars–a dangerous place to be in case of an accident, which were all too frequent in those days. Luckily, only a single man of the 90th fell to his death from the train, and the engine struck and killed a man working on a bridge near Washington. The train arrived in the capital city at 3:00 p.m., the men remaining there until the next morning. Thurston was able to visit the capitol building and commented on the sights he saw–soldiers everywhere.[12]

The battery left Washington on the morning on the twenty-ninth of February, boarding a steamboat for the short trip across and down the

---

[9]*Ricketts Diary, February 16-18, 1864*; W. H. Thurston to Laura, February 23, 1864, Thurston Papers.

[10]*Thurston to Laura, February 23, 24, 1864.*

[11]*Ricketts Diary, February 26-28, 1864*; Thurston to Laura, March 1, 1864. Ricketts recorded that the battery arrived in Baltimore at four o'clock in the morning.

[12]*Ricketts Diary, February 28-29, 1864*; Thurston to Laura, March 1, 1864.

Potomac River to Alexandria, Virginia. It was a "grand sight to behold," recorded Thurston. All sizes of vessels afloat on the blue waters of the Potomac, white tents glistening in the sun on both shores, while forts bristling with big cannon could be seen guarding the approaches to the capital. A train bound for Brandy Station pulled out of Alexandria at 10:00 a.m., arriving at its destination five hours later. It took an additional three hours for the men to leave the train, form, and march back to their old camp.[13]

The men remaining in camp while the veterans were on furlough spent most of the time preforming the usual camp duties. In February, however, the battery saw brief action at Morton's Ford. Major General Benjamin F. Butler, commanding the newly-formed Army of the James, proposed to attack Richmond by a sudden raid and free Union prisoners there. As a diversion, General Sedgwick, commanding the Army of the Potomac in Meade's absence, was ordered to draw Lee's attention.

Although Sedgwick opposed his orders, he decided to cross the Rapidan at Morton's Ford, four miles south of Stevensburg. The terrain across the river from the ford was generally flatter and allowed the attacking Union troops more room to deploy. General Caldwell, temporarily in command of the Second Corps (Warren was ill) sent Alexander Hays and his Third Division, supported by three batteries, storming across the ford on the morning of February 6. Confederate pickets were taken by surprise and Hays' men quickly crossed and deployed on the other side. One of the three batteries was Batteries F&G, commanded by Lieutenant Spence. All three batteries unlimbered above the ford, while Lieutenant Mitchell's section of Batteries F&G was sent downstream to watch the Federal left flank across the river.

Vigorous Confederate artillery fire forced Hays' infantry to halt their advance as units of Ewell's corps moved up in support. Hays' men remained pinned down all day and withdrew after dark, having suffered 255 casualties. Lieutenant Colonel Monroe, Second Corps Artillery Brigade commander, discovered the next morning that the infantry had withdrawn without anybody informing him of this. With difficulty, Mitchell's section was located and withdrawn even as enemy skirmishers, whom Mitchell believed to be friendly troops, approached the river and began firing at his guns. Luckily, only one man was wounded. General Lee reported a casualty total of fifty-seven in this brief affair.[14]

---

[13]*Ricketts Diary, February 29, 1864; Thurston to Laura, March 1, 1864.*

[14]*For the Morton's Ford engagement, see O.R., volume 33, 114-43, with Colonel Monroe's report on pages 137-38.*

Alfred Waud sketch of Ricketts' battery. March 10, 1864

(LIBRARY OF CONGRESS)

A few days after the veterans of Battery F reported for duty, Captain Ricketts, in obedience to a circular order from army headquarters, reported the number of men brought back to camp. The captain's enumeration showed that 102 officers and men had reenlisted and had gone home on furlough. Eighty-one of this number accompanied the captain, together with thirty-nine new recruits; twenty-one veterans failed to report. Of the latter, nine were absent without leave and the remaining dozen absent sick. On March 24, Ricketts forward a revised list which showed that four men were absent sick and twenty absent without leave. That same day, the captain also reported that his battery now numbered 178, a number in excess of the maximum strength allotted to a field battery. Ricketts proposed to transfer twenty-one men to Battery G. The men transferred apparently had not reenlisted, and by disposing of them, Ricketts wrote that his battery would only include veterans and the new recruits. Headquarters approved Ricketts' suggestion and the men were transferred to Battery G on March 26.[15]

But there were still too many men in the battery, which neared two hundred men before Ricketts started trimming it back. In addition to sending men to Battery G, Ricketts got permission from Second Corps Artillery Brigade commander Captain John G. Hazard to send about thirty men to Battery B, 1st Rhode Island, on a temporary basis, it seems. The men so transferred were not happy, and on April 29 addressed a petition to Governor Curtin, asking to be returned to Ricketts' command or else transferred to another Pennsylvania battery. "We are willing to fight for our own state and . . . we are willing to lay down our lives for our own state but for none other." The governor's office sent the petition to the adjutant general, who in turn sent it to General Meade. The general passed it on to General Hancock, who was dismayed by the transfer. It seems that Hazard had acted without clearing it with corps headquarters. Hancock wrote that he would not have approved the transfer, "knowing the difficulties that arise in such cases." Since there were no other Pennsylvania batteries in the corps, Hancock asked Meade to approve a transfer to another Keystone

---

[15]*John C. Caldwell to Major S. F. Barstow, March 4, 1864 (Battery F strength returned to camp); Ricketts to Major C. C. Gilbert, March 24, 1864; Ricketts to Lieutenant G. L. Dwight, March 24, 1864, all in Battery F Papers, NA. All the men who did not return to camp on schedule eventually came in. Four men, "stragglers from your company," were picked up by the Provost Marshal in Philadelphia and each was given $3.00 for transportation to Brandy Station, with the understanding that each man would have the money deducted from his pay. See Lieutenant David Weaver to Commanding Officer, Battery F, April 8, 1864, Battery F Papers, NA.*

State battery. By the time all of this took place, the disaffected men were not transferred to Battery B, 1st Pennsylvania, until December 1864.[16]

Once the battery was back in camp, Captain Ricketts asked General Hunt for new guns to replace his older, worn cannon. As winter gave way to spring, rains drenched the camps and mud was everywhere, at times so severe, wrote Thurston, that the men were doing nothing more than "cooking and feeding the horses." Captain Ricketts was on the sick list for at least ten days (March 12-21), and a few of the new recruits came down with smallpox and had to be quarantined. On March 30, Battery F moved its camp to a cleaner location. Four days later, Battery G was officially detached from F and ordered to report to Camp Barry, an artillery camp within the Washington defenses. Here, Battery G was refitted and spent the next three months garrisoning three of the forts around the city. In July, Battery G moved to the Harper's Ferry area, where it remained until April 1865. After another tour of duty in Washington, the battery was disbanded in June 1865.[17]

The month of April was a busy time for the men of Battery F. New guns were delivered early in the month and Ricketts had his command become familiar with their new weapons; the captain pronounced target practice on April 19 as "excellent." The weather at times was still rainy, which interfered with battery drill and the need to break in all the new recruits. Sergeant Thurston, writing to Laura on April 3, specified that the mud and water was "over shoe deep" at the time, "but I will not complain."[18]

The Artillery Brigade of the Second Corps received a new commander on April 3, when Colonel John C. Tidball arrived. Tidball, a captain in the 2nd United States Artillery, had led one of the horse artillery brigades, then was commissioned colonel of the 2nd New York Heavy Artillery, which was one of the artillery units pulled out of the Washington fortifications to reinforce the Army of the Potomac in the upcoming campaign. To streamline the army, General Meade discontinued the First and Third Corps. Hancock, back in command of the Second Corps, saw his corps

---

[16]*Jacob F. Morton et al to Governor Curtin, April 29, 1864, Battery F Papers, NA. Endorsements on the letter include Matt Quay, Military Secretary to the governor, May 3, 1864; Thomas M. Vincent, adjutant general's office, May 5, 1864; S. F. Barstow, army headquarters, undated; General Hancock, June 8, 1864; Major Hazard, July 4, 1864; Hancock, July 4, 1864. The men were transferred to Battery B on December 29, 1864.*

[17]*Thurston to Laura, March 10, 1864; Ricketts Diary, March 2, 12-21, 28-30, 1864; Bates, Pennsylvania Volunteers, 1:969-70.*

[18]*Thurston to Laura, April 3, 1864; Ricketts Diary, April 19, 1864.*

augmented with the addition of the Third Corps, while Warren was transferred to command of the Fifth Corps, into which the First Corps was merged. Sedgwick retained the Sixth Corps, strengthened by a division of the Third. Pleasonton was relieved of command of the Cavalry Corps, which was given to Major General Philip Sheridan, one of Grant's trusted subordinates. General Burnside, back in command of his Ninth Corps, brought his command up from Alexandria to act in concert with the Army of the Potomac. Since Burnside ranked Meade in seniority, he received his orders directly through Grant. The March 25 consolidation order did not prove popular with the two corps that were discontinued, but the order made the remaining corps more effective.[19]

Rainy weather continued to plague the army. On one occasion, an April 9 review was canceled because of the rain. Generally, soldiers viewed grand reviews with mixed emotions. The review for General Hancock on April 20 went off as planned. Wrote Thurston: "The troops made a splendid display showing how efficient in drill and discipline the American Soldier can become in so short a time." On the other hand, the battery finally got back to camp at two in the afternoon, "tired and hungry." Two days later, General Grant arrived and witnessed another review of the Second Corps, causing Thurston to record how "magnificent and grand" the scene appeared.[20]

The men of Battery F witnessed a military execution on April 25. The victim, Thomas R. Dawson of the 20th Massachusetts, had been found guilty of desertion and rape. Thurston described the scene in another letter to Laura:

> That poor man was hung at 1 o'clock.... His grave was dug at the foot of the scaffold. The troops was formed in a hollow square around the scaffold, colors unfurled to the cool still breeze. The vast assemblage stood, looking to catch the first glimpse of the prisoner. At 12 ½ A.M. [sic] on a high piece of ground in the distance I could by the aid of a field glass discern the slow approach of a wagon drawn by a beautiful pair of horses. As they neared the spot, I could see the prisoner with a white cap on, and the rope around his neck. They drove in the ring so that all could see. He sat in the wagon on a rude rough made coffin, painted dark brown. They drove around the square

---

[19]*Ricketts Diary, April 3, 1864. On April 30, the Artillery Brigade contained the following units: 6th Maine Battery; 10th Massachusetts Battery; 1st New Hampshire Battery; Battery G, 1st New York; 3rd Battalion, 4th New York Heavy Artillery; Battery F, 1st Pennsylvania; Battery A, 1st Rhode Island; Battery B, 1st Rhode Island; Battery K, 4th United States; Batteries C and I, 5th United States.*

[20]*Thurston to Laura, April 9, 20, 1864; Thurston to Laura, April 22, 1864.*

with a band in front playing the dead march untill they reached the scaffold. He looked pale and care worn, but seemed willing to die. He had but little to say. When he passed us he said good bye soldiers. Many tears trinkled down the cheeks of brave men when he made this remark, but he did not shead a tear. He mounted his scaffold firm as though nothing troubled him. The Chaplain made a touching and appropriate appeal in his behalf to the throne of Mercy, and then descended the scaffold. The Provast Marshal drawed the cap down over his face, tied the rope to the top piece, and gave him a white handkerchief to waive when he was ready. He waived his signal at 1 o'clock & five minutes, when the fatal drop fell landing his soul into the spirit world. There he hung suspended between heaven and earth untill the Surgeon pronounced life extinct. He was then cut down and put in the rough coffin and burried.

I had forgotten to write when the drop fell the prisoner fell four feet, his feet touched the ground, he struggled, the guard caught hold of the rope and pulled him from the ground. It looked to me like murder. I understand he is a member of the 19th Mass. Regt., and leaves a family to weep over his sad and disgraceful death. I cannot say he did not deserve to be hung, yet I can never forget the scene.[21]

As the month wore on, ominous signs of a movement began to spread through the camps. On the eighteenth, Thurston wrote that the sutlers were packing up to go home and civilians ordered away as well. Nine days later, Thurston penned that the battery was ordered to draw rations for twenty days. By the thirtieth, the weather boded fair and "all things seem to be ready." Wrote Thurston: "The most trying time in the history of the civil war has arrived. The destiny of the Nation clings around the next struggle. If success crowns our arms we may look for a early peace, if otherwise then all the sufferings and privation incidental to a war so mighty in propations well be naught. Our proud haughty leaders will protract the Struggle untill this fair land be deluged in blood."[22]

Sergeant Thurston was never able to send off his April 30 letter. The next day, the first of May, the battery was inspected; Thurston added a postscript to his letter to say that "every train from Washington is laden to its utmost capacity." Burnside's Ninth Corps, including a division of black soldiers, had arrived. "The army is large and in good condition," wrote

---

[21]*Thurston to Laura, April 24, 1864.* See also Alotta, Civil War Justice, *107-8,* for more details on Dawson's demise and the background to his execution. Also, for a contemporary view of the court-martial, see *Thurston to Laura, April 20, 1864.*

[22]*Thurston to Laura, April 18, 27, 30, 1864.*

Thurston. "I think victory will perch upon our Banners in the next grand Struggle." Still, the sudden deluge of work prevented Thurston from mailing his letter. A May 3 second postscript told the story: "Laura we march at 8 o'clock to knight. Do not make yourself any trouble if you don't hear from me in two or three weeks. I assure you I will write at the earliest oppertunity if my life is spared. A general order was read to us, that this was the final Struggle. Good bye God bless you and pray for me. My kind regards to your family from your devoted and true friend."[23]

---

[23]*Thurston to Laura, April 30, 1864, with postscripts.*

Chapter Nine

The Wilderness Campaign

The 1864 campaign opened on May 4, as the Army of the Potomac began moving from its camps into position to cross the Rapidan River. General Grant and his staff would accompany Meade; the general-in-chief would allow Meade, at least in theory, to control his own army but in accordance with Grant's overall strategy for this campaign. According to the plan worked out that spring, the army would cross the Rapidan at Germanna and Ely's Fords, then move through the Wilderness to the open ground beyond. The Fifth and Sixth Corps, accompanied by James Wilson's Third Cavalry Division, would cross at Germanna Ford and continue south to the Wilderness Tavern, located on the Orange Turnpike. Hancock's Second Corps, preceded by Gregg's Second Cavalry Division, and followed by the Artillery Reserve, would cross at Ely's Ford and move south to Chancellorsville.

The routes of march for day two of the movement would depend on Lee's reaction to the Yankee thrust. Lee's troops could approach the marching columns of the Army of the Potomac via the Orange Turnpike and its smaller subsidiary to the south, the Orange Plank Road, which linked up with the turnpike between Chancellorsville and the Wilderness Tavern. Burnside's Ninth Corps, acting under Grant's direct orders because Burnside outranked Meade in terms of seniority, would follow the army and protect the huge ammunition and supply trains. If all went well, cavalry would detect approaching Confederate columns, delay them, and allow the Union infantry safe passage through the tangled Wilderness before Lee could attack.[1]

Meade planned for the movement to begin during the evening of May 3-4, so that darkness would veil the approach of his army to the Rapidan fords. The Second Corps Artillery Brigade assembled near Madden's House sometime before midnight, awaiting the order to move to Ely's Ford. As the infantry divisions passed by, Colonel Tidball doled out some of his

---

[1] For the Union plans, see Edward Steere, *The Wilderness Campaign* (Harrisburg, PA: The Stackpole Company, 1960), 29-40.

batteries to each division; Battery F was detached to follow Brigadier General Gershom Mott's Fourth Division across the ford. Gregg's cavalry easily cleared out Confederate pickets at Ely's Ford, allowing the engineers to assemble two pontoon bridges. Hancock's infantry began crossing on the morning of May 4 and by mid-afternoon, the corps had assembled in the vicinity of the Chancellor House ruins, while the mounted units rode on ahead to watch the roads to the south.[2]

Captain Ricketts commented in his diary that Battery F encamped on the same ground on which it had been posted a year before, when the guns had unlimbered during the waning stages of the battle of Chancellorsville. Indeed, Lieutenant Brockway later wrote that it was a "wonderful coincidence." Continued Brockway: "The spot was full of interest, as at this point battery after battery had been massed, the horses sent to the rear and entrenchments made of logs, knapsacks, dead horses, limber-chests and whatever came to hand. . . . A few hundred yards to the front were the ruins of the Chancellor House, and over the whole country was scattered the usual debris of a battle-field. The enemy had leveled the entrenchments after Hooker's retreat."[3]

The Union army resumed its march on the morning of May 5. Hancock's Second Corps continued south, taking the road past Catharine Furnace to Todd's Tavern, where, after reception of morning orders to halt, three divisions were concentrated, with Francis C. Barlow's division in the rear near Catharine Furnace. Hancock was ordered to hold his corps in readiness to march while the generals decided what to do about the presence of Confederates to the west. "The day was fine, though intensely hot," recalled Lieutenant Brockway."[4]

In the meantime, Union cavalry tangled with Confederate cavalry and infantry on both the Orange Turnpike and Plank Road, as well as cavalry on Catharpin Road beyond Todd's Tavern. Grant and Meade were aware by this time that Lee knew the Union army was in the Wilderness, but were unsure of the enemy's positions. By late morning, elements of Warren's

---

[2]O.R., *volume 36, part 1, 507;* Ricketts Diary, May 3-4, *1864.*

[3]Ricketts Diary, May 4, 1864; Charles B. Brockway, "Across the Rapidan," Philadelphia Weekly Times, *January 7, 1882.* Brockway must have written this article just after the war because Samuel P. Bates, Pennsylvania Volunteers *1:965,* quoted from an unidentified Brockway submission to his volume. The Bates version and 1882 version are not quite the same, but very similar.

[4]O.R., *volume 36, part 1, 507;* Brockway, "Across the Rapidan"; Steere, Wilderness, *88-107.*

Fifth Corps had deployed on and south of the Orange Turnpike, facing units of Ewell's corps, while Sedgwick brought up most of the Sixth Corps in support. Worried about maintaining a link with Hancock, who was now some four miles beyond Warren's left, Meade sent Brigadier General George W. Getty's Second Division of the Sixth Corps to occupy the crossroads where the Orange Plank Road and Brock Road–the latter running north-south–intersected. Union cavalry reported that prisoners taken during the morning skirmishing were from A. P. Hill's Third Corps. Getty arrived at the crossroads as blueclad troopers were retreating through the intersection. Getty immediately deployed skirmishers, who drove the enemy back. Dead and wounded enemy skirmishers were found within thirty yards of the crossroads.[5]

Meade then sent a message to Hancock, ordering him to bring the Second Corps north to the Brock intersection and support Getty. Union infantry began moving by one o'clock, and most of the afternoon was spent in moving along narrow, dusty trails and deploying in dense underbrush. The corps march was delayed over an hour when the messenger from Meade apparently went astray in the woods and took time to find Hancock. Once the corps began moving north, Captain Ricketts received an early order directing him to report to General Getty, who had no artillery with his three brigades. Upon reporting to the general, Ricketts discovered that there was little open space to unlimber his battery. He sent Lieutenant Brockway and his two-gun section to the front and retained the remaining four guns in reserve.[6]

Brockway commented on his assignment:

I may truthfully say that I never expected to come out of the engagement alive, nor to bring any of my men out. The infantry on my right and left were to a great extent shielded by the wilderness, while I had to take the open road, and those of us who were mounted formed a very good mark and were visible to the enemy a mile off. The road was narrow–a ditch on each side–with no chance to limber up and retreat in case of accidents. I therefore had my caissons follow some distance in the rear and put the guns in echelon, or in an oblique line, in order to enable me to open with both at once. I also took the precaution of having several shells prepared, as I knew the attack would be sudden.[7]

---

[5]*Steere,* Wilderness, *131, 136-37.*

[6]O.R., *volume 36, part 1, 507;* O.R. Supplement, *volume 6, 552; Ricketts Diary, May 5, 1864; Steere,* Wilderness, *135-36, 184-96.*

[7]*Brockway, "Across the Rapidan."*

When Brockway placed his section in position, "a dead silence reigned." Sergeant Thurston, commanding one of Brockway's guns (Sergeant Frank Brockway was in charge of the other), recalled that Lieutenant Brockway told him that "should I fall do the best you can." The lieutenant could see their own skirmishers only fifty yards in front. Farther down the road, perhaps four hundred yards, were enemy soldiers, leisurely pacing back and forth, watching the Yankees.[8]

At about 3:30 p.m., the lead elements of Hancock's infantry arrived and began filing into line behind Getty's troops. The wooded terrain and lack of open spaces slowed the deployment of the corps. An impatient Meade sent a peremptory order to Getty to attack immediately; fighting on Warren's front had been going on for more than two hours and Meade wished Hancock and Getty to exert some pressure on Hill's troops and perhaps aid Warren's continued engagement. Getty's men were already in position. The Vermont Brigade of Colonel Lewis A. Grant was lined up south of the road. Brigadier General Frank Wheaton's brigade was formed on the right of the Plank Road, with Brigadier General Henry L. Eustis' Fourth Brigade on the right. As the Second Corps approached, Mott's division formed on Grant's left, while Major General David B. Birney's two brigades were divided as the attack began. Alexander Hays led his troops behind Getty's to support the right, while Brigadier General Hobart Ward's men supported the left.[9]

Lieutenant Brockway recalled that Getty's skirmishers moved forward at 4:30 p.m. "A few steps aroused the sleeping lion and the silence soon changed to a deafening roar of musketry," penned the lieutenant. Getty's entire line crashed into the Confederate battle line, composed of troops from Major General Henry Heth's Division. Although outnumbered by the Union attackers, Heth's men used the wooded terrain to advantage and fought their opponents to a standstill. Brockway advanced his guns some two hundred yards, unlimbered, and went into action, throwing percussion shells into the enemy's ranks. A 12-pounder Napoleon appeared in the road to counter Brockway's fire. "Here was a tangible enemy, and we all breathed freer in seeing something definite to fire at," he wrote. Brockway's gunners were veterans, and a shot soon exploded an enemy caisson, while shortly thereafter most of the opposing men and horses had been disabled. The Southern boys fired rounds of canister at the Federals, tearing up splinters from the plank road and occasionally knocking over a man or horse. "But

---

[8]Brockway, "Across the Rapidan"; William M. Thurston to Laura, November 14, 1864.

[9]Steere, Wilderness, *197-200, 207-8.*

our percussion shell was superior and their artillery was soon withdrawn."[10]

Heth's infantry then charged forward. As the men in blue recoiled, Brockway's guns belched forth solid shot, then switched to canister. Supporting infantry rallied behind his guns and Hancock sent forward more troops to bolster Getty's failed attack. Brockway's gunners cleared the road in front of them, but individual enemy soldiers skulked behind trees on both sides of the road, loading behind cover, then jumping into the road to fire at the artillerists. These tactics failed to drive Brockway's section back, however; the lieutenant wrote that the enemy firing was wildly inaccurate. Two hours had passed, and Brockway discovered, to his dismay, that only a single round of canister remained.[11]

Captain Ricketts, watching from the rear, sent forward Lieutenant Snider's section to relieve Brockway. Snider unlimbered his guns farther back on the road, whereupon Brockway ordered his men to attach prolonges and draw the guns off by hand after firing their last round of canister as a parting shot. Brockway may also have left a caisson behind, the horses having been disabled. Snider was not in action very long before one of his 3-inch rifles burst, breaking off a foot and a half of the muzzle.[12]

About the time Snider went into action, fresh troops arrived to bolster Heth's battered division. Major General Cadmus M. Wilcox brought his division, also of Hill's corps, to the support of Heth's brigades. When Wilcox reported to Heth that his men were arriving, Heth suggested to Wilcox that his fresh troops should attack, to which Wilcox readily assented. Brigadier General Samuel McGowan's Brigade of South Carolinians charged forward astride the Plank Road, driving back the Union infantry opposed to his fresh troops. McGowan reported that a two-gun section of artillery fired a couple of rounds at his approaching men, then was removed by hand, leaving a caisson. The Carolinians continued forward and encountered Snider's guns. One had already burst, and the

---

[10]*Brockway, "Across the Rapidan." The lone Confederate cannon was detached from the Madison Light Artillery, a Mississippi battery serving in Major William T. Poague's Battalion. Lieutenant Frank George brought this Napoleon into action against Brockway's two guns.*

[11]*Ibid.*

[12]*Ibid. In this article, Brockway does not specify to which section the burst cannon belonged. Evidence suggests Snider's; Ricketts' official report does not make it clear, nor did Sergeant Thurston, who, it seems, would have mentioned the bursting if he had witnessed it.*

Corporal Ephraim Berger, a transfer from Battery G, wears a rain cover over his forage cap.

(GARRY LEISTER COLLECTION, USAMH)I

remaining gun was unable to stem the gray tide. Snider's artillerists abandoned their guns and fled as the Confederates swept through the area.[13]

Help was on the way for Snider's beleaguered gunners. As Brigadier General John Gibbon's Second Division arrived in the rear of the fighting, his brigades moved forward to bolster the sagging Union line. Colonel Samuel S. Carroll led his brigade into the fray and encountered McGowan's advancing Carolinians. The fighting became even more fierce and confused; some units of McGowan's Brigade broke through and seized Snider's guns, while other elements of the brigade were fought to a standstill and eventually forced back. At some point during the confusion, Captain Francis Butterfield of the 8th Ohio, serving on Carroll's staff, rallied some men from the 8th Ohio and 14th Indiana and recaptured Snider's single working gun. Ricketts was about to send in his remaining section when General Hancock ordered him to gather his battery and withdraw from the fighting.[14]

The withdrawal of Ricketts' battery gave the sections a chance to regroup after the day's action. Casualties were surprisingly light—one man killed and two wounded. A dozen horses were killed and wounded. The battery expended 135 rounds of ammunition, and had lost the one gun that burst; it was buried near Todd's Tavern to prevent its capture by the enemy. The terrific struggle continued the next day, May 6, but Battery F was not engaged. Ricketts went into position somewhere near the Brock Road, behind the line of battle, but was not engaged throughout the day.[15]

The two-day struggle in the Wilderness cost the Army of the Potomac a staggering 17,666 casualties, with at least nine thousand Confederates hors de combat. But, instead of withdrawing across the Rapidan, or, as Lee suspected, heading to Fredericksburg and crossing the Rappahannock River there, Grant ordered Meade to move the army toward Spotsylvania Court House. Grant hoped to exert more pressure on the Army of Northern Virginia by sidling to the left, out into open terrain. The general expected that another battle would be fought somewhere along the North Anna

---

[13]*Brockway, "Across the Rapidan"; O.R. Supplement, volume 6, 704 (Heth's report), 775-76 (McGowan's report). In his report, McGowan did not mention the capture of any guns. Although another brigade may have seized Snider's section, it seems unlikely that another unit moved across or through McGowan's line of advance.*

[14]*O.R., volume 36, part 1, 320, 446, 448, 531-32; Brockway, "Across the Rapidan"; Steere, Wilderness, 229-30.*

[15]*Ricketts Diary, May 5, 1864; O.R., volume 36, part 1, 531-32.*

River. The Army of the Potomac would move to the southeast and continue to engage Lee's troops whenever the opportunity presented itself.[16]

Accordingly, the order of march for May 8 dictated that the army would move toward Spotsylvania Court House. Hancock's Second Corps would form the rearguard, allowing the rest of the army to move on roads behind his position. Once the roads were clear, Hancock would move the Second Corps to Todd's Tavern, where his men would form the right flank of the army. The movements that day were not as planned because the army engineers had erroneous maps that had one intersection that simply did not exist. Hancock's infantry divisions left their breastworks that morning and by noon were generally in position around Todd's Tavern. Captain Ricketts placed Battery F in position near the tavern, positioned to fire toward the front. Occasional skirmish fire broke out along the Second Corps front, but the major fighting of the day occurred at Laurel Hill, where the Fifth Corps attacked the Confederate First Corps, which had arrived in front of Spotsylvania before Warren's blueclad infantry.[17]

The fighting at Laurel Hill on the eighth touched off the Battle of Spotsylvania, which continued through May 18. On May 9, three divisions of the Second Corps moved to the southeast, taking position on Warren's right on the north side of the Po River. Mott's Fourth Division, supported by Battery F and Captain Edwin B. Dow's 6th Maine Battery, remained at Todd's Tavern, protecting the right rear. That evening, Mott received an order to move his division to the left of the Sixth Corps and connect with Burnside's right. Captain Ricketts wrote in his diary that the battery moved at three o'clock in the morning of May 10. It took the division approximately four hours to move behind the Union lines. Mott deployed his division in the vicinity of the Brown House, where he found two detached New Jersey regiments of the Sixth Corps. The Sixth Corps was now under the command of Brigadier General Horatio G. Wright; General Sedgwick had been killed on the ninth. Mott was instructed to report to Wright for additional orders, and to send skirmishers to the east to locate Burnside's right flank.[18]

Attacks by the Second and Fifth Corps against Lee's left flank failed to gain any headway. Later in the afternoon of the tenth, Colonel Emory Upton

---

[16] William D. Matter, If It Takes All Summer: The Battle of Spotsylvania *(Chapel Hill: University of North Carolina Press, 1988), 4-5, 22-23.*

[17] O.R., *volume 36, part 1, 508, 532;* Matter, Spotsylvania, *44-95.*

[18] Ricketts Diary, *May 9-10, 1864;* O.R., *volume 36, part 1, 532;* O.R. Supplement, *volume 6, 555;* Matter, Spotsylvania, *130, 138.*

led twelve picked regiments of the Sixth Corps in a massed attack against the left face of what was becoming a Confederate salient. Prior to Upton's attack, the Union high command had only a general idea of Lee's exact line of battle. Burnside, on the left, had crossed the Ni River via the Fredericksburg Road and ran up against Confederate entrenchments before reaching Spotsylvania Court House. The position of Union skirmishers, extending from Wright's left to Burnside's right, seemed to indicate that a portion of the enemy held a salient, pushing up between Burnside and the rest of the army.[19]

Colonel Upton, viewing the formidable enemy earthworks, thought that a massed attack in which the charging Yankees would not stop to fire, but continue moving until they reached the enemy line, would work. General Mott was instructed to cooperate with Upton's planned attack. But the general had conflicting orders–If Burnside was attacked before five o'clock, Mott was to move south toward the enemy and charge their works. If Burnside needed reinforcements, Mott was to send only a part of his division. The general was also cautioned to use his artillery "freely." With conflicting orders such as these, it is no wonder that the former Third Corps veterans would not live up to their previous reputation.[20]

Confused orders meant that the Union attacks scheduled for late afternoon did not go off as planned. Upton's attack went in against the western face of the Confederate salient shortly after 6:00 p.m. Although initially successful, Upton's men were forced to retreat. Mott sent in his available regiments an hour earlier. His battle line moved south through woods, driving back enemy skirmishers. As the division emerged from the woods about five or six hundred yards from the Confederate entrenchments, Southern artillery pieces opened fire, pelting the Yankees with canister. Mott's attack quickly went to pieces and the survivors turned and fled, finally reassembling near their starting point. "Motts Div. acted shamefully," penned Ricketts in his diary that night. Battery F expended twenty-eight rounds of ammunition in support of the attack. One horse was killed.[21]

The next day, May 11, Mott's division was withdrawn from the front in order to rest and regroup. Dow and Ricketts also moved to the rear and spent the day resting. By now, the Union high command had sketched out

---

[19]*Matter,* Spotsylvania, *131-55.*

[20]Ibid., *158-59.*

[21]O.R., *volume 36, part 1, 532; Ricketts Diary, May 10, 1864; Matter,* Spotsylvania, *158-61.*

the Confederate positions and determined that the vulnerable point was the salient which Mott had unsuccessfully attacked on the tenth. Grant ordered Meade to move the Second Corps to the vicinity of the Brown House and charge the enemy works at 4:00 a.m. on the twelfth. Hancock would use Barlow, Birney, and Mott in the assault, with Gibbon's division in reserve. Rain, which had begun during the night of the tenth, turned the terrain to slippery mud. Hancock's corps began moving after dark on the eleventh and was in position well before the appointed hour.[22]

Hancock's infantry began to move forward shortly after 4:30 a.m. on May 12. Although enemy pickets got off warning shots before fleeing, the mass of Union infantry pushed forward without serious opposition and crashed into and over the Confederate entrenchments at the apex of the salient. Major General Edward Johnson, a brigade commander, more than four thousand of his men, and twenty cannon, were seized by the surging blue tide. Meanwhile, in the rear, Colonel Tidball had deployed five batteries around the Landrum House, the cannon lobbing shells over the heads of their infantry some thousand yards ahead into the enemy ranks. It continued to rain, making the entire day's battle a soggy affair.[23]

Although in position during the day, Battery F seemingly failed to expend any ammunition. Hancock had established his headquarters nearby and so the men of the battery were able to see their commander throughout the day. Lieutenant Brockway, like many other Yankees in the rear, could not believe the initial success of the attack. "A moment after the charge began we beheld a crowd of men coming confusedly to the rear. I could scarcely believe the corps had broken, especially as there had been but little firing; but the gray uniforms soon dispelled the fear. They came by us in thousands, and we began to fear they would outnumber the weak guard sent with them." Brockway saw General Johnson brought in under guard. Hancock greeted him cordially. The two generals shared a drink before Hancock sent Johnson on to army headquarters.[24]

The Union breakthrough was contained and the day witnessed savage close combat as Lee's troops built a new line of works to the rear of the salient. Warren's, Wright's, and Burnside's troops all attacked during the day, and by nightfall, thousands had fallen on both sides. During the night, Lee's troops fell back to their new line. No serious action occurred on the thirteenth, as the rains continued and turned the ground into mud. In fact,

---

[22]*Matter, Spotsylvania, 183-86.*

[23]*Matter, Spotsylvania, 191-99;* O.R. Supplement, *volume 6, 555-56.*

[24]*Brockway, "Across the Rapidan."*

it rained for five straight days, forcing both armies to suspend active movements. During this time, Battery F remained in position for two more days, then on the fifteenth, the Second Corps was withdrawn as Meade and Grant redeployed the Army of the Potomac farther to the east. Birney's division was left in place to support Burnside's right, while the Second, Fifth, and Sixth Corps moved to Burnside's left. Ricketts went into park across the Ny River near the Harris House, staying here through the seventeenth.[25]

On the thirteenth, Sergeant Thurston was able to write a brief letter to Laura. "We have been fighting for 9 days," he told his sweetheart. "I will not pretend to describe the horrible scenes of the field but suffice to say it was awful. The field is covered with dead and dying we have won a cruelly fought victory. . . . I am almost tired out. We have not taken off the harness since we are marching. Our horses are tired out." Thurston surely echoed the feelings of thousands of other blue and gray veterans in hinting at the horrific casualties inflicted thus far and the seemingly endless marching and fighting, something that none of them had previously experienced.[26]

Changes in the artillery organization occurred during this time as well. On May 11, Grant had suggested to Meade that the army's Artillery Reserve be sent back to Washington, as these batteries had not been engaged because of the wooded terrain. Grant wished to save horseflesh and forage. Meade did not react, but on May 16 Grant sent his subordinate an order requiring that the reserve be sent back. When told of the order, General Hunt, the army's artillery commander, quickly came up with an alternative to avoid losing the reserve, which he had created and nurtured. Hunt recommended that each battery then with the army be downsized from six to four guns. The reserve batteries would be distributed among the three corps, each of which would have a dozen batteries. Thus, according to Hunt, the number of guns with each corps would remain about the same. He also recommended keeping six caissons with each battery to function as additional ammunition wagons. Hunt's plan was accepted and announced on May 17. Battery F lost a section and was reduced to four guns, as happened to all other six-gun batteries in the army. Each battery would have a maximum of one hundred horses.[27]

---

[25]O.R., *volume 36, part 1, 510, 532*; Matter, Spotsylvania, *271-303*.

[26]*Thurston to Laura, May 13, 1864.*

[27]*Matter, Spotsylvania, 301-2. Ricketts did not mention the reduction in either his diary or his official report. A copy of Colonel Tidball's May 17 order is in Ricketts' Papers.*

On the night of the seventeenth, the Second Corps moved back to the right again, in preparation for an attack in conjunction with the Sixth Corps. The attack went forward on May 18, but accurate Confederate artillery fire, as well as the presence of a strong abatis in front of the new Confederate line, broke up the attacking force and inflicted another thousand casualties. Battery F was in position supporting Mott's brigade (Hancock had consolidated the Third and Fourth Divisions on May 14 and placed Birney in command) but was not actively engaged during the day. Battery F was withdrawn that night and went into camp near army headquarters.[28]

The last major action at Spotsylvania occurred on May 19 as Ewell's Confederates attempted to flank the Union army on its right. The attacking Rebels encountered a newly-arrived division of heavy artillery regiments from Washington. The heavies had been issued infantry gear and were sent to reinforce the army. Although suffering heavy casualties, the Yankees blunted Ewell's assault. Warren rushed troops to help and Birney's division of the Second Corps also moved to the right.[29]

By this time, Grant had decided to leave the Spotsylvania area and continue the campaign elsewhere. General Hancock's corps was instructed to move to the southeast, staying north of the Ny River. When his troops reached the Richmond, Fredericksburg, and Potomac Railroad at Guinea Station, they were to move south along the railroad. If Lee reacted and moved to engage Hancock, the rest of the army would follow Lee and attempt to fight the Army of Northern Virginia before it could entrench. If Lee did not take the bait, the rest of the army would follow Hancock and force Lee to abandon his strong entrenchments. This was a well-conceived plan.[30]

Hancock's corps broke camp and begin moving on the night of May 20-21. After an hour's delay waiting for Brigadier General Alfred Torbert's Union cavalry to clear the roads ahead of him, Hancock pushed his men forward and shortly before dawn, Barlow's division reached Guinea Station. Union and Confederate cavalry skirmished and the infantry rested briefly before continuing onward. The Rebel troopers withdrew across the Mattapony River and the march continued. By nine o'clock, Torbert's cavalry reached Milford Station, where the Union advance encountered enemy infantry. After a 45-minute combat, Torbert's men occupied Milford

---

[28]*O.R., volume 36, part 1, 532; Matter,* Spotsylvania, *305-12.*

[29]*Matter,* Spotsylvania, *317-25.*

[30]Ibid., *312-13;* J. Michael Miller, The North Anna Campaign, "Even To Hell Itself," May 21-26, 1864 *(Lynchburg, VA: H. E. Howard, Inc., 1989), 1-7.*

as the Virginians of Brigadier General James L. Kemper's Brigade withdrew across the river. Hancock's troops later moved through the station, crossed the river, and deployed in a semi-circular line, with both flanks anchored on the Mattaponi. Battery F occupied a position on the left of the Union line, supporting the heavy artillery regiments. They were organized into a new Fourth Division, commanded by Brigadier General Robert O. Tyler, the former Artillery Reserve commander. Ricketts and two other batteries were unlimbered to support Tyler's units.[31]

Lee did not accept the Second Corps bait. Later that morning, after worrying that Grant might slip around his flank and head for Richmond, Lee decided to withdraw his army behind the North Anna River to protect Hanover Junction, an important supply depot located where two railroads came together. Throughout the afternoon, the Southern army began its withdrawal, even as Warren and the Fifth Corps crossed the Mattapony at Guinea Depot, a position closer to Hancock and threatening Lee's right flank. By nightfall on May 22, most of Lee's army was behind the North Anna, with Meade's troops following. During the twenty-second, Hancock's troops remained in position, sending out reconnaissance parties in an attempt to locate the retreating Confederates.[32]

Hancock began moving his corps southward at 5:00 a.m. on May 23. The Second Corps was charged with attacking and holding Chesterfield Ford across the North Anna. Warren moved his Fifth Corps on a parallel road, heading for Jericho Bridge. Late that morning, while halted two miles from the river, Warren interrogated a runaway slave who said that there was no Jericho Bridge. The general then realized that his maps were inaccurate and so decided to head for Chesterfield Bridge, which was an actual crossing point rather than the fictitious Chesterfield Ford. Warren also realized that his line of march would merge with Hancock's at Mount Carmel Church, so he halted to allow Hancock to proceed.[33]

Hancock sent Birney's division ahead to seize the bridge. Three Federal batteries unlimbered to support the attack, while five more batteries, Ricketts' among them, went into position farther to the left, opposite the railroad bridge. The combined barrage from these thirty-two Union guns was answered when Colonel Edward Porter Alexander brought forward several of his batteries to duel with Tidball's guns. Alexander wrote that his men had a "sharp little duel across the river with the Federal

---

[31]*Miller, North Anna, 12-22;* O.R., *volume 36, part 1, 510; Ricketts Diary, May 20, 1864.*

[32]*Miller, North Anna, 23-49.*

[33]Ibid., *50-55.*

batteries." But Birney's troops surged forward and struck the Confederate redoubt protecting the bridge, breaking four South Carolina units of Colonel John W. Henagan's Brigade, capturing seventy-three of the slower Carolinians. During the heated artillery duel, Ricketts' four guns expended 218 rounds of ammunition.[34]

Meanwhile, Warren's Fifth Corps crossed at Jericho Mill and had a sharp engagement with A. P. Hill's corps; after the fighting subsided, the Union infantry remained entrenched on the south side of the North Anna. The evening, Lee pulled his army into a v-shaped line, its apex at Ox Ford on the North Anna. Hill's corps occupied the left, Anderson the center, and Ewell on the right. Lee's men entrenched, hoping to entice the Yankees into more frontal assaults. Meanwhile, Wright brought the Sixth Corps across the river and reinforced Warren. Early the next day, May 25, Hancock crossed the river and entrenched, facing Ewell's men. Burnside brought up the Ninth Corps and formed across from Ox Ford; he also sent a division to reinforce Hancock. Battery F accompanied the corps, taking position on the left of Gibbon's division. Gibbon moved forward late in the afternoon and located the main Confederate line. After a brisk engagement with Ewell's troops, the Yankees fell back. Battery F apparently did not open fire during the day.[35]

Attacks by the Ninth Corps at Ox Ford were also repelled with comparative ease by the strongly-entrenched Confederates. Grant decided against further assaults and issued orders for another turning movement. The army would move to the east and circle around Lee's troops. Accordingly, the right wing retraced its steps across the North Anna and headed east, spearheaded by two of Sheridan's cavalry divisions, now back with the army after the raid toward Richmond. Burnside followed, and Hancock brought up the rear. The march began after dark on the twenty-sixth. Grant's objective was to move southeastward and cross the Pamunkey River, a stream formed by the junction of the North and South Anna rivers. Farther east, the Pamunkey united with the Mattapony to form the York River. Once the army neared the York, it could be supplied by ship.[36]

---

[34]*O.R., volume 36, part 1, 510-11; Ricketts Diary, May 24, 1864; Gary W. Gallagher (editor),* Fighting for the Confederacy: The Personal Recollections of General Edward Porter Alexander *(Chapel Hill: University of North Carolina Press, 1989), 388;* Miller, North Anna, *56-60.*

[35]*Miller,* North Anna, *61-120; Ricketts Diary, May 25, 1864; O.R., volume 36, part 1, 511.*

[36]*Miller,* North Anna, *130-1, 136; William Swinton,* Campaigns of the Army of the Potomac *(New York: Charles B. Richardson, 1866), 477-78.*

The Second Corps began moving only after the Sixth Corps cleared the roads, about ten o'clock in the morning of the twenty-seventh. Captain Ricketts recorded that Battery F marched eleven miles that day. Men and animals on both sides began to suffer; it had not rained since the fifteenth, and the roads were reduced to inches of dry powder by thousands of marching feet and hooves. Clouds of dust marked the paths of columns of troops. By June 1st, Sergeant Thurston could write that the "heat is excessive."[37]

On May 28th, the Second Corps crossed the Pamunkey River and went into position in the center of the Union line, the Fifth to the left and the Sixth to the right. Lee's army remained in front of the Army of the Potomac as both sides probed each other's positions. The resulting fighting on May 28-31 resulted in another stalemate, a series of engagements collectively known as the Pamunkey, Totopotomoy Creek, and Bethesda Church, while cavalry sparred at each other at Haw's Shop and other points along the lines. Battery F was not actively engaged throughout these operations. On May 29, most of the corps artillery lay in park behind the lines as the infantry developed the enemy positions; Battery F moved six miles as the lines advanced. May 30 saw two brigades attack and seize Confederate skirmish rifle pits, which were converted for Union occupation. The main enemy line, behind Totopotomoy Creek, looked too strong to attack. Colonel Tidball deployed most of the corps artillery along a low ridge behind the line of battle to support the infantry. Battery F was not engaged in the late afternoon artillery duel that day, although Ricketts' men were busy erecting earthworks in front of their cannon. Battery F's four guns finally were engaged on the thirty-first, expending nineteen rounds as Hancock's brigades searched the opposing lines. One man was wounded in Battery F.[38]

On June 1, Sergeant Thurston finally had a chance to send another letter to Laura, the first in twelve days. "The campaign thus far has been one of the most trying nature for man and beast," wrote Thurston. Rations were short and both men and animals suffered from the intense heat and dry weather. "When the troops march clouds of dust raise[,] hiding the men from each other almost suffocating them." "Don't forget to write often," the sergeant admonished his friend. "Your letters appeal me so much pleasure when I am tired and worn out almost ready to faint."[39]

---

[37]*Walker, Second Corps, 497-98; Ricketts Diary, May 27, 1864; Thurston to Laura, June 1, 1864.*

[38]*Walker, Second Corps, 498-503;* O.R., *volume 36, part 1, 532; Ricketts Diary, May 28-31, 1864;* O.R. Supplement, *volume 6, 561-2.*

[39]*Thurston to Laura, June 1, 1864.*

The first day of June saw yet more fighting along the opposing lines. That morning, the Sixth Corps withdrew from the right and began marching to Cold Harbor, as Grant ordered yet another flank movement, sidestepping the army toward the Chickahominy River. Birney withdrew his forward troops and consolidated his position. Confederate troops attacked Birney in the afternoon. "Firing quite sharp and continuous," recorded Major William G. Mitchell, one of Hancock's staff officers. At 4:50 p.m., General Gibbon sent his skirmishers forward to develop the enemy line, the Federal artillery opening fire in support. Captain Ricketts wrote that his battery was engaged all day. "Made some splendid shooting," he said, as his gunners expended 140 rounds. After dark, the corps began its own march toward Cold Harbor, Ricketts accompanying Birney's Third Division. The fighting known as Totopotomoy was over; Cold Harbor was next.[40]

Union cavalry had dueled for possession of Cold Harbor on May 31. That evening, Wright and the Sixth Corps were sent to reinforce Sheridan. At the same time, Major General William F. Smith, commanding the Eighteenth Corps, Army of the James, disembarked at White House Landing on the Pamunkey River on the thirtieth. Owing to a mistake in orders, General Smith's command moved northwest along the river rather than heading to Cold Harbor, as was intended. As a result, Smith's troops followed the Sixth Corps to the vicinity; both corps launched a late afternoon attack on June 1 that seized some of the enemy's forward works, but failed to breach Lee's main line.[41]

The Army of the Potomac spent the second day of June forming for an assault on Lee's entrenched Confederates. Hancock moved to the left of the army, with Wright on his right, followed in turn by Smith, Warren, and Burnside, the latter two corps still in the vicinity of Bethesda Church. A sharp Southern attack on Burnside's line forced that general to retract his position somewhat; a further attack on Warren, although initially successful, was repelled and the day ended with no general assault by Meade's army.[42]

The Union assault commenced about 4:30 the next morning (June 3). Although Barlow's and Gibbon's divisions made some encroachments in

---

[40]O.R., *volume 36, part 1, 366, 532;* Ricketts Diary, June 1, 1864.

[41]William F. Smith, "The Eighteenth Corps at Cold Harbor," in Robert U. Johnson and Clarence C. Buel (editors), Battles and Leaders of the Civil War, *4 volumes (New York: The Century Company, 1884-1889; reprint edition, New York: Thomas Yoseloff, 1956), 4:221-24;* Swinton, Campaigns, *481-83.*

[42]Swinton, Campaigns, *483-84.*

Alfred Waud sketch of Battery F at Cold Harbor, June 2, 1864. (LIBRARY OF CONGRESS)

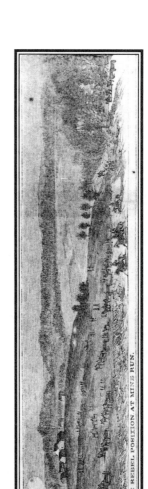

Sketch of Batteries F&G at Mine Run, November 1863. Ricketts is in center of drawing, Arnold's Rhode Island battery on left, Roe's Farm in distance. (LIBRARY OF CONGRESS)

the enemy line, they were eventually compelled to retire with heavy losses. In less than an hour's fighting, the Army of the Potomac sustained a horrific butcher's bill of some twelve thousand men, against less than fifteen hundred Confederates. That day, Captain Ricketts received orders to report to General Smith, whose corps was not adequately provided with artillery. Battery F went into position and was engaged all day, firing 230 rounds. Two horses were killed and three wounded.[43]

The repulse of the Union attack was followed by a hasty entrenching all along the line, which in places was so close to the enemy that both sides kept up a steady musketry fire. Ricketts had his men throw up earthworks to protect their guns. "All that saves my battery from being destroyed," wrote Ricketts on June 4, "is the fact of its being strongly entrenched." Enemy sharpshooters annoyed the entire army throughout the next several days, as both sides rested and refitted as best as possible under the circumstances. As Sergeant Thurston wrote a hasty letter to Laura, he commented that "Musket balls are whizzing around me as I am writing, but I have some shelter that we have thrown up and I feel safe and have undertook to write to a friend."[44]

Fighting erupted on the fifth and Battery F expended thirty-two rounds in repelling enemy forays. Skirmishing continued the next day, when both sides displayed flags of truce, allowing work parties to go between the lines to remove the wounded and bury the fast-decomposing dead. One batteryman was wounded on the sixth. Ricketts was relieved from duty with the Eighteenth Corps and returned to Hancock's position on June 8, unlimbering at four o'clock that afternoon. After darkness fell, the cannoneers went to work throwing up earthworks to protect themselves from enemy sharpshooters. Pioneers went to work felling trees in Ricketts' front to give the battery a clear field of fire toward a distant Confederate battery, some six hundred yards away.[45]

Dawn revealed Battery F to an alert enemy. Sharpshooters some three hundred yards away made life miserable for the men in blue. "Compelled to lie low," wrote Ricketts. The heavy volume of enemy fire meant that Battery F was silent throughout the day. Private William Coulter was instantly killed when struck by a bullet that came through one of the embrasures. "Everybody from general officers down have their holes in the ground,"

---

[43]O.R., *volume 36, part 1, 532; Ricketts Diary, June 3, 1864; Swinton,* Campaigns, *485-88.*

[44]*Ricketts Diary, June 4-5, 1864; Thurston to Laura, June 1, 1864, with additions.*

[45]*Ricketts Diary, June 6-8, 1864; Thurston to Laura, June 1, 1864, with additions.*

recorded the captain. Both armies began to employ mortars, which lobbed their shells in a high arc over the opposing entrenchments. "The enemy hold us hard," penned Ricketts in his diary of June 11. In many places, the lines were so close together that "a cracker can be thrown from one to the other." Neither side could successfully advance against the other. It seemed as if a stalemate had occurred.[46]

While the armies were locked in this crude trench warfare, Grant and Meade were beginning to jockey for position. The Ninth Corps was withdrawn from the right and went into line between the Fifth and Eighteenth. Then the Fifth Corps was moved into reserve. On June 7, Hancock moved the Second Corps farther to the left, toward the Chickahominy River, after which the Fifth Corps moved in behind Hancock. Grant has thus lined the army more toward the Chickahominy, in preparation for his next move, a crossing of the James River and an attack on Petersburg.[47]-

---

[46]*Ricketts Diary, June 10-11, 1864;* O.R., *volume 36, part 1, 532.*

[47]*Swinton,* Campaigns, *498.*

Chapter Ten

Petersburg

The Army of the Potomac began moving away from its Cold Harbor entrenchments after dark on June 12. Wilson's cavalry, followed by Warren and the Fifth Corps, were the first to depart. The column reached the Chickahominy at Long Bridge, where engineers erected a pontoon bridge. Wilson and Warren quickly crossed, then moved toward Richmond to cover the rest of the army. Hancock's Second Corps marched across Long Bridge next, and kept heading for Wilcox's Landing on the James River, which it reached at nightfall, after a thirty-mile march. The Sixth and Ninth Corps crossed the Chickahominy farther east at Jones's Bridge, while Smith's Eighteenth Corps marched to White House and embarked on transports for a water voyage around the Peninsula.[1]

General Lee's pickets detected the Union movement, but Lee at first was unsure of Grant's intentions. On June 5, a Federal column led by Major General David Hunter defeated a smaller Confederate force at Piedmont in the Shenandoah Valley. Hunter immediately set out for Lexington and Lynchburg. Grant, upon hearing the news, sent Sheridan with two cavalry divisions to join Hunter, but in a two-day combat around Trevilian Station (June 11-12), Confederate horsemen intercepted the Yankees and Sheridan had to retreat. Lee sent Breckinridge's division to the Valley, and on June 11, detached Jubal Early's Second Corps to repel Hunter. Thus, by the time the Army of the Potomac began moving, Lee's cavalry was elsewhere and Early on the way to Lynchburg.[2]

General Butler and the navy assembled all the ships they could, and on June 14, the transports began ferrying Hancock's troops across the wide James River to Windmill Point. That night, engineers began placing a two thousand-foot pontoon bridge across the river, which was finished early on the fifteenth, allowing wagons to cross. In the mean time, by four o'clock on the morning of the fifteenth, all the Second Corps infantry and four

---

[1]*Humphreys,* Virginia Campaign, *194-202; Ricketts Diary, June 12-13, 1864.*

[2]*Humphreys,* Virginia Campaign, *194-95.*

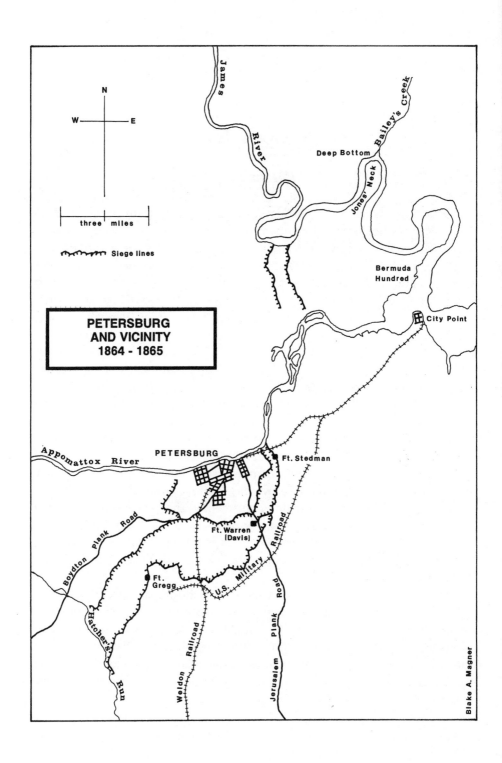

batteries had been landed on the south side of the river. The rest of the corps artillery and baggage train was ferried over throughout the day. Captain Ricketts recorded that his battery was the last unit of the corps to cross, bivouacking that night about a mile from the river.[3]

General Smith's troops landed at Bermuda Hundred on the fourteenth, and early on the fifteenth, began marching toward Petersburg. Late in the day, Smith launched a series of attacks on the undermanned outer defenses of the city, seizing a number of forts and connecting earthworks. While General P. G. T. Beauregard rushed reinforcements to the new line being erected that night, Lee hesitated to send troops from the Army of Northern Virginia. He was still unsure of Grant's objective, but did send one division back to Beauregard, which arrived after the action had ended on the fifteenth.[4]

Hancock's corps spent the day on the fifteenth marching toward Petersburg, a twenty-mile march in hot, dry, dusty weather that fatigued the troops, slowed down by faulty staff work and lack of adequate rations. The head of the corps finally arrived behind Smith's men at eleven that night, far too late to exploit Smith's earlier success. As a result, further Union attacks were delayed until the sixteenth. And then, even though Burnside arrived and Grant himself was present, no assaults took place until late in the afternoon. Grant directed the corps commanders to reconnoiter the Confederate defenses and look for likely areas of attack. The Yankee strength totaled some fifty thousand men, as opposed to only ten thousand for Beauregard.[5]

Battery F rolled toward Petersburg with the rest of the corps batteries and arrived on the field about five o'clock. Ricketts was sent to support General Barlow's division on the left of the corps line. His four guns unlimbered to the left rear of the line and at 6:00 p.m. the Federal guns opened fire, in what Captain Ricketts described as the "heaviest cannonade of the campaign." Yet, Ricketts' battery fired only ten rounds. The Union assault failed with heavy casualties, as Bushrod Johnson's and Robert Hoke's divisions beat back the fierce attacks on their lines.[6]

---

[3]*Humphreys*, Virginia Campaign, *204-5; Swinton,* Campaigns, *499-500; Ricketts Diary, June 14-15, 1864; Thurston to Laurra, June 19, 1864; O.R., volume 40, part 1, 422.*

[4]*Humphreys*, Virginia Campaign, *206-10;* Thomas J. Howe, The Petersburg Campaign: Wasted Valor, June 15-18, 1864 *(Lynchburg, VA: H. E. Howard, Inc., 1988), 21-41;* Edward G. Longacre, Army of Amateurs: General Benjamin F. Butler and the Army of the James, 1863-1865 *(Mechanicsburg, PA: Stackpole Books, 1997), 143-52.*

[5]*Humphreys*, Virginia Campaign, *210-16; Howe,* Wasted Valor, *42-51.*

[6]*Ricketts Diary, June 16, 1864; Howe,* Wasted Valor, *52-58; O.R., volume 40, part 1, 422-23.*

Early on June 17, two brigades of the Ninth Corps attacked just south of Barlow's division and seized a portion of the Confederate line. Further attacks throughout the day wrested some more terrain, but a counterattack after dark crushed one of Burnside's divisions and plugged a gap in the line. Warren brought the Fifth Corps into line on Burnside's left, but the exhausted corps was not involved in any serious fighting on the seventeenth. Battery F remained in position throughout the day but did not open fire. Simply put, the Army of the Potomac was beginning to show signs of exhaustion. Many of its best troops had been lost since the beginning of the campaign, and officer casualties were high. That evening, Hancock yielded command of the Second Corps to General Birney. His Gettysburg wound was giving him health problems, and the general decided to let the able Birney control the corps.[7]

Meade, frustrated over his army's inability to take Petersburg, ordered a general assault on June 18th. By the time the attacks began, Lee had finally realized that Grant's entire army was heading toward Petersburg, and directed Hill and Anderson to move their corps to assist Beauregard. That evening, even as his men repelled the Ninth Corps, Beauregard's engineers were erecting a new defensive line, to which his men retired later that night. When the Federal assault went forward sometime after four o'clock in the morning, the Yankees found their opponents had withdrawn to a new line. Delay followed delay as the new line was reconnoitered and the attackers realigned. When a new attack went forward after two o'clock, it was bloodily repulsed. Ricketts moved his battery to support Birney's division during the afternoon engagement. Unlimbering on a hill in rear of the infantry, Ricketts opened fire on the city, expending 362 rounds. Battery F suffered no casualties, but Sergeant Thurston wrote that an enemy shell hit the ground near his gun, exploding and showering everyone with dirt.[8]

On June 19, the day after the four-day assaults on Petersburg ended, Sergeant Thurston managed to find the time to pen another letter to Laura. "I am as poor as a shred in June," lamented the sergeant. "The cause is oweing to loss of sleep and the ardious duties the campaign has demanded and sacrifices we were compelled to make." Thurston acknowledged that "the flowers of our Army" have been sacrificed to gain the present state of affairs. "The weather is hot and dry. . . . In time of peace it was a land of pretty homes. But this war has spread desolation broadcast all over our fair land. Churches turned to hospitals and fields to graveyards." Thurston

---

[7]*Ricketts Diary, June 17, 1864;* Howe, *Wasted Valor, 62-105.*

[8]*Ricketts Diary, June 18, 1864; Thurston to Laura, June 19, 1864;* Howe, *Wasted Valor, 106-135;* O.R., *volume 40, part 1, 423.*

Private Levi S. Bowers served with Battery F throughout its entire term of service. He was one of three men from Bradford County.

(GARRY LEISTER COLLECTION, USAMHI)

believed that Richmond could not be taken without large reinforcements. The prospects for the future did not look bright, he wrote. The loss of sixty thousand men had hurt the army, in spite of what the press was telling the people back home. "I say just what I think and don't care for anyone. The people should know the truth sometimes."[9]

Grant was not yet defeated, however. The general decided that the only way to force Lee to abandon Petersburg was to cut all the railroad lines leading into the city from the south. He decided to extend the left flank of the army until it reached the Appomattox River west of Petersburg. By this maneuver, Lee's supply lines would be cut and the enemy would have to either fight or retreat. Accordingly, Meade ordered Birney and the Second Corps, supported by cavalry, to move west to the Weldon Railroad. Wright's Sixth Corps would also move up in support to extend the line to the Appomattox.[10]

Battery F remained in position supporting the Third Division (now led by General Mott) on June 19, losing one man wounded during the occasional fighting that erupted along the lines. On June 20, Colonel Tidball ordered Ricketts to detach a section and send it to the front to shell Petersburg. Brockway's section went forward and fired off sixteen rounds in conjunction with a mortar bombardment.[11]

The Second Corps withdrew from the line late on June 21 and headed west toward the Weldon Railroad. As the corps passed the left of Warren's Fifth Corps, Gibbon went into line and began entrenching, followed to the left by Mott and Barlow. Wright and two divisions of the Sixth Corps moved farther south, halting in the vicinity of Globe Tavern, a small inn adjacent to the Weldon Railroad. On June 22, A. P. Hill led two divisions against the Union encroachment on the railroad. While Wilcox's Division engaged Wright's attention, Gordon's Division found a gap between the two Union corps and piled into it, forcing back Barlow's division, whereupon Mott's troops followed. The Confederates then struck Gibbon's line from the rear and smashed his division, capturing a four-gun battery and several flags. The corps withdrew to the Jerusalem Plank Road and threw up earthworks.

---

[9]*Thurston to Laura, June 19, 1864.*

[10]*John Horn,* The Petersburg Campaign, June 1864-April 1865 *(Conshohocken, PA: Combined Books, 1993), 75-78.*

[11]*Ricketts Diary, June 19-20, 1864;* O.R., *volume 40, part 1, 423-24, 438.*

Battery F went into position on the plank road; Ricketts reported that his cannoneers threw up "very strong works during the night."[12]

The first Union attempt to gain the Weldon Railroad was a stinging defeat. The Second Corps lost four guns and seventeen hundred prisoners, then went into position astride the Jerusalem Plank Road, with the Sixth Corps on the left flank of the Union line. Battery F fired off forty-four rounds on June 23 as opposing batteries dueled with each other, the Confederates evidently probing to see what the Yankees were doing.[13]

A more serious engagement opened the next day, June 24. The apparent cause was the movement of Brigadier General Samuel W. Crawford's Fifth Corps division into position behind Gibbon's line, preparatory to relieving the Second Corps troops. Confederates noticed the movement and four batteries opened on the Yankees. In reply, Battery F, the 11th New York Battery, and 6th Maine Battery all let loose. Captain Ricketts wrote that his men were "very severely engaged with four bty's of the enemy's at from 800 to 1000 yds." Battery F expended 242 rounds, and lost one man killed and three wounded. Sergeant Thurston recalled that the action began at breakfast. The Rebel fire "upset our breakfast[.] [O]ur tents was torn to pieces, indeed a regular tear up, but we got to work and soon silenced them with but little loss." The sergeant also said that June 24 was the hottest day of the year thus far–"it seems as though the sun would melt us."[14]

Sergeant Thurston had a lot to say about the debilitated condition of the army by mid-June 1864. Water was still scarce, as no rain had fallen in any quantity since June 3. Thurston wrote that the soldiers drank water "that brute would not look at at home." Local civilians told the military that the weather and accompanying drought was the worst they could remember. Battery F boys dug a well, but the water quality was too poor to directly drink, but was useable for coffee and cooking. Any troop movement raised tremendous clouds of dust, denying any hope for secrecy. The heat and lack of water also played havoc with the horses, many of whom died.[15]

---

[12]*Ricketts Diary, June 21-22, 1864;* O.R., *volume 40, part 1, 424; Humphreys,* Virginia Campaign, *226-29.*

[13]*Ricketts Diary, June 23, 1864.*

[14]*Ricketts Diary, June 24, 1864; Thurston to Laura, June 24, 1864;* O.R., *volume 40, part 1, 424, 438, 454.*

[15]*Thurston to Laura, June 24, 27, 1864.*

As a result of the severe losses since May 5, the hot weather, and need to resupply and rest, the Union armies facing Lee and Beauregard around Richmond and Petersburg began digging more elaborate fortifications and defenses. Although historians have styled the operations around Petersburg a siege, the city was not actually closely besieged in the classical sense of the word. Communications were open with other areas of the Confederacy, but over the coming months Grant would order Meade to undertake operations against the highly-vulnerable enemy railroads. By entrenching and erecting several formidable earthwork forts, Grant intended that the siege lines could be manned by a smaller force, allowing mobile units to engage to active operations.

After dark on June 24, Ricketts' battery was relieved by Captain James Cooper's Battery B, 1st Pennsylvania, as part of a move in which Fifth Corps batteries took the place of Colonel Tidball's tired units. Some of Tidball's command remained in position supporting the Second Corps, but, by allowing several batteries to move to the rear to rest and refit, Tidball was able to rotate his batteries and thus keep fresh units in position as the others rested. Battery F moved to the rear and went into camp for eight days. The men were able to get cleaned up, seek better rations, and visit friends and relatives in other units. Sergeant Thurston was able to visit his brother Silas, serving in the 149th Pennsylvania of the Fifth Corps. However, any man wanting to leave camp had to walk; horses were weak and enemy sharpshooters sometimes fired on any visible target. Rations were now supplemented with donations from the United States Sanitary Commission, which sent Battery F a barrel of sauerkraut on the first of July, then sent various kinds of vegetables later that month. Soft bread was now issued in addition to the usual army hardtack. The weather continued hot and dry; the first soaking rain would only come on July 19.[16]

On Sunday, July 3, Battery F returned to the front line, relieving the 1st New Hampshire Battery on General Birney's line. Captain Ricketts maintained this position until the evening of the twelfth, when the entire corps, after destroying its line of entrenchments, moved to the rear and went into bivouac behind the Fifth Corps. The next day, the corps marched east to the Deserted House, where it went into camp as a reserve force. General Gibbon's division soon thereafter moved into position on the left of the line, taking with it two batteries. The rest of the corps found time to relax as the men waited for further orders. Some changes in command took place during this time. Colonel Tidball was reassigned to other duty on July 1; Major Hazard then assumed command of the Artillery Brigade. On the

---

[16]*Thurston to Laura, June 27, July 1, 19, 1864; Ricketts Diary, June 25-July 2, 1864;* Humphreys, Virginia Campaign, *243.*

Private Samuel C. Torbett sits for the photographer in front of a backdrop, his kepi clearly showing Battery F's insignia.

(GARRY LEISTER COLLECTION, USAMHI)

seventh, Lieutenant Brockway was detached from Battery F and appointed an Assistant Aide de Camp on Major Hazard's staff.[17]

The assignment of Lieutenant Brockway to the brigade staff, although meant to be temporary, effectively severed his relationship with Battery F. On August 2, Brockway requested a ten-day leave of absence "for the purpose of obtaining a set of artificial teeth." Once Brockway returned home to Bloomsburg, it appears that his health faded a bit, for on August 19, Surgeon H. C. Harrison reported that he had examined the lieutenant and found him to be suffering from bilious fever, which confined him to bed. Harrison recommended a twenty-day extension of Brockway's leave to allow him time to recuperate.[18]

On the tenth of September, Brockway wrote to Lieutenant U. D. Eddy, Major Hazard's Acting Assistant Adjutant General, to report that his leave expired on the eleventh, but the surgeon still considered him unfit for duty. Brockway was supposed to report at Annapolis for further orders; when he did, he reported to a board of surgeons for examination. They found the lieutenant still suffering from intermittent fever and thus unable to join Battery F. Brockway dutifully sent copies of the report to both Lieutenant Eddy and Lorenzo Thomas, the federal adjutant general. A month later, Brockway was still in the Officer's Hospital in Annapolis, recovering, with orders to proceed to Chicago for light duty. Surgeons still reported the officer as unfit for duty, and so, on October 22, as part of Special Orders Number 360, Brockway was mustered out of service and honorably discharged from the army.[19]

---

[17]*Ricketts Diary, July 3-12, 1864;* O.R., *volume 40, part 1, 179, 425; Brockway service record, National Archives. Colonel Tidball was temporarily assigned to West Point as commandant of the Corps of Cadets (*O.R. Supplement, *volume 7, 222).*

Shortly after Brockway was detached, Captain Ricketts wrote to Governor Curtin and recommended that William M. Shoemaker be commissioned junior first lieutenant in Battery F. When asked why he did not recommend one of the battery's officers for promotion, Ricketts replied that he wanted an officer of "ability and education." The efficiency and reputation of a battery depended "a great deal" on its officers, wrote the captain. See Ricketts to Curtin, July 15, 1864; and Ricketts to Colonel Samuel B. Thomas, September 3, 1864, both in Battery F Papers, PSA.

[18]*Brockway to Lieutenant U. D. Eddy, August 2, 1864; Leave of Absence document dated August 8, 1864; Statement of Surgeon Harrison, August 19, 1864; all in Brockway service record.*

[19]*Brockway to Eddy, September 10, 1864; Brockway to Eddy, September 14, 1864, enclosing Surgeon H. C. Harrison's report of September 9th and September 14th examination at Annapolis; Brockway to Lorenzo Thomas, September 14, 1864; Brockway to Eddy, October 11, 1864, enclosing examination of October 10th; copy of War Department Special Orders #360, October 22, 1864; all in Brockway service file.*

Battery F remained in camp behind the lines until the twenty-sixth of July. Active operations against the enemy were curtailed for various reasons. General Early's troops, after arriving at Lynchburg in time to frustrate General Hunter's attempt to seize the city, moved down the Shenandoah Valley after Hunter took his small army out of active operations by retreating across the mountains into western Virginia. Early crossed the Potomac and headed toward Washington. In response, Grant detached Wright and the Sixth Corps, and the Nineteenth Corps, coming from Louisiana to Petersburg, was rerouted to Washington. Major General Lew Wallace fought a delaying action against Early at the Monocacy River on July 9, allowing Wright's troops to reinforce the depleted Washington garrison in time to repel Early's tentative skirmishing on July 11.[20]

The departure of the Sixth Corps left the Fifth, Ninth, and Eighteenth (from left to right) manning the trench lines at Petersburg. The Second Corps was in reserve, and Butler and the Tenth Corps occupied the lines at Bermuda Hundred. Throughout the month of July, soldiers of the 48th Pennsylvania in the Ninth Corps were engaged in digging a tunnel under an opposing Confederate fort. A number of men in this regiment were coal miners, and their commander firmly believed that a mine packed with gunpowder could be exploded, creating a gap in the enemy line. Burnside gave his approval to this project, and his corps began to prepare for a massed attack once the gunpowder was exploded. The explosion was set for the morning of July 30.

As the Pennsylvanians tunneled their way forward more than five hundred feet, Battery F remained in camp, awaiting orders for another movement. The men passed the time listening to camp rumors, primarily those concerned with Early's raid across the Potomac. Sergeant Thurston echoed the frustration felt by many boys in blue about the eventual termination of the war. "They are all tired of the war," penned the sergeant, "but the pride of the American Soldier nerves him on to duty. We know that the eyes of all nations are turned toward us, and sooner than disgrace our flag we will all perish on the field."[21]

Orders finally came on July 26. Hancock, back in command of the corps, was instructed to take his corps north across the James River, supporting two of Sheridan's cavalry divisions. Recent Confederate moves in the Deep Bottom area had driven in the Union picket lines and threatened the small bridgehead north of the river. The Second Corps would cross the river and drive the enemy from New Market Heights back

---

[20]*Ricketts Diary, July 14-25, 1864.*

[21]*Thurston to Laura, July 19, 22, 1864.*

into their fortifications closer to Richmond. The cavalry division from the Army of the James would ride along in support. Two of Sheridan's divisions would use the opportunity to head north across the Chickahominy, then destroy the Virginia Central Railroad north of Richmond before returning to Deep Bottom. Additionally, Hancock's movement might draw off troops from in front of Petersburg, giving Burnside's attack a greater chance of success.[22]

The Second Corps began marching north on the afternoon of July 26. Major Hazard parceled out seven batteries to accompany the troops. Battery F, accompanied by Batteries C&I, 5th United States, followed Gibbon's Second Division. The unassigned batteries constituted the reserve of the corps and followed Gibbon's three brigades. Barlow's division led the column, followed by Mott and Gibbon. Sheridan's troopers rode behind the infantry.[23]

After a twenty-five-mile march through the night, Hancock's lead elements reached the tip of Jones Neck, a narrow peninsula of land formed by an elongated loop of the James, Two pontoon bridges spanned the river, one at Deep Bottom, and one farther east at Tilghman's Wharf. Hancock was supposed to use the upper bridge, with Sheridan crossing at Tilghman's. However, Hancock received word from the commander of the bridgehead that the enemy earthworks in his front were more formidable than previously thought. Hancock queried Meade about the situation and asked permission to cross at Tilghman's, which he thought would allow a better chance of success. Meade, unaware of the consequences of a change in plan, told Hancock to go ahead and cross at Tilghman's.[24]

Unfortunately, Hancock's decision meant that Bailey's Creek was between his corps and the Rebels in front of the bridgehead. Barlow and Mott formed and moved forward, encountering two brigades of infantry and one of cavalry. After a sharp skirmish, Union troops found a gap in the enemy line and captured a four-gun battery, chasing the enemy back across Bailey's Creek. Major General Joseph B. Kershaw rallied his men and they began to entrench on the opposite side of Bailey's Creek. The cautious Hancock, apparently worried about his flanks, brought up Gibbon's division to continue the assault. Battery F went into line with the division,

---

[22]Bryce A. Suderow, "Glory Denied: The First Battle of Deep Bottom, July 27th-29th, 1864," **North & South 3 #7** *(September 2000): 18-19;* Humphreys, Virginia Campaign, 247-48.

[23]Suderow, "Glory Denied," 21; O.R., volume 40, part 1, 425-26.

[24]Suderow, "Glory Denied," 21; Ricketts Diary, July 26, 1864.

but apparently did not see action on the twenty-seventh. Hancock frittered away the day by extreme overcaution, allowing the Confederates to rush reinforcements to oppose the Yankees.[25]

The morning of July 28 saw a Confederate counterattack against the Yankees. Lieutenant General Richard H. Anderson, commanding Lee's First Corps, sent in an attacking column against Sheridan's dismounted troopers, who repelled their assailants but lost ground. Hancock, however, failed to capitalize by not attacking. Prisoners revealed that more enemy reinforcements were coming and the Union general worried about being cut off from the bridges. Battery F was active during part of the day, expending twenty-four rounds firing at visible enemy columns across Bailey's Creek.[26]

Grant visited the front later that day and was disappointed to learn of Hancock's lack of aggressiveness. He ordered Mott's division back across the James to relieve the Eighteenth Corps, which would mass in support of Burnside's July 30 attack. Hancock's other two divisions remained in position as Lee rushed more troops to confront the Yankees. During the day on July 29, the opposing sides traded artillery fire as skirmishers were kept active. Battery F fired off eighty rounds, doing, wrote Captain Ricketts, "some splendid shooting." By nightfall on the twenty-ninth, half of Lee's available infantry was confronting Hancock.[27]

That evening, the rest of the Second Corps vacated its position behind Bailey's Creek and withdrew, marching south to act as a reserve to the day's fighting. The engagement at Deep Bottom had cost 488 Union casualties and 679 Confederates. Although successful in drawing off much of Lee's army, the feint to the north side of the James had no effect on the July 30 Mine explosion. Burnside bungled the attack badly and Lee's outnumbered veterans managed to plug the gap and inflict almost thirty-eight hundred casualties on the Union army. After watching the fiasco at the Crater, the Second Corps returned to its camps.[28]

The corps remained in camp, still acting as the army's reserve, until mid-August. By that time, General Sheridan had been detached from the army and placed in command of the troops in the Shenandoah Valley, opposing Early's Confederates. The entire Sixth Corps remained with

---

[25]Suderow, "Glory Denied," 22-23, 26-27; Ricketts Diary, July 27, 1864.

[26]Suderow, "Glory Denied," 27-30; Ricketts Diary, July 28, 1864.

[27]Suderow, "Glory Denied," 30-31; Ricketts Diary, July 29, 1864.

[28]Suderow, "Glory Denied," 31-32; Ricketts Diary, July 30, 1864.

Private Charles Shipman poses in front of a photographer's backdrop.
(GARRY LEISTER COLLECTION, USAMHI)

Sheridan, and two of the army's three cavalry divisions were sent to him as well. Worried that Lee was sending reinforcements to Early, Grant directed the Second Corps to move north of the James at Deep Bottom and attack the enemy lines. By doing so, Grant hoped, Lee would be unable to detach any more troops to the Valley.[29]

To keep the movement secret, or at least divert Confederate intelligence, the infantry of Hancock's command was marched to City Point, where the men embarked on transport vessels. It was hoped that the direction of march would fool the Rebels into thinking the Second Corps was going to Washington. The artillery of the corps, accompanied by Gregg's cavalry, marched north to Jones' Neck. Major Hazard was temporarily away from the army on leave, so Captain A. Judson Clark of Battery B, New Jersey Light Artillery, was in command of the Second Corps Artillery Brigade.[30]

The movement began on August 12, when the Second Corps left camp, the infantry heading toward City Point and the artillery rolling north, crossing the Appomattox River and bivouacking a couple of miles farther north on the road leading to Jones' Neck. The batteries remained in camp throughout the day on the thirteenth as the infantry loaded on transports. "A mysterious move," was how Captain Ricketts described his battery's new camp. Tight security was, at least thus far, concealing the objective of the expedition from friend and foe alike.[31]

General Butler contributed the entire Tenth Corps, now led by General Birney, to the movement north of the James. Birney's divisions began crossing the James at the upper pontoon bridge around midnight and were ready for action as August 14 dawned. Birney's initial attacks on the enemy opposing the bridgehead were very successful, capturing six cannon, two mortars, and several hundred prisoners. But the Second Corps was late in disembarking and Birney received orders from Hancock not to advance without his support.[32]

As Birney's troops advanced to the assault, Captain Clark assigned batteries to the three infantry divisions of the Second Corps. Battery F, together with Clark's own Battery B, New Jersey Light Artillery, rolled across the lower pontoon, then waited until Mott's Third Division was

---

[29]*Humphreys,* Virginia Campaign, *267-68.*

[30]O.R., *volume 42,, part 1, 54, 405;* Humphreys, Virginia Campaign, *268.*

[31]*Humphreys,* Virginia Campaign, *268; Ricketts Diary, August 12-13, 1864.*

[32]*Longacre,* Army of Amateurs, *196-99.*

ashore. Mott anchored Hancock's left flank, taking position behind Bailey's Creek as the rest of the corps lined up to Mott's right. Batteries F and B unlimbered near the Potteries (a site just north of Tilghman's Gate) and dueled with enemy artillery throughout the day. Captain Clark reported that the two batteries "had no difficulty in silencing" the enemy artillery. Battery F expended 119 rounds during the day. Hancock's corps made no substantial attacks during the day, as it appeared that the Rebels were in more force than was originally believed.[33]

Hancock, frustrated by the apparent strength of the enemy in his front, decided to turn the Rebel left flank. Accordingly, he ordered General Birney to disengage his corps and move to the right of the line and launch an attack at Fussell's Mill. Birney's troops had to recross the James at the bridgehead, then cross at the lower pontoon bridge. All this took many hours, the march slowed by a nocturnal heavy rain, which was followed by a steamy, humid morning on August 15. As a result, the day was spent in getting Birney's troops into position. Fighting continued all along the line, as skirmishers and artillery kept busy throughout the day. Battery F fired off sixty-two rounds.[34]

At some point during the fighting, Sergeant Thurston's cannon was disabled and had to be replaced. Still, the sergeant found time during the desultory firing to compose a letter to Laura. He had become so accustomed to shells 'whizzing and bursting" that they were second nature. But the noise from the shells fired by the Union gunboats in the James was something else. "All day they make as much noise as a horse and cart flying through the air, and make holes in the earth large enough to put half a dozen men in." The hot and dry weather plagued the men engaged in combat. "The air is filled with bare smiles from dead horses and men, enough to sicken the strongest man." The springs and wells north of the James seemed to be caked with mud, "not fit for a horse." Thurston also wrote that he was sick, barely able to sit in the saddle, "but I worried it through."[35]

Birney's attack force was finally in position by about noon on the sixteenth. During the day, the Second Corps skirmished with the enemy across Bailey's Creek in an effort to pin the Rebels in front and prevent

---

[33]O.R., *volume 42, part 1, 405-6;* Humphreys, Virginia Campaign, *269-70;* Longacre, Army of Amateurs, *199-200.*

[34]Longacre, Army of Amateurs, *200;* O.R., *volume 42, part 1, 406;* Ricketts Diary, August 15, 1864.

[35]Thurston to Laura, August 15, 1864.

them from reinforcing their left opposite Birney. Brigadier General Regis de Trobriand, commanding Mott's First Brigade, reported that his efforts were "assisted materially by a steady shelling of the enemy's position by Ricketts' (Pennsylvania) battery and one of the gun-boats in the river." Battery F fired 188 rounds during the day. Birney's afternoon attack seized the enemy skirmish line and penetrated their main line of fortifications before being thrown back by enemy reinforcements.[36]

By nightfall of the sixteenth, Hancock realized that he was not going to be able to breach the Confederate line. Too many reinforcements had moved to block the Union advance. During the day on the seventeenth, the two forces skirmished, Battery F expending thirteen rounds. The Union force remained in position on the eighteenth as well, during which Ricketts' cannon belched forth eighty-four rounds. A late afternoon Confederate attack on Birney's corps was repelled. After dark, Mott's division was relieved and ordered back across the James to its old position. Battery F and New Jersey Battery B accompanied the infantry. Hancock, although frustrated in his attempt to drive toward Richmond, had indeed prevented reinforcements from going to the Valley to support Early's troops.[37]

Mott's division moved into position lately vacated by a portion of the Fifth Corps, which moved to the Weldon Railroad and fought a battle that lasted from August 18 to the 21, leaving the Yankees in possession of a portion of the railroad. However, the Rebels still could run trains up the railroad a few miles to the south, unload the cars, and transport supplies into their lines. Therefore, Hancock was ordered to take two divisions and Gregg's cavalry south to Reams' Station, then destroy the railroad as far as Rowanty Creek, some thirteen miles south of the Union left flank. This would force the enemy to send their wagons on a thirty-mile trek to use the rail line farther south.[38]

Hancock's two divisions, accompanied by the cavalry, arrived at Reams' Station on August 23 and by nightfall on the twenty-fourth, had ripped up the track for several miles. On August 25, the corps was assailed by A. P. Hill's troops. The line was flanked and the Second Corps was driven from its position, losing more than two thousand men captured, along with nine cannon and twelve flags. Battery F, meanwhile, went into position on

---

[36]*Ricketts Diary, August 16, 1864;* O.R., *volume 42, part 1, 358;* Longacre,. Army of Amateurs, *201-2.*

[37]*Longacre,* Army of Amateurs, *202-3;* Ricketts Diary, August 17-18, 1864.

[38]*Humphreys,.* Virginia Campaign, *272-78.*

the right of the Jerusalem Plank Road. Ricketts' guns were active only on August 21, firing forty-four rounds.[39]

Thereafter, Battery F remained in the same position through the fourteenth of September. The battery caissons were parked in the rear to keep them out of the line of fire, leaving the limbers to provide ammunition. The battery's four cannon fired occasionally; Major Hazard reminded all his battery commanders that they were to open fire whenever they saw any Confederates working on their entrenchments, and reply to any Southern artillery fire. Battery F's guns were active on September 4, 5, 8, 9, 11, 13, and 14, expending a total of 307 rounds of ammunition.[40]

The firing on September 5 followed a general order for all Union batteries to fire a salute of thirty-four guns in honor of General Sherman's capture of Atlanta. Sergeant Thurston recorded that the salute began at midnight. "[I]t was a grand sight the air for the distance of 15 miles was filled with bursting shells, to which the Rebels replied briskly. They looked like so many firey dragons flying to and fro, if you have seen fire balls tossed you can form some idea of the scene."[41]

On September 15, Captain John E. Burton's 11th New York Battery relieved Battery F as the two batteries changed positions. Battery F moved into a small earthwork known as Fort Warren, located near the Jones House to the left of the Jerusalem Plank Road. Ten days later, on September 25, the battery's location was again changed. Ricketts moved his four guns into Batteries 10 and 11, relieving the 1st Connecticut Battery of the Tenth Corps. This movement occurred as part of a general redeployment in which the Second Corps replaced the Tenth and occupied the right of the line from the Appomattox River westward to link up with the Ninth Corps. The section of Battery F in Battery 11 was moved the next day into Fort Stedman. On September 27, Major Hazard issued Special Orders Number 160, instructing five Second Corps batteries, including Battery F, to increase their strength to six guns. Each battery commander was authorized to requisition the cannon, associated wheeled vehicles, and horses, to comply with this order.[42]

---

[39]Ibid., 279-83; Ricketts Diary, August 20-25, 1864.

[40]Ricketts Diary, August 26-September 14, 1864; Circular from Major Hazard dated August 30, 1864, copy in Ricketts Papers.

[41]Thurston to Laura, September 8, 1864.

[42]O.R., volume 42, part 2, 838, 1016, 1040; Ricketts Diary, September 14, 25, 1864; Special Orders Number 160, September 27, 1864, copy in Ricketts Papers. Fort Warren's name was later changed to Fort Davis. The army commanders decided that forts would be named after officers killed in battle, so all forts with names of officers yet living were changed.

Life for the troops on the front lines sometimes became unbearable. Enemy sharpshooters were a constant threat. "We dare not put our heads above our works," wrote Sergeant Thurston, "so sure as we do a hundred bullets come whizzing uncomfortably near our heads." Rations were the usual army fare, supplemented by whatever was available. Thurston complained that as autumn approached, vegetables were issued less frequently, although soft bread continued to be available. The weather also began to turn cooler, which led to the "ague" among many soldiers. It was not until November 5 that Major Hazard could report to his battery commanders that the surplus camp and garrison equipage turned in at Brandy Station last May was ready for distribution.[43]

On the tenth of October, Sergeant Thurston included the following description of Battery F's position in a letter to his sweetheart:

We are on the front line and dare not leave one moment. The wind flows and dust blows, tis almost impossible for me to write, but you must excuse the dirt as I cannot avoid it. We are surrounded by a beautiful grove of tall oaks, but they have been completely riddled with shot and shell. Not one tree but what is shattered with a hundred of these missiles. It looks as though man could not live here for one moment. But our works are so good that only a chance shot reaches us. Mortar shells come tumbleing in but they do but little damage save a big noise when they explode. I have seen them come and bury in the earth that you could scarcely find them, tearing holes in the ground large enough to bury a good sized man. It looks dangerous but does not frighten us so much as some of the timid and faint hearted. There is more noise in huge shells than danger, but the whiz of the rifle ball tells more different. We cannot see them but must depend upon good luck, or a kind providence to escape their spitefull coming. I so often think we never see our real danger, at least we don't seem to appreciate it.[44]

On October 12, Captain Ricketts left for home and a twenty-day sick leave. He had applied earlier in the month, when Surgeon John W. Allen of the 148th Pennsylvania examined the captain and found him suffering from chronic diarrhea. Surgeon Allen recommended the leave to allow Ricketts time to heal. The captain arrived in Bloomsburg on October 15, the last day of the Columbia County Fair. After visiting with friends and acquaintances

---

[43]*Thurston to Laura, September 3 (food), 10 (sharpshooters), 12 (quoted passage, food, weather, ague), 27 (sharpshooters), October 5 (ague), 1864; Circular from Major Hazard, November 5, 1864, Campbell Papers.*

[44]*Thurston to Laura, October 10, 1864.*

Bugler William Warnick served throughout the war. He was a 19-year-old boatman from Philadelphia.

(PRIVATE COLLECTION)

for a few days, the captain was taken sick on the twenty-third and was bedridden for four days before he was able to rise and walk about. The cause seemed to be a kidney stone and its attendant pain. An army surgeon and local doctor both recommended an additional thirty days' leave. Ricketts went to Harrisburg later and on December 1 received his commission as major of the 1st Pennsylvania Artillery. The new major also secured commissions for Brockway as captain, Campbell and Wireman as 1st lieutenants, and Thurston as 2nd lieutenant. Major Ricketts arrived at City Point on December 3rd; the new officers were mustered into their new grades somewhat later, as soon as they could locate a mustering officer.[45]

While Captain Ricketts was home on leave, Battery F continued to serve on the front lines at Petersburg. Lieutenant Campbell was in charge of Battery F during Ricketts' leave. Remarked Thurston, "I think we will have a nice time since the Boss has gone." The battery remained in line until the evening of October 24, when both sections were relieved and sent to the rear for rest. Thereafter, the battery remained in a state of readiness in case of emergency. Major Hazard issued orders for Battery F, as well as Batteries C&I, 5th United States Artillery, to have their horses hitched at five o'clock each morning, then on November 7, instructed Campbell to have one section only ready to report to Brigadier General Nelson A. Miles, commanding the First Division of the Second Corps, for further orders.[46]

While the battery was parked in the rear, the officers and men could talk about the upcoming presidential election, scheduled for November 8. Several states, among them Pennsylvania, made provisions to allow the soldiers to vote while on active duty. Sergeant Thurston was a Democrat and supported General McClellan, chosen as the party's candidate. However, said Thurston, "Lincoln will be elected as sure as can be." Many soldiers had seen friends and family killed and maimed during three years of war, and wished to see the conflict through to the end. They did not want a dishonorable peace. "The men in the Army say we have fought too long and hard to shrink from the contest now. . . . If we lose the election, I still will support our cause. It is the duty of every patriot though we may differ as regardless politics." When the election was held, Battery F tallied sixty-nine votes for Lincoln and forty-six for McClellan.[47]

---

[45]*Ricketts Diary, October 12-December 6, 1864; Statement of Surgeon John W. Allen, October 6, 1864, and Statements of Surgeon W. W. Rislin and Dr. D. W. Montgomery, both in Ricketts Service File, NA.*

[46]*Thurston to Laura, October 12, 1864; Special Orders #178, Artillery Brigade, Second Corps, October 24, 1864, copy in Campbell Papers; O.R., volume 42, part 3, 346, 524, 546*

[47]*Thurston to Laura, October 16, 1864; O.R., volume 42, part 3, 560.*

Battery F went back into line on November 8, relieving Batteries C&I, 5th United States, in a new fortification near the Avery House. Once in position, the men began building winter quarters, generally log cabins with tents for roofs. By early November 1864, the veterans of Battery F were impervious to the daily shelling. "We can go to sleep as though nothing has happened," wrote Sergeant Thurston. The battery drilled twice a day, weather permitting. The United States Sanitary Commission doled out presents for the veterans. Thurston received two towels, a pair of socks, and a pair of slippers.[48]

Documents for the period of late November indicate that Battery F's efficiency declined while Captain Ricketts was on leave. Each month, a board of officers inspected the batteries of the corps and wrote a report to indicate the strengths and weaknesses of each battery. On November 22th, Lieutenant C. A. Clark filed his report. Of Battery F, he had much to say:

> Battery F, 1st Pa. Arty. requires immediate attention. The supply of clothing for the men is neither uniform nor complete, the harness appears to be neglected, and the police of camp and quarters is by no means creditable. The general appearance of the Battery plainly indicates that it requires the careful attention of an energetic commanding officer, to bring it up to the proper standard. Capt. Ricketts of this Battery has been absent sick some forty (40) days and at present the Battery is in the command of a second lieutenant who is the only officer present with the battery. These facts may in a measure account for the present condition of the Battery, taking also into consideration the constant service it has performed since the opening of the campaign.[49]

On the last day of November, the Second Corps infantry evacuated their positions on the right of the line and were replaced by the Ninth Corps, with the Second Corps moving into position farther to the left, along the line previously held by the Ninth Corps. Some of the Second Corps batteries remained in position. When Major Ricketts returned to duty in early December, he was assigned to command the Second Corps batteries still in place along the Ninth Corps line. These batteries included Battery F, the 6th Maine Battery, the 3rd New Jersey Battery, Battery G, 1st New York, and Company C, 4th New York Heavy Artillery. These five batteries occupied the line from Battery Number 5 to Fort Morton. Major Ricketts

---

[48]Thurston to Laura, November 11, 1864; O.R., volume 42, part 3, 562.

[49]November 22, 1864, report, enclosed with November 24, 1864, circular from Major Hazard, both in Ricketts Service File, NA.

was involved in this capacity until December 23, when he was relieved from duty and assigned to the Artillery Brigade, Ninth Corps.[50]

---

[50]*Circular, Artillery Brigade, Ninth Corps, December 5, 1864;, and Special Orders #203, Artillery Brigade, Second Corps, December 5, 1864, copies of both in Campbell Papers;* O.R., *volume 41, part 1, 43;* O.R., *volume 43, part 3, 813, 1078 (Special Orders #220, Artillery Brigade, Second Corps, December 26, 1864, relieving Ricketts from command of the Second Corps batteries on the Ninth Corps front). See also Ricketts Diary, December 23, 1864, in which he wrote that he was assigned to duty with the Ninth Corps.*

Chapter Eleven

1865

The advent of 1865 found Battery F still occupying Fort Stedman and Batteries 11 and 14. Lieutenant Campbell was in command. Lieutenant Thurston was home on leave, with Lieutenants Frank Brockway and Henry Wireman present for duty. "All quiet along the lines," recorded Brockway in his diary. "Will I live to fill this book? That is the question. There is many battles that are to be fought, many lives are to be lost and many homes will be left dessolute. Am I to survive this war? With the help of God I will. If my time is up, I will not."[1]

Lieutenant Thurston returned to camp on January 8, a week late on reporting. However, it was not the lieutenant's fault. On January 5, he and a lieutenant from the 36th Wisconsin were issued orders to escort seventy-eight enlisted men from the Army of the Potomac and ten from the Army of the James to City Point from Camp Distribution. The usual mail boat bound for City Point was laid up for repairs, forcing Thurston to wait until the next day. Then, the ship his detachment was on encountered heavy fog and had to stop for the night. The captain then ran his ship onto a sand bar and was finally freed on the seventh. As the ship left the Potomac and steamed into the Chesapeake Bay, she ran into strong winds, "shaking her poor stern to stern." Seasickness quickly overwhelmed the passengers, and when the ship docked at City Point at four o'clock in the morning of January 8, a happier set of men never existed.[2]

By the time Thurston returned to duty, it seems that all was not well in Battery F. On January 5, Major Ricketts went along the line, inspecting the batteries under his command. When he stopped in

---

[1]*Frank Brockway Diary, January 1, 1865.*

[2]*Special Orders #5, Headquarters Rendezvous Distribution, January 5, 1865, Thurston Papers; Thurston to Laura, January 8, 1865.*

Fort Stedman to visit Lieutenant Brockway, the major was evidently disappointed that brother Charles had declined the captaincy of Battery F. Back in December, when Ricketts was able to obtain his promotion to major, he sought a captain's commission for his old friend Charles Brockway, who, even though he was at home, was probably the best choice to succeed Ricketts in command of the battery. When apprized of the situation, Brockway replied that he was "never in such a quandary." He confessed that command of Battery F "would be my highest pride," but since leaving the army he had entered into some business arrangements which would be difficult to leave without financial loss. Therefore, Brockway declined the commission.[3]

On January 5, Brockway wrote to Major Ricketts and said that the temptation was very strong to hop on the next train and come to the front. But he also heard that some members of the battery, led by Sergeant Mowrer and Artificer Jacob M. Harman, had gotten up a petition against Brockway's appointment, a sentiment shared by Lieutenant Colonel Brady. In spite of Ricketts' continued support of his candidacy, Brockway consistently decided against returning to Battery F.[4]

The January weather in 1865 seems to have been warmer than in past years. On the tenth, Lieutenant Brockway wrote that it rained hard all day, with "mud up to our necks." The rain soaked through the tent canvas used as a roof in Brockway's cabin, wetting his bed and leaving him soaked as well. By the time the storm ended on the eleventh, part of the earthworks caved in and the bombproof leaked like a sieve "inside and out." Major Ricketts sent orders for the soldiers to fix the damage to Fort Stedman; the major sent up a shipment of lumber to be used in the repairs.[5]

But it was still winter and the nights got cold. Lieutenant Thurston, writing on January 14, complained that two blankets were not enough to keep warm after the fire went out. He usually shared a cabin with Lieutenant Wireman, but the two officers were then a mile apart, their sections occupying two separate batteries. "Lieutenant Campbell is back in camp with the horses and balance

---

[3] *Frank Brockway Diary, January 5, 1865; Ricketts Diary, January 5, 1865; Charles Brockway to Ricketts, December 3, 1864, Brockway Papers.*

[4] *Charles Brockway to Ricketts, January 5, March 9, 1865, Brockway Papers.*

[5] *Frank Brockway Diary, January 10, 11, 13, 1865.*

of the company about one mile. I have my horse brought up twice a day and then I ride back to camp to get my meals. Here we all meet, have a little chat eat grub and return to the front."[6]

Army life went on, day after day. The pickets of both armies were usually shooting at each other, and the artillery joined in on occasion. On January 18, Brockway's and Wireman's sections received orders to return to camp after dark, after which Wireman and Sergeant Mowrer started for home on furloughs.[7]

Lieutenant Thurston's two guns remained in Battery 14. On January 23, they engaged in a lively artillery duel with the enemy, in the midst of a day-long rain storm. Thurston noticed that the Rebels were erecting tents along their lines, which made a tempting target. "I opened on them putting several holes through causing them to pull down in a hurrah," bragged the lieutenant. The enemy soon commenced firing at Thurston's section with a battery of mortars, "quite careless," as the Yankee soldiers remarked. Some shells landed quite near the battery, but caused no harm. Just for good measure, Thurston sent two percussion shells into Petersburg during the firing, "causing quite a stir among the inhabitants." Thurston proudly declared that the Rebels quit erecting tents after the duel.[8]

Later in the month, rumors of peace flew along the lines. In late December, Francis P. Blair, Sr., an influential Democrat, had sought out the president and asked him for permission to travel to Richmond to discuss peace with the Confederacy. Lincoln agreed and Blair went to Richmond in January. They agreed that a Confederate delegation would go through the lines to speak with Union authorities about a proposed peace. Davis authorized three commissioners–Vice President Alexander Stephens, R. M. T. Hunter of Virginia, and former Supreme Court Justice John A. Campbell–to negotiate.

On January 29, Confederates displayed a flag of truce in front of the Ninth Corps. Permission was sought for the commissioners to come through the lines, which was granted. The three men rode a carriage through the lines on January 31 and were conveyed to

---

[6]*Thurston to Laura, January 15, 1865. Lieutenant Brockway's section still occupied Fort Stedman.*

[7]*Brockway Diary, January 18, 1865; Thurston to Laura, January 20, 1865.*

[8]*Thurston to Laura, January 24, 1865.*

Four members of Battery F strike a pose while playing cards. Left to right: Captain John F. Campbell, 2nd Lieutenant George W. Mourer, Private John F. Weaver, and Private S. Priestley Harder.

(WILLIAM GLADSTONE COLLECTION, USAMHI)

Fort Monroe, where Secretary of State William H. Seward received them and listened to their proposals. On February 3, Lincoln himself arrived and told the Rebels that the United States must be reestablished in order for there to be peace. The Southerners wanted a peace between the two countries so that the French intervention in Mexico could be dealt with. But, since the South was not a separate country in Lincoln's eyes, this was not possible. The conference broke up with nothing being agreed upon. The Confederates went back to Richmond on February 4.[9]

Lieutenant Thurston had a firsthand view of the Confederate commissioners, who entered the Union lines "not two hundred yards from my command." Major General John G. Parke and some staff officers met the commissioners, placed them in a splendid carriage drawn by four gray horses, and conveyed them to a waiting railway train on the military railroad that ran behind the Union lines. "Upon their arrival cheer after cheer filled the air from both armies," penned Thurston. Colonel William J. Bolton, commanding the 51st Pennsylvania, through whose regiment the commissioners passed, recorded that all firing ceased and a general sense of "good feeling" pervaded the siege lines.[10]

But the good feeling did not last long. General Grant let it be known that he would not compromise any planned military operations while the peace commissioners conferred at Fort Monroe. Although Lieutenant Brockway recorded no activity along the lines, Colonel Bolton reported that the enemy opened fire in front of Fort Stedman on February 1, and then again on the fourth after the commissioners had returned.[11]

On February 5, two divisions of the Second Corps, the entire Fifth Corps, and a division of the Ninth Corps moved to the left, intent on interdicting Confederate supply wagons traveling on the Boydton Plank Road. The Yankees extended their lines to Hatcher's Run, and in fighting that lasted through February 7, managed to hold their lines and repel the Southern attackers. Although Battery

---

[9]*The chronology of the peace commission is found in E. B. Long,* The Civil War Day by Day *(Garden City, NY: Doubleday & Company, Inc., 1971), 616, 622-23, 625, 626, 629-30, 632-634.*

[10]*Thurston to Laura, January 31, 1865; Richard A. Sauers (editor),* The Civil War Journal of Colonel William J. Bolton, 51st Pennsylvania, April 20, 1861-August 2, 1865 *(Conshohocken, PA: Combined Publishing, 2000), 242-44.*

[11]*Brockway Diary, January 31-February 5, 1865; Sauers,* Bolton Journal, *244.*

F was not engaged in this movement, the four guns held in reserve behind the lines were ordered to be ready to move at a moment's notice. Four days of rations were issued on the fifth as the men and horses were readied to move if needed. The engagement at Hatcher's Run ended in a storm on the seventh and led to the Yankee left remaining in place along the run. Lieutenant Wireman returned from his furlough on the seventh and Mowrer on the ninth.[12]

The remaining days of February slipped by, one by one. Lieutenant Thurston's two guns remained in position, firing occasional shots at the enemy. Rain and snow interfered with normal military operations on many days. On February 10, there was a drill for the two sections in camp. The next day, Irish-born Patrick Curry got drunk in the evening and was tied to a limber wheel until midnight. On Sunday, February 12, Battery F had a regulation Sunday inspection, a "cold and windy" day. Monthly inspection took place on the twentieth, followed by a standing gun drill the next day and another drill on the twenty-seventh. Otherwise, the battery remained in camp as the men discussed rumors and camp talk. Cannon salutes honored the captures of Charleston and Wilmington and Washington's birthday.[13]

March 1st saw Battery F mustered for pay. The paymaster arrived in the afternoon and paid the officers and men. Lieutenant Campbell and some officers from the 200th Pennsylvania got together and became "beastly drunk and raised hell all night.' Campbell called Wireman some "hard names" and tried to start a fight. Campbell left camp on a furlough on March 5 and was absent until April 2. He had requested a furlough on March 1, needing twenty days to visit a sick sister. Campbell said his father had died last fall and he needed to also go home to settle the estate. During his absence, Lieutenant Wireman was the senior officer in command of the battery.[14]

Charles Brockway paid a surprise visit to Battery F on March 2.

---

[12]*Brockway Diary*, February 5-9, 1865; *Ricketts Diary*, February 5-8, 1865. On February 6, Brockway penned the following in his diary: "I think we will not pull out. We are not considered competent to participate in an engagement. Very well. They may think it as long as they choose."

[13]*Brockway Diary*, February 10-28, 1865; Thurston to Laura, February 23, 25, 1865.

[14]*Brockway Diary*, March 1, 5, April 2, 1865; O.R., volume 46, part 2, 843; Campbell request of March 1, 1865, Campbell service file, NA.

Corporal John W. Bullock. He wears service stripes on both sleeves of his artillery jacket. English-born Bullock transferred from Battery G and was a carpenter by profession.

(GARRY LEISTER COLLECTION, USAMHI)

He came to retrieve the body of William Stewart, who had died of disease some six weeks hence. A detachment of the battery rode a rail car down to Parke's Station, found the body, and brought the coffin back. Brockway, accompanied by Lieutenant Campbell, started for home on the fifth.[15]

On March 9, Lieutenant Brockway received orders to move the center section into Battery 10. Brockway moved after dark and went into position. The men were awake and at their posts at five in the morning. The lieutenant recorded that the "bullets come in here rather sharp." Mice and rats were in "abundance" in the earthworks. Two men–Corporal Joseph Strong and Private James Graves–began quarreling on the twelfth but would not fight each other. "Bad boys" said Lieutenant Brockway. Lieutenant Wireman dropped by for a visit one evening and played twenty-three games of uchre with Brockway. On the fifteenth, Brockway's men presented him with a silver bridle, breast strap, and spurs. "That shows they still like me," commented Brockway.[16]

Battery F received marching orders on March 15. That evening, Brockway's section pulled out of Battery 10 and moved back to the caisson park. The battery broke camp the next morning at seven o'clock and moved eight miles to the left, erecting a new camp near Patrick's Station, a stop on the United States Army Military Railroad. This new station was near the Hatcher's Run battlefield. The battery also heard word that two guns were to be turned in and only four guns would remain. "This will knock me out of a commission," rued Brockway. "Fate is against me, it seems. Well, I can serve as Sergt. untill my time is out."[17]

March 17 was Saint Patrick's Day, and, as usual, the Irish Brigade whooped it up. Lieutenant Brockway went to see the usual horse race and the number of ladies present. For most of the men, the day was spent in putting up tents and cleaning the new campground. March 18 saw a monthly inspection by Lieutenant Colonel Hazard. The colonel instructed Brockway's section to

---

[15]*Brockway Diary, March 2-5, 1865.*

[16]Ibid., *March 9-15, 1865. Lieutenant Thurston also received a silver bridle from his men about this same time. See Thurston to Laura, March 8, 1865.*

[17]*Brockway Diary, March 15-16, 1865; Thurston to Laura, March 16, 19, 1865.*

demonstrate dismounting a piece and slinging the barrel. "Hazard allowed I was d——md well drilled. Quite a compliment."[18]

Battery F was reviewed by Second Corps commander Andrew A. Humphreys on March 19, and then had another drill on the twentieth. Tempers flared during the drill when Lieutenants Brockway and Wireman got into an argument; Wireman desisted after Brockway produced a drill manual and proved he was right. Battery F relieved the 10th Massachusetts Battery temporarily and occupied the Bay Stater's position on the twenty-second and twenty-third so the 10th could participate in a review.[19]

The morning of March 25 brought a surprise Confederate attack that broke the monotony of the waiting along the siege lines. General Lee determined to break through the Union lines and ordered Major General John B. Gordon to lead a picked force to assail the Yankees. Gordon's men moved forward and captured Fort Stedman and Batteries 9, 10, and 11, punching a temporary hole in the Ninth Corps line. General Meade was at City Point. General Parke, in command of the army, ordered up reinforcements, but the Ninth Corps contained the attack. Brigadier General John F. Hartranft led a division of six new Pennsylvania regiments into the fray, driving back the enemy and retaking the fort. Major Ricketts assisted Colonel Tidball during the action in placing batteries in positions to enfilade the enemy positions. Gordon's men had to abandon their gains and withdraw, losing perhaps two thousand prisoners.[20]

During the day, Humphreys received permission to engage the enemy to his front. The Second Corps picket line, heavily reinforced, charged forward and drove back the entrenched Confederate picket line. Battery F was on alert behind the lines, but was not engaged during the day.[21]

Battery F then returned to camp but did not remain there long.

---

[18]*Brockway Diary, March 17-18, 1865; Thurston to Laura, March 16, 1865, with supplement dated March 17. For details on dismounting a piece, see* Instruction for Field Artillery, *134-35. Lieutenant Thurston remarked that Colonel Hazard praised Battery F "in consequence of the good appearance of our Baty and soldierly bearing of the men & cleanliness of our camp." See Thurston to Laura, March 19, 1865.*

[19]*Brockway Diary, March 19-23, 1865; Thurston to Laura, March 19, 1865.*

[20]*Humphreys,* Virginia Campaign, *316-120; Ricketts Diary, March 25, 1865.*

[21]*Humphreys,* Virginia Campaign, *320-21; Brockway Diary, March 25, 1865.*

The men had just unhitched the horses when orders were received to move to the left. The battery went into a fort near Hatcher's Run, relieving two New York batteries of the Fifth Corps, which was pulled out of line and sent to the left. Grant, upon hearing of Gordon's repulse, ordered Meade to launch an offensive. Grant correctly reasoned that Lee was now weak in numbers and that a Federal attack might break the lines and force Lee to evacuate Petersburg and Richmond. He also wished to ensure that Lee did not evacuate the lines, steal a march, and join forces with General Joseph E. Johnston in North Carolina.[22]

Accordingly, part of the Army of the James moved to the left of the line, where Sheridan's cavalry and the Fifth Corps formed the main striking force. As the troops moved, the men of Battery F cleaned their new home. Lieutenant Thurston reported that the battery received a surgeon's certificate from Lieutenant Campbell. He was sick and would not return to duty just yet. Thurston also had heard that Campbell had gotten married since he was at home. High water on the Susquehanna River also seemingly hampered Campbell's ability to return to Virginia.[23]

Battery F moved yet again on March 29, this time taking position in Fort Gregg, a newer earthwork fort on the left of the line, near Hatcher's Run. Fighting erupted during the day as Warren's Fifth Corps encountered enemy infantry, with Humphreys moving up in support. Lieutenant Thurston wrote that the sounds of battle could be heard, and the wounded began coming in "large numbers. But rain began coming down that night, the creeks quickly filled, and road movement was only possible after sweating and wet soldiers helped corduroy the low spots in the rutted mud.[24]

The rain continued all day on the thirtieth and finally cleared that night. Battery F remained in Fort Gregg, listening to the sounds of battle to the west. Sheridan left Dinwiddie Court House and moved north, only to be forced back. Warren and Humphreys continued to advance, but the mud made the going very slow. Fighting continued on March 31, as Warren's men fought their way up the White Oak Road, and Sheridan was again repelled, but

---

[22]*Humphreys, Virginia Campaign, 322-24.*

[23]*Brockway Diary, March 28, 1865; Thurston to Laura, March 19, 27, 1865.*

[24]*Thurston to Laura. March 30, 1865; Brockway Diary, March 29, 1865.*

ascertained the Confederate positions at the vital Five Forks crossroads.[25]

The climax of the Union movement occurred on April 1, as the Fifth Corps and Sheridan's cavalry smashed Major General George Pickett's Confederates defending Five Forks, capturing perhaps four thousand of the enemy. To take advantage of the situation on the enemy right, Grant ordered an attack on April 2. The Ninth Corps fought its way into the enemy lines in its front, while the Sixth Corps made a decisive breakthrough along its front. Lee ordered an evacuation of Petersburg and Richmond, for his army was broken and could only be saved by retreating across the Appomattox River. In the midst of these victorious operations, Lieutenant Campbell finally rejoined the battery on April 2.[26]

Major Ricketts spent the night of the second in Fort Rice. "At daylight saw our troops advance over Cemetery Hill without opposition. Ricketts took charge of three batteries and at noon followed the Ninth Corps into Petersburg. Battery F was still in Fort Gregg, but late on April 2 was ordered to join the Ninth Corps. Brockway and Sergeant John A. McFarland managed to have themselves detached on Ricketts' staff and accompanied the major into Petersburg, the coveted prize of the last nine months. Otherwise, no one was allowed into the city without a valid pass. Brockway commented on the widespread belief of the black population that the year of jubilee had finally arrived.[27]

As the Army of the Potomac moved after Lee, Battery F was transferred to the Artillery Reserve and left in Petersburg. On April 4, the battery received an order to send forty horses to the Second Corps. Sergeant Charles G. Matthews led the detachment, the men all armed with revolvers, to find Humphreys and the Second Corps early on April 5. Other detachments of the battery cleaned up abandoned ordnance from the Rebel earthworks. The rest of the battery received teams of horses from City Point and moved down toward the supply base, going into camp "outside of the fortifications" that evening. All sorts of rumors were beginning to reach the battery. Lee had surrendered, many said. Sheridan had captured fifteen thousand prisoners, said another. When some

---

[25]*Brockway Diary, March 30-31, 1865.*

[26]*Brockway Diary, April 1- 2, 1865.*

[27]*Ricketts Diary, April 3, 1865; Brockway Diary, April 3, 1865*

prisoners passed by the camp, it did look as if the Confederacy was 'going down."[28]

On Saturday, the eighth of April, the battery went down to a nearby creek and the officers and men washed themselves. From all appearances, the men concluded that they would stay in their present location for some time, so they began to beautify the camp. They replanted wild flowers as well as small cedar and spruce trees. Then came the grand news of Lee's surrender on the ninth. The reserve artillery batteries fired off a hundred gun salute. That night, Captain Campbell got drunk celebrating the victory. Life in camp quickly became dull and boring. The officers spent much time going to City Point in hopes of finding a mustering officers so their promotions could take effect. Most of the battery sat around in camp, writing letters to loved ones, playing games, and wishing for money so they could visit the sutlers.[29]

News of President Lincoln's assassination angered the officers and men of Battery F. Lieutenant Brockway thought that the guilty party should be burned at the stake. Lieutenant Thurston probably best expressed the sentiments of that faction of the army who may not have voted for Lincoln:

> I suppose you have heard of the assassination of the President which is a sad calamity to our Nation at this time. The soleum duties that devolved upon the chief magistrate of the Nation I fear will not be ably fulfilled by Johnson. I must confess I never liked Lincoln, still I have learned to believe that he was honest and his whole heart and soul was enlisted in the cause of our policy, and all his statesmanship. Some cowardly ruffian has murdered him. It has cast a gloom over the Army and the Nation. I feel to knight like exterminating every Rebel in this South.[30]

Battery F moved its camp on April 18 to a field covered with grass, "which pleases the men all to pieces." News of the capture of Mobile and Johnston's surrender to Sherman in North Carolina cheered the men, for it now seemed that the war was generally over.

---

[28]*Brockway Diary, April 4-7, 1865;* O.R.., *volume 46, part 1, 661 (Hunt's report detailing the formation of the Artillery Reserve and its camps);* O.R. Supplement, *volume 7, 758.*

[29]*Brockway Diary, April 8-15, 1865; Thurston to Laura, April 12, 1865.*

[30]*Brockway Diary, April 16, 1865; Thurston to Laura, April 18, 1865.*

Private Cyrus Jones, a blacksmith from Lancaster, transferred from Battery G.
(RONN PALM COLLECTION, USAMHI)

"The weather is splendid and we have good times," penned Lieutenant Thurston. Indeed, whenever there was free time, the officers were able to ride around the countryside. The battery was resupplied with all new horses, so drilling had to commence in earnest to ensure that the new animals were ready, just in case.[31]

One of the few highlights of life at this time took place on April 21. In a brief ceremony, the officers and men presented Major Ricketts with a sword and sash, sword belt, and bridle. During the Appomattox Campaign, Ricketts assisted in handling the corps Artillery Brigade and scouring the countryside to bring in abandoned Confederate cannon. He was able to spend some time with paroled Confederate officers, talking with them about Gettysburg and other battles. The Ninth Corps was ordered to Washington for added security, and began arriving at City Point on April 21. On the twenty-third, General Meade ordered Major Ricketts detached from the Ninth Corps and sent to report to Brigadier General William Hays, commanding the Artillery Reserve. The major became Hays' chief of staff and inspector general.[32]

There was little of importance for Ricketts to do. He mustered five batteries for pay on the thirtieth. Visits to Richmond and Petersburg were always for pleasure. In Battery F, the officers requested furloughs to go home to see their families. Lieutenant Brockway received a leave and departed for home on April 28. Battery drill ended the same day when the order was received to turn in all the battery horses. But still the men were getting impatient. The war was over, so why drill now? Brockway put laggards who refused to attend drill on extra duty. Flags remained at half mast and cannon still fired salutes to honor the martyred president. Officers were required to wear black crepe on the left arms as tokens of respect. Flags were draped with black crepe.[33]

Battery F apparently did not turn in its horses, for on May 3, the Artillery Reserve broke camp and began a northward march that would take it to Washington. The batteries crossed the Appomattox River at Broadway Landing, then moved across the pontoon bridge over the James River at Aiken's Landing, camping on Cox's Farm just north of Dutch Gap. The batteries moved a further fifteen miles

---

[31]*Thurston to Laura, April 18, 24, 1865; Brockway diary, April 18-21, 1865.*

[32]*Ricketts Diary, April 4-23, 1865.*

[33]*Brockway Diary, April 22-28, 1865; Ricketts Diary, April 28-May 2, 1865; Thurston to Laura, April 27, 1865.*

on May 4, passing through Richmond. By nightfall on the fifth, the artillery was in camp adjacent to the Pamunkey River. The next day, May 6, the batteries crossed the Pamunkey and encamped. The march continued on the seventh. After fording the Mattapony River, the reserve camped at Bowling Green after a 24-mile trek. The batteries moved twenty-two miles on the eighth, camping near Fredericksburg. May 9 was cold, windy, and rainy, so after twenty miles, the command encamped at Aquia Creek. Evening of the tenth found the batteries five miles beyond Dumfries; the day was cold and cloudy. On the eleventh, the route of march went through Wolf Run Shoals and Fairfax Courthouse, to a camp near Annandale. The night brought another cold storm. As a result, May 12 was a day of inactivity as the Fifth Corps passed the artillery.[34]

The artillery march ended on May 13, when the batteries left Annandale and moved to new camps near Fairfax Seminary. Battery F named its bivouac Camp Barr. Situated on a hill overlooking the Potomac River valley, Camp Barr afforded a vista of the river and its heavy ship traffic. The surrounding hillsides were white with tents. The Second and Fifth Corps were now concentrated near the artillery, and news circulated through camp that Sherman's western soldiers were also marching north to the capital city. Drilling continued to keep the men busy and maintain discipline, but by the time Lieutenant Brockway returned to camp on May 19, the cannon had been turned in to the Washington Arsenal.[35]

During the next days, Battery F's officers visited Washington, went to see friends in other units, and tried to maintain discipline among their sometimes unruly artillerists. The Artillery Reserve did not take part in the Grand Review of May 23, when the Army of the Potomac paraded down Pennsylvania Avenue. Brockway remained in charge of the camp while the rest of the officers were to see the event. Major Ricketts rode in Colonel Tidball's staff as part of the Second Corps Artillery Brigade. When Sherman's troops paraded on May 24, many Eastern officers crowded the avenue to watch the spectacle of the western units and their eccentricities.[36]

On May 25, Battery F received a circular order to prepare the final muster rolls of all the one-year men in the battery so they

---

[34]*Ricketts Diary*, May 3-12, 1865.

[35]*Brockway Diary*, May 19, 1865; Thurston to Laura, May 12, 1865; *Ricketts Diary*, May 13, 1865.

[36]*Brockway Diary*, May 20-24, 1865; *Ricketts Diary*, 23-24, 1865.

could be discharged from service. They were mustered out of service on May 28. On the first of June, Battery F marched to the Washington Depot and boarded a train for Baltimore, then went on to Harrisburg, where the unit arrived at daylight on June 2. After debarking, the battery formed and marched through the city to Camp Return, located adjacent to Camp Curtin just north of the city. Admiring citizens presented the officers with bouquets of flowers and cheered as the veterans marched past the assembled crowds. Once in camp, the old, worn tents were turned in and A-tents issued to the battery.[37]

Once in camp, the officers again took liberties as quickly as they could. Brockway went home for a brief visit from June 3-5. When he returned, only Captain Campbell remained. Lieutenant Thurston had also apparently gone home, while Mowrer and Wireman were both absent. Mowrer requested a leave after he received news that his mother was "dangerously ill." Thurston returned on the seventh; Wireman took up residence at the Lochiel House in the city. The men stuck in camp began to resent the liberties their officers were taking. Several wound up in the guard house for being rowdy.[38]

Finally, on June 8, the muster rolls were finished and were submitted to the proper authorities for approval. But the mustering officer pronounced the rolls imperfect and a hurried call was made to the clerks to correct the rolls. When the men saw Battery B being mustered out, they began cursing the officers "in all kind of ways." Rain descended in torrents during the day; lightning struck a telegraph pole adjacent to the camp. Everybody was miserable.[39]

June 10 was the final day for Battery F as a unit in the service of the United States. The rolls were accepted and the battery was mustered out of service, to date from June 9. Lieutenant Mowrer returned in time for the ceremony. "The boys tore the tent down over him" and then went for Captain Campbell, but he backed them down. "They had better not tackle me," agonized Lieutenant Brockway. The paymaster was still to appear so the boys had to remain in camp. "Demoralized mob," penned Brockway.[40]

---

[37]*Brockway Diary, May 25-June 2, 1865; Thurston to Laura, May 28, June 2, 1865; Mowrer to Campbell, May 28, 1865, Mowrer service file, NA.*

[38]*Brockway Diary, June 3-8, 1865; Thurston to Laura, June 7, 1865*

[39]*Brockway Diary, June 8, 1865.*

[40]Ibid., *June 10, 1865.*

Private Henry C. McClintock, a gentleman by occupation, enlisted at Williamsport.
(GARRY LEISTER COLLECTION, USAMHI)

The paymaster came on the eleventh and paid off the enlisted men. Now everyone could go home but the officers, who still had to wait for their pay. Meanwhile, Brockway went into the city and went shopping. He picked out a suit of clothes but had to wait for pay day before purchasing his new civilian duds. He received his money on the twelfth. Lieutenant Thurston went home, accompanying Captain Campbell's wife. The captain had to wait to settle the battery account books. Brockway left Harrisburg on June 13, taking his horse on a northbound train from Marysville to Sunbury.[41]

Major Ricketts was still in Washington. He and a party of officers and women went to visit Mount Vernon on June 1st. Mrs. Herbert, a descendant of Lord Halifax, guided the party through the house and tomb, "explaining to us everything of interest. We lunched on the lawn and returned to camp at dark. Very much pleased with our excursion & with one another." On Sunday, June 4, Ricketts attended the Episcopal Church in Alexandria, the very same in which George Washington once sat. The major attended a number of parties and watched the review of the Sixth Corps on June 8. Ricketts left Washington in mid-June and went home for a short while, then returned to camp. He was mustered out of service on July 3. The entire complement of Battery F was now discharged from military service.[42]

Battery F had compiled a solid record of service during its three years and eleven months of service. It fought in 56 engagements and was underfire 131 times. The battery roster totaled 349 officers and men. Casualties, as recorded by the War Department, were as follows:

	Officers	enlisted men
killed and died of wounds	1	16
wounded	3	40
died of disease	-	10
captured or missing	1	12
total casualties	5	78[43]

---

[41] Ibid., *June 11-13, 1865.*

[42] *Ricketts Diary, June 1-July 3, 1865.* "Sketches of Prominent Democrats," *The Four Quarters, July 1, 1871;* "Death of Charles B. Brockway," Columbia County Republican, *January 5, 1888.*

[43] F. Charles Petrillo, *Ghost Towns of North Mountain* (Wilkes-Barre, Pa.: Wyoming Historical and Geological Society, 1991), 61. As noted on the battery monument at Gettysburg. See also Nicholson, *Pennsylvania at Gettysburg,* 2:1069.

Chapter Twelve

Postwar Memories

The officers and men of Battery F went home in June 1865. The war was over and everyone could now try to resume their civilian pursuits. Charles Brockway resumed his law studies, finished them, and was admitted to the bar. In 1867, he bought *The Columbian*, a Democratic newspaper published in Bloomsburg, and became its chief editor. Brockway sold the paper in 1870 and entered politics. He served in the Pennsylvania state legislature from 1872 to 1874, representing Bloomsburg. Brockway married and fathered three children. The war had severely damaged his health, however, and the young Democrat was never the same. In late 1887, Brockway's health began a long decline from which he never recovered. He died in his Bloomsburg home on January 3, 1888.

Frank Brockway went home and engaged in a number of different occupations. He was a justice of the peace in Salem Township, Columbia County, for fourteen years, but worked primarily as a farmer. He married Cora Campbell in 1868 and produced five children, only one of whom lived past his maturity. In 1872, Brockway became a brick manufacturer, retiring in 1909. Frank Brockway passed away in September 1940, age ninety-five, perhaps one of the last survivors of Battery F.[1]

The battery's first captain, Ezra Matthews, relocated to Philadelphia and established a banking and brokerage firm. He married a Philadelphia woman in 1871 and fathered two children. Matthews joined the Pennsylvania National Guard with the rank of captain in May 1876. He was promoted to lieutenant colonel and inspector of the guard's First Brigade within the year. In 1877, Matthews was promoted to brigadier general and commanded the First Brigade. His troops played a prominent part in the fighting with steel industry strikers in Pittsburgh later that year. Matthews

---

[1] J. H. Battle (editor), History of Columbia and Montour Counties, Pennsylvania *(Chicago: A. Warner & Company, 1887), 1088-89.*

resigned his commission in December 1877. Two years later, he was reappointed to the guard as a lieutenant colonel and ordnance officer of the division, a position he held until he resigned in 1884. Matthews became a companion of the Military Order of the Loyal Legion of the United States. He attended the order's annual meeting in 1885, which was held at the Union League of Philadelphia. The captain came down with a bad cold and died from its effects on November 7.[2]

Colonel Ricketts came home in July 1865 and resumed his study of law, but did not stay very long at it, preferring instead to become a land speculator. In September 1869, the colonel purchased his father's interest in the sportsman's lodge known as Long Pond Tavern, and its accompanying five thousand acres. Ricketts continued to buy virgin timber land, using tax sales, and eventually controlled more than eighty thousand acres (a hundred square miles), straddling the counties of Luzerne, Sullivan, and Wyoming. He married Elizabeth Reynolds (a direct descendant of the Mayflower Reynolds) in October 1868, producing three children. Bruce and Elizabeth built themselves a comfortable summer mansion on North Mountain, where Ricketts often entertained family and friends after the timber business played out in 1913.

The colonel was nominated by the Democratic Party as lieutenant governor in 1886, but the party lost the election; Ricketts carried his home county of Luzerne by a wide margin. The colonel served as the Receiver of Taxes in Wilkes-Barre from 1898 through 1902. He was active in the Grand Army of the Republic and remained keenly interested in his comrades of Battery F. Ricketts died from the Spanish influenza outbreak on November 13, 1918; a broken-hearted Elizabeth followed him six days later. The couple are buried side by side in a private family plot on North Mountain, said to be their favorite place in the wilderness. In time, part of the colonel's vast holdings became Ricketts Glen State Park.[3]

---

[2]*Obituary,* Grand Army Scout and Soldiers Mail, *November 14, 1885;* In Memoriam, Ezra Wallace Matthews *(MOLLUS, 1885); MOLLUS File on Matthews, Civil War Library and Museum, Philadelphia.*

[3]Peter Tomasak, "Hiking with History in Ricketts Glen State Park," Pennsylvania State Parks *4 #2 (Spring 1994): 2-3;* "Col. Ricketts Dead," Wilkes-Barre Record, *November 14, 1918;* "Colonel Ricketts of This City is Claimed By Death," *Wilkes-Barre* Times Leader, *November 13, 1918;* "Last of Her Family. Sudden Passing of Mrs. R. Bruce Ricketts—Distinguished Patriots and Pioneer Business Men Among Ancestors," *Wilkes-Barre Record, November 20, 1918.*

Battery F&G reunion and dedication of the monument on East Cemetery Hill. Shown are members who made it to Gettysburg for the official dedication which was on July 2, 1894. This photo was taken on July 4, 1894. Ricketts is standing in the direct middle. Other members have not been identified. (JEFF KOWALIS)

Many of the battery's veterans maintained a lively interest in the history of their unit and stayed in touch with each other in the years after the war. In 1887, enough interest was generated to form a reunion committee to plan annual reunions so that the men and their families could gather and keep the history of Battery F alive. The first reunion took place in Harrisburg on Thursday, October 27, 1887. Twenty-three veterans, Colonel Ricketts among them, met in the post room of Grand Army of the Republic Post 58 of Harrisburg. The veterans elected officers for the coming year, and decided that each member would pay a dollar annually to help defray expenses of the association. George E. Heinbach, then a resident of Lewistown, was elected president. Mason B. Hughes of Shickshinny became vice president, and Joel H. Schmehl of Reading took over the duties of secretary and treasurer. A committee was appointed to adopt an appropriate badge for future use by the members of the association. Before ending the brief one-day reunion, members voted to hold the second reunion at Gettysburg on July 2, 1888, the twenty-fifth anniversary of the battery's stand on East Cemetery Hill.[4]

The members of Battery F also appointed a committee to select the design for a monument to be erected on the Gettysburg battlefield. Earlier that year, the Pennsylvania General Assembly passed legislation that set aside funds to be used to mark the positions of all Pennsylvania units engaged in the battle of Gettysburg. Each unit would receive fifteen hundred dollars from the commonwealth to help with the cost of its monument. A five-man commission would oversee each unit's monument design. The five commissioners included John P. Taylor (1st Pennsylvania Cavalry), John P. S. Gobin (47th Pennsylvania, a unit not in the battle), John P. Nicholson (28th Pennsylvania), Samuel Harper (139th Pennsylvania), and R. B. Ricketts (Battery F). These five men would serve without salary. After Major Harper died in 1889, he was replaced by William R. Hartshorne (13th Pennsylvania Reserves) in 1891.[5]

The second annual reunion of Battery F was held in the

---

[4]"Ricketts' Brave Boys," Harrisburg Morning Call, *October 28, 1887;* "The Ricketts Battery," Harrisburg Patriot, *October 28, 1887;* Ricketts' Battery; Abstract of Proceedings of Meeting Held on Thursday, October 27, 1887, Together With Roster of the Survivors of the Battery *(n.p., n.d.).*

[5]Nicholson, Pennsylvania at Gettysburg, *1:v-vii.*

Gettysburg Courthouse on July 2, 1888. Colonel Ricketts was absent, but thirty men attended the reunion. The same officers were unanimously re-elected for the coming year. After the usual business was conducted, the members present decided to convene in Wilkes-Barre on the first Tuesday of October 1889 for the third reunion.[6]

But changes took place in 1889 that scuttled the plans for an October reunion date. The Pennsylvania General Assembly decided to have a grand celebration at Gettysburg, during which the majority of state monuments being erected would be dedicated. Furthermore, fifty thousand dollars was appropriated to pay the costs of transportation for those veterans who had actually been in the 1863 battle. After some delay, "Pennsylvania Days" were set for September 11-12, 1889.[7]

Accordingly, Battery F decided to meet in Gettysburg on September 11. At some point prior to that time, the battery association, which had yet to decide on a monument design, corresponded with Battery G's association and decided to hold a joint reunion. Since the batteries had been consolidated during the Gettysburg Campaign, the two associations also determined to erect a joint monument as well. The September 11 meeting drew forty-two men from Batteries F and G. Each association elected its own officers. Ricketts' men re-elected George Heinbach as president and Joel Schmehl as secretary/treasurer; William H. Trump, the battery's former 1st Sergeant, took over as vice president. The men voted to hold the 1890 reunion in Reading.[8]

Reunions in subsequent years were held in a number of locations from which battery members had enlisted. The battery monument was officially dedicated on July 2, 1894, although it had been erected at least by 1893. Located in the midst of the battery position on East Cemetery Hill, the monument was carved from a single large slab of blue westerly granite by the Smith Granite Company, at a cost of some three thousand dollars. The eleven-foot-long by nine-feet-high granite depicts, in bas relief, one of the battery's 3-inch Ordnance Rifles being served by two gunners. The

---

[6]*Manuscript account of reunion proceedings, Gettysburg, July 2, 1888.*

[7]*Nicholson,* Pennsylvania at Gettysburg, *1:vi-vii.*

[8]*Roster of Battery F and G, First Pennsylvania Light Artillery, and Abstract of Proceedings of Meeting Held on Wednesday, Sept. 11, 1889 (n.p., n.d.).*

reverse lists each battery's strength and casualties, together with a brief description of the consolidated battery's role at Gettysburg.[9]

The monument erected by the veterans of Batteries F and G was not without controversy, however. Although the design of the monument itself was left to the monument committee, and although it was approved by the state commission, the inscription was in part based on information supplied by the federal War Department, Ricketts voiced an objection to the misstatement that Battery F was recruited in Schuylkill County. The matter seemingly was referred to the War Department, but something happened that derailed any correction to the monument. In August 1915, Ricketts received the new edition of *Pennsylvania at Gettysburg* and noted that the error was still there. Worse, Battery F was supposedly organized at Williamsport, Pennsylvania, in December 1861. Mystified, Ricketts wrote to Colonel John P. Nicholson and asked him where this information was obtained. Nicholson replied that his source was the *Official Army Register*. Nicholson also remarked that he had wondered what decision the War Department had reached back in the 1890s, when Nicholson had asked for a clarification on the controversy.[10]

Ricketts then wrote to Pennsylvania Adjutant General Thomas J. Stewart and asked him about the early records of Battery F. Stewart checked through the state's files and found that the battery's alphabetical roll clearly showed that the complement of Battery F came from many different counties; Captain Matthews apparently was the only one from Schuylkill County. Furthermore, the battery was mustered into service on August 5, 1861. Stewart checked the *Official Army Register* and found that Hampton's Independent Battery F was organized at Williamsport, Maryland, in December 1861. Here was the error in the Official Army Register–Nicholson had confused Hampton's Battery F with Ricketts' Battery F! Nicholson looked at the wrong page, for Battery

---

[9]Frederick W. Hawthorne, Gettysburg: Stories of Men and Monuments as Told by Battlefield Guides *(Hanover, PA: The Sheridan Press for the Association of Licensed Battlefield Guides, 1988), 105.*

[10]*Ricketts to Nicholson, August 17, 1915; Nicholson to Ricketts, August 19, 1915, copy of both in Ricketts Papers.*

Ricketts Monument at Gettysburg. This photo was taken on July 4, 1894. Left to right: Frank Ricketts (Brother), R. Bruce Ricketts, Sheldon Reynolds, George Murray Reynolds (Brother-in-laws); sitting left to right Benjamin Reynolds (Brother-in-law), William R. Ricketts (colonel's only son).

(CHESTER SIEGEL)

F's information on page 813 was correct; he had copied information from page 817, which listed Hampton's battery.[11]

Ricketts also had to defend himself against the charge that he did not command Batteries F&G at Gettysburg. This rather strange tale emerged in March 1893. Two articles appeared in Wilkes-Barre papers. Both were unsigned, and both stated that Ricketts was on staff duty during the battle and that the Brockway brothers led the battery during the fight. These articles produced a storm of indignation. Colonel Ricketts himself wrote a rebuttal, including a copy of his official report in the article. Other veterans rallied to his defense, and as the story spread to New York papers, veterans such as Colonel Richard Coulter (11th Pennsylvania of the First Corps) and William Beidelman (the mayor of Easton and a veteran of the 153rd Pennsylvania, Eleventh Corps) sent letters of support. Colonel Wainwright submitted a letter, as did a number of Battery F survivors. In the end, the plot to attack Colonel Ricketts failed miserably.[12]

The annual battery reunions continued every year. In 1913, the fiftieth anniversary of the battle of Gettysburg, the commonwealth of Pennsylvania sponsored a giant reunion of as many surviving Civil War veterans as could be found across the country. Thousands attended. The survivors of Batteries F&G met on East Cemetery Hill on July 2. Forty-five men gathered, and heard a letter of regret from Colonel Ricketts read aloud. Mail sent to thirteen other comrades during the year was returned, and seventeen veterans had answered the last call, further reducing the number of survivors. Colonel Ricketts was again elected president of the association, with James F. Kennedy elected to represent Battery F.[13]

---

[11]*Stewart to Ricketts, October 13, 1915, copy in Ricketts Papers.*

[12]*"Captain Ricketts at Gettysburg,"* Wilkes-Barre Leader, *March 27, 1893; "Col. Ricketts' Denial,"* Wilkes-Barre Press, *March 29, 1893; "More Vindication for Ricketts,"* Wilkes-Barre Telegram, *April 2, 1893; "On Cemetery Hill,"* Wilkes-Barre Leader, *April 10, 1893. Frank Brockway was named as the author of these scathing articles in "The Passing Throng,"* Bloomsburg *Morning Press, December 16, 1938. Frank was indignant that most of the credit for the battery's success as a unit was given Ricketts leaving his brother Charles Brockway out of the picture.*

[13]*Proceedings of Survivors' Association, Batteries F and G, First Artillery, P.R.V.C., 52nd Anniversary and 27th Reunion, Gettysburg, Pa., July 2, 1913 (n.p., n.d.).*

The 1914 reunion was held in Wilkes-Barre on September 4. Earlier that year, Secretary Luther Seiders, who held this position for twenty-eight years, had gone to Harrisburg; on June 15, Flag Day, he participated in the parade and ceremonies which retired the commonwealth's Civil War flags to specially-built cases in the Capitol Rotunda. Seiders carried the regimental color of the 1st Pennsylvania Artillery that hot afternoon. Nineteen veterans attended the Wilkes-Barre reunion, during which Henry Wireman was elected president of Battery F.[14]

Reunions after 1914 saw a steady decline as the aged veterans passed away. The 1915 reunion was held at the city of Shamokin, in Northumberland County. Only five veterans–Henry Wireman, George W. Mowrer, Isaac Rake, Jacob S. Yordy, Luther Seiders–attended. Mail of nine veterans had been returned by the Post Office, and another dozen men had died since the last reunion. Ten veterans were present in Wilkes-Barre for the 1916 reunion. Seiders announced the usual return of mail (six men) and reported the deaths of eleven others. He reported further that there were now fifty-five survivors of Battery F yet living and thirty-nine men from Battery G.[15]

As the twentieth century progressed, Civil War veterans became fewer and fewer. The last national reunion was held at Gettysburg in 1938, the seventy-fifth anniversary of the battle. In 1956, Albert Woolson of the 1st Minnesota Heavy Artillery died; he was the last bona fide Civil War veteran. Without extensive research, we do not know the name of the last survivor of Battery F. Even though the men are all gone, their monuments remain, as well as the stories of their heroism and sacrifice for a cause in which each and every one, regardless of politics, believed.

---

[14]*Sauers,* Advance the Colors, *1:33-34, 38; "Visiting War Veterans," Wilkes-Barre Record, September 5, 1914.*

[15]Survivors' Association, Batteries F and G, First Artillery, P.R.V.C., *proceedings for 1915 and 1916 (n.p., n.d.).*

Colonel Ricketts' frock coat, artillery sword and slouch hat.
(LUZERNE COUNTY HISTORICAL SOCIETY)

Battery F
Roster

The roster of Battery F appearing below is based on that contained in volume 1 of Samuel P. Bates' *History of Pennsylvania Volunteers*. Further annotations, additions, and corrections have been gleaned from battery papers in both the Pennsylvania State Archives and National Archives, as well as other sources listed in the Bibliography for this book. Battery F's company books were lost at Second Manassas and thus the original records for the battery are incomplete. There are 349 names on this list, seven more than credited to Battery F by the War Department.

Names preceded by an asterisk (*) were omitted in Bates' roster. Dates for muster in for some of the 1861 enlistees seem to be in error, a common practice when Bates faced the absence of good records. Those men are identified by question marks for dates of enlistment. In these cases, the original records had been lost and Bates had available only the 1864 re-enlistment dates.

Most of those who were enlisted in Battery F in 1864 were drafted, and were sometimes credited to townships and counties different from where they lived in order to receive bounty money and help fill that locale's quota.

Captain
Ezra W. Matthews. Mustered in 7/8/61. Promoted to Major, 4/11/63. Enlisted at Pine Grove, Schuylkill County, age 25, teacher.

Robert Bruce Ricketts. Mustered in 7/8/61. Promoted to 1st Lieutenant, 8/5/61. Promoted to Captain, 3/16/63. Promoted to Major, 12/1/64. Brevet Colonel, 3/13/65. Mustered out of service, 6/5/65. Enlisted from Columbia County, age 22, law student.

John F. Campbell. Mustered in 7/8/61. Promoted to Corporal, 8/1/61. Promoted to Sergeant, 1/3/63. Promoted to 2nd Lieutenant, 5/20/64. Promoted to 1st Lieutenant, 12/2/64. Promoted to Captain, 4/17/65. Mustered out with battery, 6/9/65. 11/63: Enlisted at Danville, Montour County, age 22, miller.

1st Lieutenant

Elbridge McConkey. Mustered in 7/8/61. Promoted to 1st Lieutenant, 8/5/61. Resigned, 2/20/62. Enlisted from Chester County.

Henry L. Godbold. Mustered in 7/8/61. Died 9/22/62, of wounds received at Rappahannock Station, 8/23/62. Enlisted from Dauphin County.

Charles B. Brockway. Mustered in as Sergeant, 7/8/61. Promoted to 2nd Lieutenant, 2/28/62. Promoted to 1st Lieutenant, 3/16/63. Brevet Captain, 3/13/65. Captured at Second Manassas, 8/30/62. Discharged, 10/22/64, expiration of term. Enlisted at Bloomsburg, Columbia County, age 21, law student. Brevet captain for gallantry at Second Manassas, 7/16/67.

Henry Wireman. Mustered in 7/8/61. Promoted to Corporal, 7/1/62. Promoted to Sergeant, 1/1/63. Promoted to 1st Lieutenant, 12/6/64. Mustered out with battery, 6/9/65. 11/63: Enlisted at Danville, Montour County, age 20, gentleman.

William M. Thurston. Mustered in 7/8/61. Promoted to Corporal, 7/1/62. Wounded at Gettysburg, 7/2/63. Promoted to Sergeant, 7/3/63. Promoted to 2nd Lieutenant, 12/6/64. Promoted to 1st Lieutenant, 4/22/65. Mustered out with battery, 6/9/65. 11/63: Enlisted at Sunbury, Northumberland County, age 25, blacksmith.

2nd Lieutenant

Truman L. Case. Mustered in 7/8/61. Discharged as supernumerary officer, 2/4/63, as per Special Orders #57, War Department. Enlisted at Montrose, Susquehanna County.

Francis H. Snider. Mustered in as Ordnance Sergeant, 7/8/61. Reduced to the ranks, 4/22/62. Promoted to Sergeant, [?/?/62]. Wounded at Mine Run, 11/27/63. Promoted to 2nd Lieutenant, 1/31/64. Discharged 10/8/64. Enlisted at Philadelphia.

George W. Mowrer. Mustered in 7/8/61. Promoted to Sergeant, 11/1/62. Promoted to 2nd Lieutenant, 4/22/65. Mustered out with battery, 6/9/65. 1/64: Enlisted at Danville, Montour County, age 19, student.

Franklin P. Brockway. Mustered in 1/1/62. Promoted from Corporal to Sergeant, 4/4/64. Promoted to 2nd Lieutenant, 12/21/64 (mustered as such, 4/22/65). Mustered out with battery, 6/9/65. Enlisted at Berwick, Columbia County, age 18, farmer.

1st Sergeant
William H. Trump. Mustered in 7/8/61. Promoted from Corporal to Sergeant, 4/14/64. Mustered out with battery, 6/9/65. Enlisted at Danville, Montour County, age 19, student. Residence was at Espy, Columbia County.

Quartermaster Sergeant
Stephen E. Ridgeway. Mustered in 12/30/61. Promoted to Corporal, 8/17/63. Promoted to Sergeant, 4/6/65. Mustered out with battery, 6/9/65. Enlisted at Danville, Montour County, age 19, student.

Sergeant
Morgan Bahn. Mustered in 7/29/61. Transferred from Battery G at re-enlistment. Promoted from Corporal to Sergeant, 5/20/64. Mustered out with battery, 6/9/65. 11/63: Enlisted from York County, age 24, carpenter.

Jesse Chamberlain. Mustered in 7/16/61. Transferred from Battery G at re-enlistment. Mustered out with battery, 6/9/65. 1/64: Enlisted at Pine Grove, Schuylkill County, age 24, laborer.

Henry A. Conrad. Mustered in 7/10/61. Discharged on surgeon's certificate, 1/15/64. Enlisted at Harrisburg, Dauphin County.

Myron French. Mustered in 7/8/61. Promoted to Sergeant sometime after

The Antietam. Killed at Gettysburg, 7/2/63. Enlisted at Jackson, Susquehanna County. After the war in Jackson, Pa., a GAR post was named after him.

Smith L. French. Mustered in 7/8/61. Promoted to Corporal, 4/4/64. Promoted to Sergeant, [4/7/65]. Mustered out with battery, 6/9/65. Enlisted at Jackson, Susquehanna County, age 18, farmer.

Franklin M. Haines. Mustered in 7/24/61. Promoted to Corporal, 8/1/63. Promoted to Sergeant, ?/?/??. Transferred from Battery G at re-enlistment. Mustered out with battery, 6/9/65. 1/64: Enlisted at Alexandria, Huntingdon County, age 24, tinsmith.

Charles G. Matthews. Mustered in 1/21/64. Promoted to Sergeant, 3/1/64. Mustered out with battery, 6/9/65. Enlisted at Philadelphia, age 31, armorer.

John A. McFarland. Mustered in 7/8/61. Promoted to Corporal, 8/1/63. Promoted to Sergeant, ?/?/??. Mustered out with battery, 6/9/65. Enlisted at Williamsburg, Blair County, age 18, laborer.

William B. Mellick. Mustered in 7/8/61. Wounded at Front Royal, VA, 6/9/62. Discharged on surgeon's certificate, 7/18/62.

Corporal
Ephraim Berger. Mustered in 12/24/61. Transferred from Battery G at re-enlistment. Mustered out with battery, 6/9/65. Enlisted from Northampton County, age 20, boatman.

Delos D. Bryant. Mustered in 7/8/61. Discharged on surgeon's certificate, 5/19/62.

John W. Bullock. Mustered in 11/24/62. Transferred from Battery G at reenlistment. Mustered out with battery, 6/9/65. Born in England, enlisted from Scranton, Luzerne County, age 21, carpenter.

John H. Christian. Mustered in 7/8/61. Wounded at Gettysburg, 7/2/63. Mustered out, 8/8/64. Enlisted at Danville, Montour County.

Franklin Houser. Mustered in 1/27/62. Promoted to Corporal, 8/26/64. Mustered out with battery, 6/9/65. Enlisted at Berwick, Columbia County, age 26, tailor.

George E. Heinbach. Mustered in 8/5/61. Transferred from Battery G at reenlistment. Promoted to Corporal, 5/20/64. Mustered out with battery, 6/9/65. 12/63: Enlisted at Ickesburg, Perry County, age 21, laborer.

Albert Herbein (also as Herbine). Mustered in 8/5/61. Transferred from Battery G at re-enlistment. Promoted to Corporal, 4/4/64. Mustered out with battery, 6/9/65. 1/64: Enlisted from Cumberland County, age 21, chair maker.

James F. Kennedy. Mustered in 7/8/61. Promoted to Corporal, 4/7/65. Mustered out with battery, 6/9/65. Enlisted at Williamsburg, Blair County, age 19, farmer. Detailed to Brigade Hospital as per Special Orders #157, 9/19/64.

Oscar G. Larrabee. Mustered in 7/8/61. Captured at Second Manassas, 8/30/62. Captured at Gettysburg, 7/2/63. Promoted to Corporal, 4/4/64. Mustered out with battery, 6/9/65. 1/64: Enlisted at Jackson, Susquehanna County, age 21, teacher.

Leon Eugene C. Moore. Mustered in 3/17/62. Transferred to Battery G, 3/26/64. Enlisted at Minersville, Schuylkill County. Died in Los Angles, California, in 1927.

Mark O'Brian (Also spelled O'Brien). Mustered in 7/8/61. Mustered out with battery, 6/9/65. 12/63: Born in Canada, enlisted at Philadelphia, age 24, laborer.

William H. Patterson. Mustered in 7/8/61. Wounded at Bristoe Station, 10/14/63. Transferred to Battery G, 3/26/64. Enlisted at Jackson, Susquehanna County.

Joseph Peterson. Mustered in 8/5/61. Mustered out with battery, 6/9/65. 12/63: Born in New Jersey, enlisted at Philadelphia, age 23, farmer.

Abraham Rudisill. Mustered in 8/5/61. Transferred from Battery G at re-enlistment. Mustered out with battery, 6/9/65. 12/63: Enlisted at Hanover, York County, age 55, tailor.

William H. Shoop. Mustered in 7/8/61. Transferred to Battery G, 3/26/64. Enlisted at Hollidaysburg, Blair County.

Joseph Strong. Mustered in 7/8/61. Captured at Second Manassas, 8/30/62. Mustered out with battery, 6/9/65. 12/63: Enlisted at Williamsport, Lycoming County, age 24, lawyer.

William Umberhower (also as Umbenhower). Mustered in 7/20/61. Transferred from Battery G at re-enlistment. Promoted to Corporal, 4/4/64. Mustered out with battery, 6/9/65. 1/64: Enlisted at Pine Grove, Schuylkill County, age 21, miner.

Bugler
William L. Warnick. Mustered in 7/8/61. Mustered out with battery, 6/9/65. 12/63: Enlisted at Philadelphia, age 19, boatman.

James W. Francis. Mustered in 2/9/64. Mustered out with battery, 6/9/65. Enlisted at Reading, Berks County, age 18, painter.

Artificer
Jacob S. Yordy. Mustered in 7/8/61. Mustered out with battery, 6/9/65. 1/64: Enlisted at Rushville, Northumberland County, age 23, wheelwright.

Jacob M. Harman. Mustered in 3/9/64. Mustered out with battery, 6/9/65. Enlisted at Philadelphia, age 26, harness maker.

Private
George W. Ackerman. Mustered in 2/6/64. Mustered out with battery, 6/9/65. Enlisted from Dauphin County, age 19, boatman.

William Amon (also as Ammon). Mustered in 2/9/64. Transferred to Battery B, 12/29/64 (with Battery B since 7/11/64). Enlisted at Reading, Berks County, age 19, miner.

Elijah Y. Anderson. Mustered in 7/8/61. Killed at Gettysburg, 7/2/63. Enlisted at Harrisburg, Dauphin County.

George W. Angstadt. Mustered in 2/4/64. Transferred to Battery B, 12/29/64 (with Battery B since 7/11/64). Enlisted at Reading, Berks County, age 19, laborer.

Cyrus B. Appleman. Mustered in 3/15/64. Wounded at Totopotomoy Creek, 5/31/64. Mustered out with battery, 6/9/65. Enlisted from Columbia County, age 34, moulder.

John Ardes. Mustered in 7/19/61. Transferred to Battery A, 12/29/64. Born in England, enlisted from Delaware County, age 24, dyer.

William Arsta. Mustered in 7/19/61. Transferred from Battery G at re-enlistment. Mustered out with battery, 6/9/65. 12/63: Born in Germany, enlisted from York County, age 25, farmer.

William Bailer (also as Bayler). Mustered in 9/1/64. Mustered out with battery, 6/9/65.

Thomas Ball. Mustered in 3/25/64, in Battery G. Transferred to Battery F, ?/?/??.

George E. Barnes. Mustered in 3/18/64. Transferred to Battery A, 12/27/64. Enlisted from Chester County, age 19, carpenter.

John Bartle (also as Bartte). Mustered in 7/8/61. Deserted 9/16/62, near Keedeysville, MD. Age 45, blacksmith.

Owen (also as Orren) E. Bartlett. Mustered in 8/5/61. Mustered out with battery, 6/9/65. 11/63: Enlisted from Bradford County, age 38, laborer. Detailed as hospital attendant at Brigade Hospital, 5/2/64.

John Bassing. Mustered in 2/10/64. Mustered out with battery, 6/9/65. 12/64: Born in Germany, enlisted at Danville, Montour County, age 33, laborer.

Samuel Bassler. Mustered in 2/13/64. Transferred to Battery A, 12/29/64.

*John J. Bechtold (also as Bechtolus). Mustered in 12/24/63. Transferred to Battery G, 3/28/64. Born in Germany, enlisted at Lancaster, Lancaster County, age 41, saddler.

Francis E. Benedict. Mustered in 7/13/61. Wounded at Antietam, 9/17/62. Discharged on surgeon's certificate, date unknown. Enlisted at Jackson, Susquehanna County.

William Bennett. Mustered in 9/1/61. Transferred to Battery A, 12/27/64.
William O. Bingham. Mustered in 7/8/61. Transferred to Battery G, 3/26/64.

Enlisted at Danville, Montour County.

Enoch Blackman. Mustered in ?/?/61. Mustered out with battery, 6/9/65. 1/64: Enlisted at Philadelphia, age 22, sailor.

Charles Blakeny (also as Blakeney). Mustered in 7/8/61. Discharged on surgeon's certificate, 11/15/63. Enlisted at Williamsburg, Blair County, age 25, boatman.

William Blessing. Mustered in 8/22/61. Transferred from Battery G at reenlistment. Mustered out with battery, 6/9/65. 11/63: Enlisted at Harrisburg, Dauphin County, age 19, blacksmith.

Peter Bonney. Mustered in 8/22/61. Transferred from Battery G at reenlistment. Mustered out with battery, 6/9/65. 12/63: Born in Prussia, enlisted at Scranton, Luzerne County, age 32, shoemaker.

Levi S. Bowers. Mustered in 7/8/61. Mustered out with battery, 6/9/65. 11/63: Enlisted at Springfield, Bradford County, age 22, saddler.

Frank M. Bradigan. Mustered in 8/6/61. Transferred from Battery G at reenlistment. Mustered out with battery, 6/9/65. 1/64: Enlisted at Pine Grove, Schuylkill County, age 21, laborer.

Stewart F. Branton (also as Brantner and Branton). Mustered in 2/23/64. Mustered out with battery 6/9/65. Enlisted at Williamsburg, Blair County, age 20, farmer.

Charles Briner. Mustered in 2/3/64. Transferred to Battery A, 12/27/64. Enlisted from Berks County, age 18, laborer.

Henry W. Brown. Mustered in 1/26/64. Mustered out with battery, 6/9/65. Enlisted at Harrisburg, Dauphin County, age 18, laborer.

Daniel Bubb. Mustered in 7/8/61. Absent sick at muster out. Discharged 7/27/65. Enlisted at Danville, Montour County, age 20, farmer.

Carpenter Buckalew. Mustered in 3/15/64. Absent sick, from 4/12/64 through at least 10/31/64. Mustered out with battery, 6/9/65. Enlisted at Scranton, Luzerne County, age 20, boatman.

Jacob Burge. Mustered in 8/26/61. Transferred from Battery G at re-enlistment. Mustered out with battery, 6/9/65. Detailed to Brigade Hospital, as per Special Orders #157, 9/19/64. 12/63: Enlisted at Lock Haven, Clinton County, age 20, laborer.

Hugh Burns (Also spelled Byrnes). Mustered in 7/26/61. Transferred from Battery G at re-enlistment. Mustered out with battery, 6/9/65. 1/64: Born in Ireland, enlisted at Lancaster, Lancaster County, age 37, miner.

Henry W. Call. Mustered in 2/2/64. Mustered out with battery, 6/9/65. Enlisted from Berks County, age 20, shoemaker.

Simon S. Campbell. Mustered in 2/1/64. Mustered out with battery, 6/9/65. Enlisted at Middletown, Dauphin County, age 18, machinist.

Henry J. Carson. Mustered in 7/11/61. Transferred from Battery G at re-enlistment. Mustered out with battery, 6/9/65. 11/63: Enlisted at Pittsburgh, Allegheny County, age 19, laborer.

Peter V. Cassiday. Mustered in 7/8/61. Discharged on surgeon's certificate, 11/29/62. Enlisted at Hollidaysburg, Blair County.

William Chamberlain. Mustered in 2/26/64. Mustered out with battery, 6/9/65. Enlisted at Lock Haven, Lycoming County, age 17, laborer.

John H. Christian. Mustered in 7/8/61. Discharged 8/6/64. Enlisted at Danville, Montour County, age 23. Rank listed as corporal at muster out.

Benneville Christman. Mustered in 2/3/64. Transferred to Battery B, 12/29/64 (with Battery B since 7/11/64). Enlisted at Reading, Berks County, age 20, shoemaker.

Charles H. Clark. Mustered in 7/8/61. Transferred to Battery G, 3/26/64. Enlisted at Susquehanna Depot, Susquehanna County.

John Clements. Mustered in ?/?/61. Mustered out with battery, 6/9/65. 1/64: Born in Ireland, enlisted at Philadelphia, 31, laborer.

Samuel Clere (Also as Clere and Clone). Mustered in 7/8/61. Wounded at Front Royal, VA, 6/13/62. Discharged on surgeon's certificate, 2/24/63. Enlisted at Hollidaysburg, Blair County.

Richard J. Colden. Mustered in 9/4/62. Transferred to Battery G, 3/26/64.

Martin Conners. Mustered in 8/22/64. Transferred to Battery A, 12/27/64.

William Coulter. Mustered in 7/8/61. Killed at Cold Harbor, 6/64. 11/63: Enlisted at Greenfield, Mercer County, age 19, farmer.

John J. Coyn (also as Coin). Mustered in 5/30/64. Mustered out with battery, 6/9/65. Enlisted at Scranton, Luzerne County, age 19, miner.

Patrick Curry. Mustered in 7/8/61. Wounded at Second Manassas, 8/30/62. Mustered out with battery, 6/9/65. 1/64: Born in Ireland, enlisted at Philadelphia, age 24, laborer.

Jacob Davis. Mustered in 2/8/64. Transferred to Battery B, 12/29/64 (with Battery B since 7/11/64). Enlisted at Halifax, Dauphin County, age 19, cabinet maker.

Theophilus Davis. Mustered in 2/2/64. Mustered out with battery, 6/9/65. Enlisted at Middletown, Dauphin County, age 20, laborer.

William B. Davis (also as Darr). Mustered in 7/8/61. Mustered out with battery, 6/9/65. 11/63: Enlisted at Carlisle Cumberland County, age 24, boatman.

William N. Davis. Mustered in 11/8/61. Transferred from Battery G at re-enlistment. Mustered out with battery, 6/9/65. 1/64: Enlisted at Allentown, Lehigh County, age 23, laborer.

Moses Dell. Mustered in 7/8/61. Wounded at Antietam, 9/17/62. Mustered out 7/11/64, expiration of term. Enlisted at Hollidaysburg, Blair County.

John A. Dennan. Mustered in 1/30/64. Mustered out with battery, 6/9/65.

Cornelius S. Dibble. Mustered in ?/?/61. Mustered out with battery, 6/9/65. 12/63: Enlisted from Union Township, Susquehanna County, age 20, farmer.

John Diebler (also as Deibler). Mustered in 12/18/61. Mustered out with battery, 6/9/65. Enlisted at Shamokin, Northumberland County, age 25, mason.

Burton W. Dix. Mustered in 7/8/61. Mustered out with battery, 6/9/65. 12/63: Enlisted at Jackson, Susquehanna County, age 26, farmer.

John Dodson. Mustered in 9/1/64. Mustered out with battery, 6/9/65. Born in England, enlisted at Norristown, Montgomery County, age 25, laborer.

Seymore Dorrey (Also as Doney). Mustered in 7/8/61. Deserted 7/22/62. Killed at Antietam, 9/17/62. Enlisted at Williamsport, Lycoming County, age 18, laborer.

Joseph F. Dow. Mustered in 2/2/64. Not on muster out roll.

John H. Downing. Mustered in 7/8/61. Mustered out with battery, 6/9/65. 1/64: Enlisted at McConnellsburg, Blair County, age 27, boatman.

Patrick Doyle. Mustered in 1/16/64. Mustered out with battery, 6/9/65.

George E. Dutcher. Mustered in 3/9/64. Transferred to Battery A, 12/27/64. Enlisted at Scranton, Luzerne County, age 18.

Whit B. Easterbrook (Also as Eastbrook). Mustered in 7/8/61. Discharged on surgeon's certificate, date unknown, but sometime before 7/15/62. Enlisted at Jackson, Susquehanna County.

Eli F. Eastman. Mustered in 7/8/61. Captured at Second Manassas, 8/30/62. Transferred to Battery G, 3/26/64. Enlisted at Jackson, Susquehanna County.

George Eden. Mustered in 9/1/64. Transferred to Battery A, 12/27/64. Born in England, enlisted at Norristown, Montgomery County, age 32.

Jackson Engart (Also as Edgart). Mustered in 7/8/61. Deserted, date unknown (name appears on a desertion list dated 7/15/62). Enlisted at McConnellstown, Huntingdon County, age 33, laborer.

Samuel Esterline. Mustered in 2/6/64. Mustered out with battery, 6/9/65. Enlisted at Reading, Berks County, age 18, laborer.

Charles F. Farron. Mustered in 2/22/64. Mustered out with battery, 6/9/65.

George Fields. Mustered in 3/27/62. Wounded at Antietam, 9/17/62. Discharged on surgeon's certificate, 3/15/63. Enlisted at Philadelphia.

Benjamin Fink. Mustered in 8/18/64. Transferred to Battery A, 12/27/64. Enlisted at West Chester, Chester County, age 18, laborer.

James H. Fisher. Mustered in 2/3/64. Mustered out with battery, 6/9/65. Enlisted at Reading, Berks County, age 26, carpenter.

Simon Floray. Mustered in 7/8/61. Captured at Second Manassas, 8/30/62. Mustered out, 8/31/64, expiration of term. Enlisted at Williamsport, Lycoming County, age 18.

Henry Foster. Mustered in 8/21/64. Transferred to Battery A, 12/27/64. Born in England, age 24, machinist. 1888–residence in Philadelphia.

Enoch Fox. Mustered in 7/8/61. Died, 8/19/61.

Jacob Fox. Mustered in 7/8/61. Died of typhoid fever at Lincoln General Hospital, Washington, D.C., 10/10/64. 11/63: Enlisted at Mifflinville, Mifflin County, age 31, laborer.

Thomas E. Frame. Mustered in 7/8/61. Absent sick from 4/20/64 through at least 10/31/64, with syphilis. Mustered out with battery, 6/9/65. 12/63: Enlisted at Danville, Montour County, age 22, tailor.

William Frederick. Mustered in 7/8/61. Mustered out with battery, 6/9/65. 11/63: Enlisted at Hollidaysburg, Blair County, age 23, laborer.

*Barney Freese. Mustered in ?/?/61. Enlisted at Bloomsburg, Columbia County, age 26, laborer.

Merritt C. French. Mustered in 7/8/61. Deserted, 10/9/62. Enlisted at Jackson, Susquehanna County, age 21, farmer.

Francis Frew. Mustered in 2/23/64. Not on muster out roll. Enlisted at Greensburg, Westmoreland County, age 17, laborer.

Henry Frick. Mustered in 2/8/64. Not on muster out roll. Born in Germany, enlisted at Easton, Northampton County, age 30, farmer.

Aaron B. Galloway. Mustered in 9/7/61. Discharged on surgeon's certificate, 8/8/62. Enlisted from Susquehanna County.

Matthew Garrett. Mustered in 9/1/63. Transferred to Battery G, 3/26/64. 1898–residence in Philadelphia.

Maynard Gates. Mustered in 7/8/61. Transferred to Battery G, 3/26/64. Enlisted at Jackson, Susquehanna County.

Charles Gearinger (Also as Garringer). Mustered in 2/21/64. Died at Douglas General Hospital, Washington, D.C., 9/11/64. Enlisted at Danville, Montour County, age 22, roller.

John Gehring (also as Gehrung and Geahring). Mustered in 2/5/64. Mustered out with battery, 6/9/65. Born in Germany, enlisted at Reading, Berks County, age 37, blacksmith.

Tilghman (Also as Tillman and Tilman) Geiser. Mustered in 7/8/61. Discharged on surgeon's certificate, 7/1/62. Enlisted at Williamsburg, Blair County, age 20, boatman.

Henry Gelp. Mustered in 7/19/61. Transferred from Battery G at re-enlistment. Mustered out with battery, 6/9/65. Born in Germany, enlisted at Harrisburg, Dauphin County, age 42, mason.

William George. Mustered in 8/22/61. Transferred from Battery G at re-enlistment. Discharged on surgeon's certificate, date unknown. 1/64: Enlisted from Juniata County, age 23, shinglemaker.

Frederick Gerau (Also as Geraw). Mustered in 9/16/61. Transferred from Battery G at re-enlistment. Mustered out with battery, 6/9/65. 12/63: Born in Prussia, enlisted at Philadelphia, age 43, soldier.

Leonard Getz (Also as Geitz and Gets). Mustered in 2/2/64. Transferred to Veteran Reserve Corps, 12/28/64. Enlisted from Lancaster County, age 34, gas fitter.

Melwood C. Gillespie. Mustered in 7/1/61. Promoted to 2nd Lieutenant, Battery G, 6/12/63. Enlisted at Williamsport, Lycoming County, age 28.

John M. Given. Mustered in 7/8/61. Wounded and captured at Gettysburg, 7/2/63. Not on muster out roll; supposed to have died in enemy hands. Enlisted at Harrisburg, Dauphin County.

Harrison Goins. Mustered in. Mustered out, 5/26/62, expiration of term.

Henry W. Gossler. Mustered in 2/1/64. Absent sick from 4/9/64 through at least 10/31/64. Mustered out with battery, 6/9/65. Enlisted from Berks County, age 33, moulder.

William Gottschall. Mustered in 2/6/64. Mustered out with battery, 6/9/65. Enlisted at Middletown, Dauphin County, age 22, laborer.

James Graves. Mustered in 9/1/64. Mustered out with battery, 6/9/65. Born in England, enlisted at West Chester, Chester County, age 35, laborer.

Frederick Gray. Mustered in 2/6/64. Mustered out with battery, 6/9/65. Enlisted at Danville, Montour County, age 20, laborer.

Samuel Gray. Mustered in 7/8/61. Mustered out with battery, 6/9/65. 12/63: Enlisted at Danville, Montour County, age 21, teamster.

Lee Greenwood. Mustered in 7/8/61. Discharged on surgeon's certificate, 1/13/63. Enlisted at Jackson, Susquehanna County.

Jacob G. Greib. Mustered in 9/8/64. Transferred to Battery A, 12/27/64. Enlisted at Harrisburg, Dauphin County, age 23, timer(?).

Isaac Grimes. Mustered in 2/2/64. Transferred to Battery B, 12/29/64 (with Battery B since 7/11/64). Enlisted from Berks County, age 18, laborer.

Jacob Haag. Mustered in 7/8/61. Promoted to 1st Sergeant from Sergeant, 3/1/64. Mustered out with battery, 6/9/65. 12/63: Born in Germany, enlisted at Danville, Montour County, age 40, mason.

Charles A. Haines. Mustered in 1/19/64. Not on muster out roll. Born in England, enlisted at Philadelphia, age 24, carpenter.

Bennett Hall. Mustered in 9/5/64. Mustered out with battery, 6/9/65. Enlisted from Bucks County, age 39, potter.

William Halligan. Mustered in 1/29/64. Transferred to Battery B, 12/29/64 (with Battery B since 7/11/64). Enlisted at Lancaster, Lancaster County, age 18, laborer.

Peter Hammil. Mustered in 7/8/61. Not on muster out roll.

S. Priestley Harder. Mustered in 12/31/61. Promoted to Corporal, 4/4/64. Mustered out 1/23/65, as per Special Order #35. Enlisted at Danville, Montour County, age 20, plasterer.

John A. Hart. Mustered in 7/8/64. Mustered out, expiration of term. Enlisted at Williamsport, Lycoming County, age 23, blacksmith.

Charles Hawk (also as Hauck). Mustered in 2/5/64. Transferred to Battery B, 12/29/64. Born in Germany, enlisted at Reading, Berks County, age 29, saddler.

Jacob O. Heinbach. Mustered in 2/17/64. Mustered out with battery, 6/9/65. Enlisted at Harrisburg, Dauphin County, age 21, carpenter.

John Henry. Mustered in 7/8/61. Wounded at Rappahannock Station, 8/23/62. Transferred to Battery G, 3/26/64. Enlisted at Williamsport, Lycoming County.

Peter Henry. Mustered in 7/8/61. Discharged on surgeon's certificate, 11/21/61.

Rudolph Henry. Mustered in 2/4/64. Mustered out with battery, 6/9/65. Born in Germany, enlisted at Reading, Berks County, age 34, shoemaker.

Henry J. Herman. Mustered in 2/3/64. Absent sick in Mower General Hospital, at muster out, 8/12/65. Enlisted at Reading, Berks County, age 31, butcher.

Daniel T. Herter. Mustered in 7/8/61. Not on muster out roll.

John F. Hickman. Mustered in 5/16/61. Transferred from Battery G at reenlistment. Mustered out with battery, 6/9/65. 1889–residence in Philadelphia.

Samuel K. Hilands. Mustered in 11/22/63. Mustered out with battery, 6/9/65. Enlisted at Williamsburg, Blair County.

Adam Hildebrandt. Mustered in 9/13/61. Transferred from Battery G at reenlistment. Mustered out with battery, 6/9/65. 1/64: Enlisted from Lancaster County, age 19, laborer.

Henry Hildebrandt. Mustered in 9/13/61. Mustered out with battery, 6/9/65. 12/63: Enlisted from Lancaster County, age 38, weaver.

Samuel R. Hilins (Also as Hilings). Mustered in 7/8/61. Not on muster out roll. Enlisted at Williamsburg, Blair County, age 18, farmer.

Daniel Hindel (also as Heindel). Mustered in 7/29/61. Transferred from Battery G at re-enlistment. Absent sick since 8/1/64. Died at Philadelphia, 10/25/64. 12/63: Enlisted from York County, age 26, laborer.

William P. Hinkle (also as Hinckle). Mustered in 7/8/61. Discharged on surgeon's certificate, 7/11/62. Enlisted at Williamsport, Lycoming County.
John F. Hinman (Also as Hindman). Mustered in 5/19/63. Transferred to Battery G, 3/26/64. Enlisted at Reading, Berks County, age 22, turner.

Samuel Hoffmaster. Mustered in 2/2/64. Mustered out with battery, 6/9/65. Enlisted from Berks County, age 20, blacksmith.

John Hogan. Mustered in 8/1/61. Transferred from Battery G at reenlistment. Mustered out with battery, 6/9/65. 12/63: Enlisted at Germantown, Perry County, age 22, farmer.

George Horning. Mustered in 8/20/64. Transferred to Battery A, 12/27/64. Enlisted at Lancaster, Lancaster County, age 26, laborer.

John Houser. Mustered in 3/14/64. Mustered out with battery, 6/9/65. Enlisted at Harrisburg, Dauphin County, age 36, laborer.

Mason B. Hughes. Mustered in 2/27/64. Mustered out with battery, 6/9/65. Enlisted at Philadelphia, age 21, student.

John Hugheston. Mustered in 7/8/61. Not on muster out roll. Listed as being in Insane Asylum, 7/15/62. Enlisted at Harrisburg, Dauphin County, age 23, farmer.

Isaac P. Hummel. Mustered in 2/12/64. Transferred to Battery B, 12/29/64 (with Battery B since 7/11/64). Enlisted at Reading, Berks County, age 21, shoemaker.

Alexander Jackson. Mustered in 10/29/61. Not on muster out roll.

James Jackson. Mustered in 2/12/64. Mustered out with battery, 6/9/65.

Henry S. Jenkins. Mustered in 6/4/64. Mustered out with battery, 6/9/65. 1888–residence in Harrisburg, Dauphin County.

Richard Jenkins. Mustered in 2/2/64. Mustered out with battery, 6/9/65. Enlisted at Harrisburg, Dauphin County, age 22, puller (?).

Cyrus Jones. Mustered in 9/3/61. Transferred from Battery G at re-enlistment. Mustered out with battery, 6/9/65. 1/64: Enlisted at Lancaster, age 31, blacksmith.

Henry Jones. Mustered in 3/2/64. Not on muster out roll.

Joshua Keller. Mustered in 2/16/64. Mustered out with battery, 6/9/65. Enlisted from York County, age 20, farmer.

Samuel W. Kiler (also as Kyler). Mustered in 7/8/61. Mustered out with battery, 6/9/65. Enlisted at Williamsburg, Blair County, age 18, farmer.

Peter Killian (Also as Killion). Mustered in 11/3/61. Wounded at Antietam, 9/17/62; died of wounds, 10/10/62. Enlisted at Williamsport, Maryland.

Thomas E. Kinney. Mustered in 7/24/61. Not on muster out roll. Enlisted at Hollidaysburg, Blair County.

William T. Kinney. Mustered in 7/8/61. Mustered out with battery, 6/9/65. 12/63: Enlisted at Bellsville, Blair County, age 26, farmer.

Henry Kissell (also as Kissel). Mustered in 2/22/64. Mustered out with battery, 6/9/65. Enlisted from Clinton County, age 19, laborer.

William Kline. Mustered in 2/19/64. Absent sick at muster out.

Henry Koons. Mustered in 2/16/64. Died 1/2/65. Enlisted from York County, age 19, farmer.

Michael Krebbs (also as Krepps). Mustered in 7/18/61. Transferred from Battery G at re-enlistment. Mustered out with battery, 6/9/65. 1/64: Enlisted from York County, age 21, plasterer.

Lewis Kretz (also as Kratz). Mustered in 2/6/64. Transferred to Battery B, 12/29/64 (with Battery B since 7/11/64). Enlisted at Reading, Berks County, age 18, laborer.

Daniel L. Kuhns (also as Kuntz). Mustered in 9/30/61. Transferred from Battery G at re-enlistment. Mustered out with battery, 6/9/65. 1/64: Enlisted at Strasburg, Lancaster County, age 27, laborer.

Velosco (Also as Velasco) O. Lake. Mustered in 7/8/61. Wounded at the Wilderness, 5/5/64. Mustered out with battery, 6/9/65. 11/63: Enlisted at Jackson, Susquehanna County, age 18, farmer.

James Laneous (Also as Lanious). Mustered in 9/13/61. Transferred from Battery G at re-enlistment. Mustered out with battery, 6/9/65. 1/64: Enlisted at Lancaster, age 19, laborer.

Alfred W. Larrabee. Mustered in 7/8/61. Discharged on surgeon's certificate, 3/5/63. Enlisted at Jackson, Susquehanna County.

J. Wesley Larrabee. Mustered in 8/31/64. Mustered out with battery, 6/9/65. Enlisted from Susquehanna County, age 18, farmer.

John Latshaw. Mustered in 2/3/64. Mustered out with battery, 6/9/65. Enlisted at Reading, Berks County, age 25, farmer.

George D. Laube. Mustered in 7/8/61. Wounded at Antietam, 9/17/62; died of wounds, 9/17/62.

*David Laughlin. Deserted, 2/14/62.

John Laughlin. Mustered in ?/?/61. Mustered out with battery, 6/9/65. 1/64: Born in Ireland, enlisted at Philadelphia, age 18, brickmaker.

William Lehman. Mustered in 2/25/64. Transferred to Battery B, 12/29/64 (with Battery B since 7/11/64).

Henry Lutz. Mustered in 2/8/64. Mustered out, 6/21/65. Enlisted at Reading, Berks County, age 32, butcher.

John H. Maffitt. Mustered in 2/22/62. Transferred to Battery G, 3/26/64. Born at Hagerstown, MD, age 27. Enlisted at Hagerstown, Maryland.

John Marquart (Also as Marquet). Mustered in 2/2/64. Mustered out with battery, 6/9/65. Enlisted from Berks County, age 17, boatman.

Augustus P. Martin. Mustered in 7/8/61. Wounded at Rappahannock Station, VA, 8/21/62. Discharged on surgeon's certificate, 12/8/62. Enlisted at Williamsport, Lycoming County.

Orrin Mattison (also as Matterson). Mustered in 7/8/61. Discharged on surgeon's certificate, 12/5/61. Mustered in 8/12/64. Mustered out with battery, 6/9/65. Enlisted at Jackson, Susquehanna County, age 42, farmer.

David P. Maynard (also as Manard). Mustered in 9/11/61. Captured at Second Manassas, 8/30/62. Discharged on surgeon's certificate, [2/26/63]. Enlisted from Susquehanna County, age 23, laborer.

Alexander McBride. Mustered in 1/25/64. Not on muster out roll. Born in Ireland, enlisted at Philadelphia, age 31, laborer.

Henry C. McClintock. Mustered in 7/8/61. Mustered out with battery, 6/9/65. 11/63: Enlisted at Williamsport, Lycoming County, age 20, gentleman.

Neal McCollum (also as McCollem). Mustered in 7/8/61. Deserted, 5/17/63, Belle Plain, VA. On 7/15/62 list as under charges for general court martial, but escaped. Enlisted at Harrisburg, Dauphin County, age 20, laborer.

Patrick McGinley. Mustered in 1/27/64. Transferred to Battery A, 12/27/64. Born in Ireland, age 19, laborer.

Michael McGoldrick. Mustered in 1/3/64. Killed at the Wilderness, 5/5/64. 1/64: Enlisted at Philadelphia, age 20, sailor.

H. Peter McKinney (also as McKenney). Mustered in 2/2/64. Transferred to Battery A, 12/27/64. Enlisted at Lancaster, age 18, moulder.

Patrick McKinney. Mustered in 1/1/64. Transferred to Battery A, 12/27/64.

James B. McLain. Mustered in 7/24/61. Transferred from Battery G at re-enlistment. Mustered out with battery, 6/9/65. 1/64: Enlisted from Franklin County, age 27, farmer.

Alexander E. McMurtrie. Mustered in 7/8/61. Discharged on surgeon's certificate, date unknown. Enlisted at Williamsport, Lycoming County.

John S. McVey. Mustered in 3/3/64. Mustered out with battery, 6/9/65. Enlisted at Philadelphia, age 18, student.

Joseph Micho. Mustered in 7/8/61. Transferred to Battery G, 3/26/64. 2/64: Enlisted at Williamsport, Lycoming County, age 22, lawyer.

Samuel Miller. Mustered in 12/11/61. Transferred from Battery G at re-enlistment. Mustered out with battery, 6/9/65. 12/63: Enlisted at Bethlehem, Northampton County, age 28, laborer.

John C. Mills. Mustered in 7/8/61. Died at Baltimore, 12/29/61.

William Minier (also as Menier). Mustered in 12/21/61. Mustered out with battery, 6/9/65. Enlisted at Shamokin, Northumberland County, age 18, farmer.

William Mohr. Mustered in 2/9/64. Mustered out with battery, 6/9/65. Enlisted at Reading, Berks County, age 25, collier.

John W. Moore. Mustered in 2/20/64. Transferred to Battery B, 12/29/64 (with Battery B since 7/11/64). Enlisted at Williamsburg, Blair County, age 18, laborer.

William Morrison. Mustered in 2/10/64. Mustered out with battery, 6/9/65. Enlisted at Danville, Montour County, age 17, farmer. Listed as a musician.

Jacob F. Morton. Mustered in 2/5/64. Transferred to Battery B, 12/29/64 (with Battery B since 7/11/64). Enlisted at Reading, Berks County, age 18, laborer.

Frederick Mosel (also as Mosil). Mustered in 7/8/61. Mustered out with battery, 6/9/65. 12/63: Enlisted from Blair County, age 24, laborer.

Samuel Mowry (also as Mowery). Mustered in 7/8/61. Deserted, 6/29/63. Discharged, 8/5/64. Enlisted at Harrisburg, Dauphin County, age 28, blacksmith.

George A. Musseno (also as Masseno). Mustered in 2/2/64. Transferred to Battery B, 12/29/64 (with Battery B since 7/11/64). Enlisted from Berks County, age 21, brakeman.

Andrew S. Myers. Mustered in 7/16/61. Transferred from Battery G at re-enlistment. Mustered out with battery, 6/9/65. 1/64: Enlisted at Pine Creek, Lycoming County, age 23, carpenter.

John K. Myers. Mustered in 2/16/64. Mustered out with battery, 6/9/65. 1888–residence in Homer City, Indiana County.

Patrick F. Nealon. Mustered in 1/13/64. Transferred to Battery B, 12/29/64 (with Battery B since 7/11/64). Born in Ireland, enlisted at Carbondale, Luzerne County, age 21, laborer.

Francis Need (also as Neid and Nied). Mustered in 7/8/61. Captured at Gettysburg, 7/2/63. Discharged, 5/31/64. 1898–residence in Danville, Montour County. Appears as corporal on 4/23/63 roster.

Abraham P. Neff. Mustered in 2/24/64. Mustered out, 7/3/65. Enlisted at Greensburg, Westmoreland County, age 29.

Charles Nimis. Mustered in 2/5/64. Mustered out with battery, 6/9/65. Born in Germany, enlisted at Reading, Berks County, age 30, shoemaker.

Andrew Nipple. Mustered in 7/8/61. Not on muster out roll.

William Nolan. Mustered in 1/18/64. Mustered out with battery, 6/9/65.

Henry F. Nuss. Mustered in 7/29/61. Mustered out with battery, 6/9/65. 12/63: Enlisted at Danville, Montour County, age 19, blacksmith.

Timothy O'Bryan. Mustered in 2/2/64. Transferred to Battery B, 12/29/64 (with Battery B since 7/11/64). Born in New Jersey, enlisted at Reading, Berks County, age 24, laborer.

*Lewis J. Olden. Enlisted ?/?/61. Wounded at the Wilderness, 5/5/64. 11/63: Enlisted at Philadelphia, age 28, baker.

Andrew B. Oliver. Mustered in 2/8/64. Transferred to Battery B, 12/29/64 (with Battery B since 7/11/64). Enlisted at Philadelphia, age 23, bookbinder.

Robert Orange. Mustered in ?/?/61. Captured at Second Manassas, 8/30/62. Mustered out with battery, 6/9/65. Born in England, enlisted at Philadelphia, age 46, weaver.

Pesarius (Also as Pesarious and Pasarivous) Parker. Mustered in ?/?/61. Mustered out with battery, 6/9/65. 1/64: Enlisted at Philadelphia, age 21, driver.

Samuel Perry. Mustered in 3/16/64. Transferred to Battery B, 12/29/64 (with Battery B since 7/11/64). Enlisted at Scranton, Luzerne County, age 18, boatman.

Edwin H. Peter. Mustered in 2/2/64. Transferred to Battery B, 12/29/64 (with battery B since 7/11/64). Enlisted at Reading, Berks County, age 19, shoemaker.

Joseph Peterman. Mustered in 7/8/61. Discharged on surgeon's certificate, 4/2/63. Enlisted at Philadelphia.

James H. Phillips. Mustered in 2/9/64. Wounded 8/23 or 8/25/64. Absent sick at muster out, 7/6/65, in Campbell Hospital, Washington, D.C. Mustered out, 7/9/65. Enlisted at Reading, Berks County, age 20, laborer.

Hiram M. Pidcoe (also as Pidcoke). Mustered in ?/?/61. Transferred from Battery G at re-enlistment. Mustered out with battery, 6/9/65. 11/63: Enlisted at Williamsport, Lycoming County, age 22, plasterer.

James M. Pidcoe (also as Pidcoke). Mustered in 9/5/64. Mustered out with battery, 6/9/65. Enlisted at Williamsport, Lycoming County, age 31, farmer.

William G. Pinkerton. Mustered in 9/13/61. Transferred from Battery G at re-enlistment. Mustered out with battery, 6/9/65.

Henry Pool. Mustered in 12/11/61. Died at Hancock, MD, 1/62.

Thomas W. M. Potts. Mustered in 2/16/64. Absent sick, at Satterlee General Hospital, at muster out, 6/5/65. Enlisted at Philadelphia, age 44.

William Powell. Mustered in 7/8/61. Wounded at Antietam, 9/17/62. Discharged on surgeon's certificate, 2/10/63. Enlisted at Bloomsburg, Columbia County.

James Powryne. Mustered in 7/8/61. Killed at Gettysburg, 7/2/63. Enlisted at Starucca, Wayne County.

James W. Quinn. Mustered in 7/8/61. Mustered out with battery, 6/9/65. 1/64: Enlisted at Lancaster, age 35, shoemaker. Died in Lancaster, 8/9/65.

Isaac Rake. Mustered in 7/1/61. Transferred to Battery G, 3/26/64. Enlisted at Danville, Montour County, age 24, laborer.

John G. Rake. Mustered in 12/30/61. Mustered out with battery, 6/9/65. 1/64: Enlisted at Danville, Montour County, age 26, laborer.

Gideon Rauenzahn (also as Rauengahn and Raungahen). Mustered in 2/2/64. Mustered out with battery, 6/9/65. Enlisted from Berks County, age 20, mason.

John Ray. Mustered in 2/4/64. Mustered out with battery, 6/9/65. Enlisted at Reading, Berks County, age 21, laborer.

John T. Reed. Mustered in 12/18/61. Transferred to Battery G, 3/26/64. Enlisted at Shamokin, Northumberland County, age 21.

Francis Remlin (Also as Remline). Mustered in 7/5/61. Not on muster out roll. 12/63: Born in Germany, enlisted at Bloomsburg, Columbia County, age 26, laborer.

John Rife. Mustered in 8/22/64. Transferred to Battery A, 12/27/64.

James H. Riggin. Mustered in 11/1/61. Captured at Second Manassas, 8/30/62. Killed at Gettysburg, 7/2/63. Enlisted at Philadelphia.

Thomas Riley (also as Reilly). Mustered in 8/31/64. Transferred to Battery A, 12/27/64. Born in England, enlisted at Philadelphia, age 25, finisher.

Josiah R. Roberts. Mustered in 2/10/64. Mustered out with battery, 6/9/65. Enlisted at Danville, Montour County, age 18, student.

James Robinson. Mustered in 7/8/61. Killed at Rappahannock Station, 8/21/62.

William Robinson. Mustered in 5/25/63. Transferred to Battery G, 3/26/64.

John Rogers. Mustered in 4/22/61. Mustered out, 5/26/62, expiration of term.

George Roland. Mustered in 2/3/64. Transferred to Battery B, 12/29/64 (with Battery B sine 7/11/64). Enlisted at Reading, Berks County, age 21, moulder.

Ezra L. Romig (also as Romag). Mustered in 2/9/64. Mustered out with battery, 6/9/65. Enlisted at Reading, Berks County, age 26, helper.

John Roney. Mustered in 2/7/64. Mustered out with battery, 6/9/65.

William Roney. Mustered in 1/1/64. Mustered out with battery, 6/9/65. 1/64: Enlisted at Philadelphia, age 19, brickmaker.

Joseph Ropp. Mustered in 4/22/61. Mustered out, 5/26/62, expiration of term.

Benjamin Ross. Mustered in 8/10/64. Transferred to Battery A, 12/27/64.

John Rouke. Mustered in 7/8/61. Mustered out 7/11/64, expiration of term. In McClellan Hospital in Washington, D.C., since 5/4/64. Enlisted at Williamsburg, Blair County, age 27.

Joseph Ruth. Mustered in 2/3/64. Transferred to Battery B, 12/29/64 (with Battery B since 7/11/64). Enlisted at Reading, Berks County, age 25, shoemaker.

Oscar G. Sampson. Mustered in 9/7/61. Discharged on surgeon's certificate, date unknown. On sick list at Hancock, MD, 2/30/62. As nurse in Baltimore hospital on 7/15/62 list. Enlisted from Susquehanna County.

Washington T. Sampson. Mustered in 7/8/61. Deserted, 8/5/61, at Harrisburg, PA. Enlisted at Thompson, Susquehanna County, age 26, farmer.

George Sampsel (also as Samsel). Mustered in 3/16/64. Not on muster out roll. Enlisted at Scranton, Luzerne County, age 18, laborer.

David P. Sanders. Mustered in 3/1/62. Deserted, 9/10/62.

Charles N. Savage. Mustered in 1/1/62. Deserted, 10/11/62. Enlisted at Danville, Montour County, age 18, puller. Charge of desertion removed on 1/24/94; discharged 10/11/62.

Joel H. Schmehl. Mustered in 2/8/64. Mustered out with battery, 6/9/65. Enlisted at Reading, Berks County, age 18, shoemaker.

Adam Schwalb. Mustered in 2/8/64. Transferred to Battery B, 12/29/64 (with Battery B since 7/11/64. Born in Germany, enlisted at Reading, Berks County, age 18, laborer.

Raymond T. Scott. Mustered in 7/8/61. Mustered out, 7/16/64, expiration of term. Enlisted at Jackson, Susquehanna County, age 35. Transferred from Veteran Reserve Corps for muster out. Listed as quartermaster sergeant at time of muster out.

Luther Seiders. Mustered in 5/25/63. Transferred to Battery G, 3/26/64. 1888–residence in Reading, Berks County.

Michael U. Seiders. Mustered in 5/21/63. Transferred to Battery G, 3/26/64.

Benjamin F. Shaffer. Mustered in ?/?/61. Mustered out with battery, 6/9/65. 1/64: Enlisted at Lancaster, age 27, farmer. Worked as wagoner.

Frank Shaw. Mustered in 1/22/64. Not on muster out roll. Enlisted at Philadelphia, age 25, sailor.

John Shelhorn (Also as Shellhorn). Mustered in 2/2/64. Mustered out with battery, 6/9/65. Born in Germany, enlisted at Reading, Berks County, age 42, ostler.

Peter Shenfelder. Mustered in 5/26/63. Discharged on surgeon's certificate, 12/22/63. Enlisted at Reading, Berks County, age 16, laborer.

Thomas Shepherdson (also as Shipperson). Mustered in 9/1/64. Mustered out with battery, 6/9/65. Born in England, enlisted at West Chester, Chester County, age 34, paddler.

Eli Sherwood. Mustered in 9/1/64. Mustered out with battery, 6/9/65. 1888–residence in Berwick, Columbia County.

Charles Shipman (Also as Shipnor, Shipney, and Shipner). Mustered in 7/8/61. Mustered out with battery, 6/9/65. Enlisted at Danville, Montour County, age 28, farmer.

*Gilmore W. Shirey. Mustered in 8/22/61. Transferred from Battery G at re-enlistment. Admitted to Filbert Street Hospital in Philadelphia, 3/2/64. Deserted from hospital, 8/7/64. 12/63: Enlisted from Clearfield County, age 18, farmer.

John Shirman. Mustered in 2/10/64. Mustered out with battery, 6/9/65. Born in Germany, enlisted at Danville, Montour County, age 28, laborer.

James Shoemaker. Mustered in 1/22/62. Not on muster out roll. On sick list at Falmouth, VA, 5/24/62. Enlisted at Bloomsburg, Columbia County, age 25.

John Shoemaker. Mustered in 1/22/62. Discharged on surgeon's certificate, date unknown. On 7/15/62 sick list. Enlisted at Bloomsburg, Columbia County.

*David Shoup. Enlisted at Hagerstown, Maryland, 3/24/62, by Captain Matthews.

Charles H. Sibley. Mustered in 7/8/61. Transferred to Battery G, 3/26/64. Enlisted at Philadelphia.

Henry C. Simler (also as Sembler and Semler). Mustered in ?/?/61. Wounded at Cold Harbor, 6/7/64. Admitted to McClellan General Hospital in Philadelphia on 7/29/64. Deserted from hospital, 10/1/64. Mustered out with battery, 6/9/65. 12/63: Enlisted at Philadelphia, age 19, book binder.

J. Forest Simpson. Mustered in 7/8/61. Wounded and captured at Second Manassas, 8/30/62. Mustered out with battery, 6/9/65. 12/63: Enlisted at Hollidaysburg, Blair County, age 18, laborer.

David Slaughter. Mustered in 7/8/61. Deserted, 2/14/62. On 7/15/62 sick list; home on furlough, claimed to have received discharge. Enlisted at Silver Springs, Cumberland County, age 36, carpenter.

George Smith. Mustered in 2/3/64. Not on muster out roll. Enlisted at Lancaster, Lancaster County, age 39, laborer.

James Smith. Mustered in 3/7/64. Not on muster out roll. Enlisted at Harrisburg, Dauphin County, age 29, machinist.

Upton (Also as Uplin) G. Snively. Mustered in 2/25/62. Discharged on surgeon's certificate, 7/12/62. Enlisted from Franklin County, age 22.

Joseph Soll. Mustered in 4/22/61. Mustered out, 5/26/62, expiration of term.

William H. Steever. Mustered in 7/21/61. Transferred from Battery G at re-enlistment. Mustered out with battery, 6/9/65. 1/64: Enlisted from Cumberland County, age 24, farmer.

John Stevenson. Mustered in 2/28/64. Transferred to Battery A, 12/27/64. Enlisted at Jersey Shore, Lycoming County, age 18, laborer.

Fernando Stewart. Mustered in 7/8/61. Deserted, 7/22/62. Enlisted at Williamsport, Lycoming County, age 24, lumberman.

*William Stewart. Mustered in 7/8/61. Died of disease, 1/?/65. Enlisted at Williamsburg, Blair County, age 17, laborer.

David Stout. Mustered in 3/15/64. Transferred to Battery B, 12/29/64 (with Battery B since 7/11/64). Enlisted at Scranton, Luzerne County, age 16, boatman.

Richard S. Stratford. Mustered in 7/8/61. Mustered out with battery, 6/9/65. 12/63: Born in England, enlisted from Wayne County, age 34, laborer.

Joseph Strecker. Mustered in 2/2/64. Not on muster out roll. Enlisted from Berks County, age 44, ostler.

John Swander. Mustered in 2/8/64. Transferred to Battery B, 12/29/64 (with Battery B since 7/11/64).

Oney F. Sweet. Mustered in ?/?/61. Mustered out with battery, 6/9/65. 1/64: Enlisted at Gibson, Susquehanna County, age 20, clerk.

Pardon (Also as Gordon) Tabor. Mustered in 7/8/61. Mustered out with battery, 6/9/65. 12/63: Born in New York, enlisted at Starucca, Wayne County, age 31, teamster.

McGloray (also as McClera) Thibault. Mustered in 7/8/61. Transferred to Battery G, 3/26/64. Enlisted at Williamsport, Lycoming County.

Richard Thomas. Mustered in 8/20/64. Mustered out with battery, 6/9/65. Born in England, enlisted from Berks County, age 31, paddler.

Charles Thompson. Mustered in 2/29/64. Deserted 3/1/64. Enlisted from Philadelphia, age 23, laborer.

Edward Thompson. Mustered in 12/26/61. Killed at Antietam, 9/17/62. Enlisted at Danville, Montour County, age 21.

Bernard Tiffany. Mustered in 8/1/61. Discharged on surgeon's certificate, 2/24/63. Enlisted at Jackson, Susquehanna County.

Henry M. Tiffany. Mustered in 12/11/61. Captured at Second Manassas, 8/30/62. Died from spotted fever while at home on furlough, 2/64. 12/63: Enlisted at Jackson, Susquehanna County, age 32, laborer.

John Tomes. Mustered in 8/25/64. Transferred to Battery A, 12/27/64. Enlisted at Philadelphia, age 38, moulder.

Samuel C. Torbert (also as Torbett). Mustered in 7/8/61. Mustered out with battery, 6/9/65. 12/63: Enlisted at Jersey Shore, Lycoming County, age 26, saddler.

Eli Trine. Mustered in 2/2/64. Transferred to Battery B, 12/29/64 (with Battery B since 7/11/64). Enlisted at Lancaster, Lancaster County, age 30, laborer.

*John C. Truman, enlisted ?/?/61. Mentioned in order of 9/62, when detached for recruiting.

Ephraim Uhler. Mustered in 7/18/61. Transferred from Battery G at re-enlistment. Mustered out with battery, 6/9/65. 1/64: Enlisted at Pine Grove, Schuylkill County, age 24, laborer.

James H. Van Horne. Mustered in 2/24/64. Wounded at Petersburg, 6/19/64. Absent, sick, at muster out. Enlisted at Williamsport, Lycoming County, age 21, blacksmith.

William Van Orsdall. Mustered in ??. Mustered out with battery, 6/9/65.

Benjamin Vanhorn. Mustered in 7/8/61. Deserted at Belle Plain, VA, 2/16/63. Scheduled for execution, 2/26/64. Special Order #86, 3/3/64, sentenced Vanhorn to hard labor at Dry Tortugas for remainder of term of service. Mustered out with battery, 6/9/65. 63: Enlisted at Williamsport, Lycoming County, age 19, laborer.

John W. Wagner. Mustered in 7/8/61. Mustered out with battery, 6/9/65. 12/63: Born at Rome, Italy, enlisted at Uniontown, Juniata County, age 30, laborer.

William W. Wapples (also as Waples). Mustered in 2/2/64. Died from bilious cholic near Petersburg, 8/20/64. Born in New Jersey, enlisted at Danville, Montour County, age 29, contractor.

John W. Watts. Mustered in 7/8/61. Transferred to Battery G, 3/26/64. Enlisted at Danville, Montour County, age 22, miner.

John F. Weaver. Mustered in 7/8/61. Detached as regimental hospital steward.

Anthony Webber (also as Weber). Mustered in 2/5/64. Mustered out with battery, 6/9/65. Enlisted at Reading, Berks County, age 18, laborer.

Daniel T. Webster. Mustered in 2/17/64. Transferred to Battery A, 12/27/64. Enlisted from Bradford County, age 18, farmer.

Orlando T. Weiting (also as Weitung). Mustered in 1/4/64. Mustered out with battery, 6/9/65.

John W. Wemuag. Mustered in 1/25/64. Mustered out with battery, 6/9/65.

Peter Wenrick. Mustered in 8/20/61. Transferred from Battery G at re-enlistment. Mustered out with battery, 6/9/65. 12/63: Enlisted at Harrisburg, Dauphin County, age 29, laborer.

Lewis Widner (also as Weidner). Mustered in 2/3/64. Transferred to Battery B, 12/29/64 (with Battery B since 7/11/64). Enlisted at Reading, Berks County, age 40, carpenter.

Thomas Wildsmith. Mustered in 9/1/64. Mustered out with battery, 6/9/65. Born in England, enlisted at Norristown, Montgomery County, age 43, heater.

Nicholas Wingert. Mustered in 2/5/64. Mustered out with battery, 6/9/65. Enlisted at Reading, Berks County, age 19, boiler maker.

William T. Wissinger. Mustered in 3/8/64. Mustered out with battery, 6/9/65.

Joseph Wolff (also as Wolf). Mustered in 7/19/61. Transferred from Battery G at re-enlistment. Mustered out with battery, 6/9/65. 12/63: Born in Prussia, enlisted from York County, age 30, farmer.

William Wolff (Also as Wolf). Mustered in 7/19/61. Transferred from Battery G at re-enlistment. Mustered out with battery, 6/9/65. 12/63: Enlisted from York County, age 21, farmer.

William R. Wood. Mustered in 9/1/64. Mustered out with battery, 6/9/65. Enlisted at West Chester, Chester County, age 28, miner.

Jacob Wormest. Mustered in 2/5/64. Mustered out, 6/21/65. Enlisted at Reading, Berks County, age 45, shoemaker.

Charles F. Worthline. Mustered in 2/4/64. Absent, sick, at muster out.

John Wright. Mustered in 9/1/64. Mustered out with battery, 6/9/65. Born in Scotland, enlisted at West Chester, Chester County, age 37, engineer.

John Writzel (also as Weitzel). Mustered in 2/3/64. Mustered out with battery, 6/9/65. Enlisted at Reading, Berks County, age 20, laborer.

William F. Yerger. Mustered in 2/5/64. Mustered out with battery, 6/9/65. Enlisted at Reading, Berks County, age 18, butcher.

*Franklin Young. Mustered in 3/16/64. Transferred to Battery B, 12/29/64 (with Battery B since 7/11/64). Enlisted at Scranton, Luzerne County, age 17, boatman.

Statistical Summary

The following table summarizes the counties of residence for the officers and men of Battery F, broken down further by year of enlistment. The column labeled "Bty G" includes those men who transferred from Battery G when re-enlisting in 1863-1864. There were no new enlistments added to Battery F in 1865.

County	1861	1862	1863	Bty G	1864	Total
Unknown	22	2	1	2	22	49
Allegheny	-	-	-	1	-	1
Berks	-	-	4	-	43	47
Blair	18	-	1	-	2	21
Bradford	2	-	-	-	1	3
Bucks	-	-	-	-	1	1
Chester	1	-	-	-	6	7
Clearfield	-	-	-	1	-	1
Clinton	-	-	-	-	1	1
Columbia	6	4	-	-	2	12
Cumberland	2	-	-	2	-	4
Dauphin	7	-	-	3	12	22
Delaware	1	-	-	-	-	1
Franklin	-	1	-	1	-	2
Huntingdon	1	-	-	1	-	2
Indiana	-	-	-	-	1	1
Juniata	1	-	-	1	-	2
Lancaster	3	-	1	5	6	15
Lehigh	-	-	-	1	-	1
Luzerne	-	-	-	2	8	10
Lycoming	14	-	-	2	5	21
Mercer	1	-	-	-	-	1
Mifflin	1	-	-	-	-	1
Montgomery	-	-	-	-	3	3
Montour	19	1	-	-	7	27
Northampton	-	-	-	2	1	3
Northumberland	5	-	-	-	-	5
Perry	-	-	-	2	-	2
Philadelphia	15	1	1	2	15	34
Schuylkill	1	1	-	4	-	6
Susquehanna	25	-	-	-	1	26
Wayne	3	-	-	-	-	3
York	-	-	-	7	2	9
State of Maryland	1	2	-	-	-	3
Total	149	12	8	39	141	349

Occupations

Of the 349 names on the roster, the occupations of 236 officers and men have been identified. These are listed below:

armorer	1		lumberman	1
baker	1		machinist	2
blacksmith	10		mason	4
boatman	12		miller	1
boiler maker	1		miner	6
bookbinder	2		moulder	5
brakeman	1		ostler	2
brickmaker	2		paddler	2
butcher	3		painter	1
cabinet maker	1		plasterer	3
carpenter	9		potter	1
chair maker	1		puller	1
clerk	1		roller	1
collier	1		saddler	4
contractor	1		sailor	3
driver	1		shingle maker	1
dyer	1		shoemaker	11
engineer	1		soldier	1
farmer	35		student	8
finisher	1		tailor	3
gas fitter	1		teacher	2
gentleman	2		teamster	2
harness maker	1		timer	1
heater	1		tinsmith	1
helper	1		turner	1
laborer	71		weaver	2
lawyer	1		wheelwright	1

Bibliography

Unpublished Primary Sources

Antietam Papers. Dartmouth College.

Antietam Studies. Record Group 94. Records of the Office of the Adjutant General. National Archives.

Barnett, James. Papers. Western Reserve Historical Society.

Battery F, 1st Pennsylvania Light Artillery. Papers. Record Group 19. Department of Military Affairs. Pennsylvania State Archives.

Battery F, 1st Pennsylvania Light Artillery. Papers. Record Group 94. Records of the Office of the Adjutant General. National Archives.

Beem, David E. Papers. Indiana Historical Library.

Brockway, Charles B. Papers. Harold Kashner.

Brockway, Frank. Papers. Frank Wright.

Campbell, John F. Papers. Ken and Sue Boardman.

Compiled Service Records. Record Group 94. Records of the Office of the Adjutant General. National Archives.
    Brockway, Charles B.
    Campbell, William F.
    Case, Truman L.
    Godbold, Henry L.
    Matthews, Ezra J.
    McConkey, Elbridge.
    Mowrer, George.
    Ricketts, Robert B.
    Snider, Francis H.
    Thurston, William H.
    Warnick, William W.
    Wireman, Henry.

Daniel, John W. Papers. University of Virginia.

Military Order of the Loyal Legion of the United States. Membership Files.
  Matthews, Ezra J.
  Ricketts, Robert B.

Patterson, William H. Papers. United States Army Military History Institute.

Ricketts, Robert Bruce. Papers. Mr. Chester Siegel.

Ricketts, Robert Bruce, Civil War Diary's. Luzerne Co. Historical Society

Rothermel, Peter F. Papers. Pennsylvania State Archives.

Seymour, Isaac. Journal. William L. Clements Library, University of Michigan.

Thurston, William H. Papers. Garry Leister.

Published Primary Sources

Bates, Samuel P. *History of Pennsylvania Volunteers, 1861-5*. 5 volumes. Harrisburg: B. Singerly, State Printer, 1869-1872.

Broadfoot Publishing Company. *Supplement to the Official Records of the Union and Confederate Armies*. 95 volumes. Wilmington, NC: Broadfoot Publishing Company, 1994-1999.

Brockway, Charles B. "Across the Rapidan." Philadelphia *Weekly Times*, January 7, 1882.

Brockway, Charles B. Letters to *Columbia Democrat*, 1861-1863.

Caines, E. H. C. "A Gettysburg Diary. Carroll's Brigade and the Part It Played in Repulsing the 'Tigers'." *National Tribune*, December 23, 1909.

Christian, John H. Letters to the Danville *Intelligencer*, October 18, November 15, 1861.

Fritz, Levi J. Letter to the *Montgomery Ledger*, November 24, 1863.

Gallagher, Gary W. (editor). *Fighting for the Confederacy: The Personal Recollections of General Edward Porter Alexander*. Chapel Hill: University of North Carolina Press, 1989.
Instruction for Field Artillery. Philadelphia: J. B. Lippincott & Company, 1863.

Kimball, Nathan. "Fighting Jackson at Kernstown." In Robert U. Johnson and Clarence C. Buel, *Battles and Leaders of the Civil War*. 4 volumes. New York: The Century Company, 1884-1888, 2:302-13.

Ladd, David and Audrey (editors). *The Bachelder Papers*. 3 volumes. Dayton, OH: Morningside House, 1994-1995.

Military Order of the Loyal Legion of the United States. Commandery of Pennsylvania. *In Memoriam: Ezra Wallace Matthews*. Philadelphia, 1885.

Moore, Leon Eugene C. "Charge of the Louisiana Tigers at Gettysburg." *National Tribune*, August 5, 1909.

Nevins, Allan (editor). *A Diary of Battle: The Personal Journals of Colonel Charles S. Wainwright, 1861-1865*. Reprint edition, New York: Da Capo Press, 1998.

Nicholson, John P. (editor). *Pennsylvania at Gettysburg: Ceremonies at the Dedication of the Monuments Erected by the Commonwealth of Pennsylvania to Mark the Positions of the Pennsylvania Commands Engaged in the Battle*. 2 volumes. Harrisburg: E. K. Meyers, State Printer, 1893.

Rudisill, James J. *The Days of Our Abraham, 1811-1899*. York, PA: The York Printing Company, 1936.

Sauers, Richard A. (editor). *The Civil War Journal of Colonel William J. Bolton, 51st Pennsylvania, April 20, 1861-August 2, 1865*. Conshohocken, PA: Combined Publishing, 2000.

Smith, William F. "The Eighteenth Corps at Cold Harbor." In Robert U. Johnson and Clarence C. Buel, *Battles and Leaders of the Civil War*. 4 volumes. New York: The Century Company, 1884-1888, 4:221-30.

Sweet, Oney F. "Ricketts's Battery." *National Tribune*, April 29, 1909.

Thomas, Mary W., and Sauers, Richard A. (editors). *The Civil War Letters of First Lieutenant James B. Thomas, Adjutant, 107th Pennsylvania.* Baltimore: Butternut & Blue, 1995.

Thurston, William H. "A Ricketts Batteryman Supports Carroll's Brigade Claim." *National Tribune*, October 13, 1892.

United States War Department. *The War of the Rebellion: A Compilation of the Official Records of the Union and Confederate Armies.* 70 volumes in 128 parts. Washington: Government Printing Office, 1880-1901.

Unit Histories

Locke, William. *The Story of the Regiment.* New York: James Miller, Publisher, 1872. [11th Pennsylvania]

Walker, Francis A. *History of the Second Army Corps in the Army of the Potomac.* New York: Charles Scribner's Sons, 1886.

Secondary Studies

Alotta, Robert I. *Civil War Justice: Military Executions Under Lincoln.* Shippensburg, PA: White Mane Press, 1989.

Battle, J. H. (editor). *History of Columbia and Montour Counties, Pennsylvania.* Chicago: A. Warner & Company, 1887.

Busey, John W., and Martin, David W. *Regimental Strengths and Losses at Gettysburg.* Hightstown, NJ: Longstreet House, 1986.

"Capt. Ricketts at Gettysburg." *Wilkes-Barre Leader*, March 27, 1893.

"Col. Ricketts Dead." *Wilkes-Barre Record*, November 14, 1918.

"Col. Ricketts' Denial." Wilkes-Barre *Press*, March 29, 1893.

"Colonel Ricketts of This City is Claimed by Death." Wilkes-Barre *Times-Leader*, November 13, 1918.

"Death of Charles B. Brockway." *Columbia County Republican*, January 5, 1888.

Fishel, Edwin C. *The Secret War for the Union*. Boston: Houghton Mifflin Company, 1996.

Hall, Clark B. "Season of Change: The Winter Encampment of the Army of the Potomac, December 1, 1863-May 4, 1864." *Blue & Gray Magazine* 8 #4 (April1991): 8-22, 48-62.

Hawthorne, Frederick W. *Gettysburg: Stories of Men and Monuments as Told by Battlefield Guides*. Hanover, PA: The Sheridan Press for the Association of Licensed Battlefield Guides, 1988.

Henderson, William D. *The Road to Bristoe Station*. Lynchburg, VA: H. E. Howard, Inc., 1987.

Hennessy, John J. *Historical Report on the Troop Movements for the Second Battle of Manassas, August 28 Through 30, 1862*. Denver Service Center, National Park Service, 1985.

_____. *Return to Bull Run: The Campaign and Battle of Second Manassas*. New York: Simon & Schuster, 1993.

Horn, John. *The Petersburg Campaign, June 1864-April 1865*. Conshohocken, PA: Combined Books, 1993.

Howe, Thomas J. *The Petersburg Campaign: Wasted Valor, June 15-18, 1864*. Lynchburg, VA: H. E. Howard, Inc., 1988.

Humphreys, Andrew A. *From Gettysburg to the Rapidan: The Army of the Potomac July, 1863, to April, 1864*. New York: Charles Scribner's Sons, 1883.

_____. *The Virginia Campaign of 1864 and 1865*. New York: Charles Scribner's Sons, 1883.

In Memoriam, Ezra Wallace Matthews. N.p., n.d.

Kimmel, Ross M. "Men and Materiel." *America's Civil War* 14 #3 (July 2001): 12, 14, 16, 78.

Lash, Gary G. *The Gibraltar Brigade on East Cemetery Hill*. Baltimore: Butternut & Blue, 1995.

"Last of Her Family. Sudden Passing of Mrs. R. Bruce Ricketts–Distinguished Patriots and Pioneer Business Men Among Ancestors." *Wilkes-Barre Record*, November 20, 1918.

Long, E. B. *The Civil War Day by Day*. Garden City, NY: Doubleday & Company, Inc., 1971.

Longacre, Edward G. *Army of Amateurs: General Benjamin F. Butler and the Army of the James, 1863-1865*. Mechanicsburg, PA: Stackpole Books, 1997.

Matter, William D. *If It Takes All Summer: The Battle of Spotsylvania*. Chapel Hill: University of North Carolina Press, 1988.

Miller, J. Michael. *The North Anna Campaign: "Even To Hell Itself."* Lynchburg, VA: H. E. Howard, Inc., 1989.

"More Vindication for Ricketts." Wilkes-Barre *Telegram*, April 2, 1893.

Obituary of Ezra W. Matthews. *Grand Army Scout and Soldiers Mail*, November 14, 1885.

"On Cemetery Hill." *Wilkes-Barre Leader*, April 10, 1893.

"The Passing Throng." Bloomsburg *Morning Press*, December 16, 1938.

Pennsylvania Artillery. Battery F. *Ricketts' Battery; Abstract of Proceedings of Meeting Held on Thursday, October 27, 1887, Together with Roster of the Survivors of the Battery*. N.p., n.d.

Pennsylvania Artillery. Batteries F and G. *Proceedings of Survivors' Association, Batteries F and G, First Artillery, P.R.V.C, 52nd Anniversary and 27th Reunion, Gettysburg, Pa., July 2, 1913*. N.p., n.d.

_____. *Roster of Battery F and G, First Pennsylvania Light Artillery, and Abstract of Proceedings of Meeting Held on Wednesday, Sept. 11th, 1889*. N.p., n.d.

_____. *Survivors' Association, Batteries F and G, First Artillery, P.R.V.C., Shamokin, Pa., September 3 and 4, 1915*. N.p., n.d.

_____. *Survivors' Association, Batteries F and G, First Artillery, P.R.V.C., Wilkes-Barre, Pa., September 1st and 2d, 1916.* N.p., n.d.

Petrello, F. Charles. *Ghost Towns of North Mountain.* Wilkes-Barre, Pa.: Wyoming Historical Geological Society, 1991.

Pfanz, Harry. *Gettysburg–Culp's Hill & Cemetery Hill.* Chapel Hill: University of North Carolina Press, 1993.

Rankin, Thomas M. *Stonewall Jackson's Romney Campaign, January 1-February 20, 1862.* Lynchburg, VA: H. E. Howard, Inc., 1994.

"The Ricketts Battery." *Harrisburg Patriot*, October 28, 1887.

"Ricketts' Brave Boys." *Harrisburg Morning Call*, October 28, 1887.

Robertson, James I., Jr. "Stonewall in the Shenandoah: The Valley Campaign of 1862." *Civil War Times Illustrated* 11 (May 1972): 3-49.

Sauers, Richard A. *Advance the Colors! Pennsylvania Civil War Battleflags.* 2 volumes. Lebanon, PA: Sowers Printing Company for the Pennsylvania Capitol Preservation Committee, 1987-1991.

Sears, Stephen W. *Chancellorsville.* Boston: Houghton Mifflin Company, 1996.

_____. *Landscape Turned Red: The Battle of Antietam.* New Haven, CT: Ticknor & Fields, 1983.

"Sketches of Prominent Democrats." *The Four Quarters*, July 1, 1871.

Steere, Edward. *The Wilderness Campaign.* Harrisburg, PA: Stackpole Company, 1960.

Stocker, Rhamanthus M. *Centenial History of Susquehanna County, Pa.* Philadelphia: R. T. Peck & Company, 1887

Suderow, Bryce A. "Glory Denied: The First Battle of Deep Bottom, July 27th-29th, 1864." *North & South* 3 #7 (September 2000): 17-32.

Swinton, William. *Campaigns of the Army of the Potomac.* New York: Charles B. Richardson, 1866.

Tomasak, Peter. "An Encounter with Battery Hell." *The Gettysburg Magazine* #12 (January 1995): 30-41.

_____. "Hiking with History in Ricketts Glen State Park." *Pennsylvania State Parks* 4 #2 (Spring 1994): 2-3.

"Visiting War Veterans." *Wilkes-Barre Record*, September 5, 1914.

Wahn, Vorin E., Jr. *Fiasco at Fredericksburg*. University Park: Pennsylvania State University Press, 1961.

Warner, Ezra J. *Generals in Blue*. Baton Rouge: Louisiana State University Press, 1964.

Index

This Index includes people and places directly associated with Battery F. Common names such as Lee and Meade are included when mentioned prominently. A 158 n37 means that the subject in question is on page 158, note 37.

Abbott, R. O., 80

Abercrombie, John J., 9, 10, 17, 18, 21, 23

Aiken's Landing, VA, 212

Aldie, VA, 17, 83

Alexander, Edward Porter, 167-68

Alexandria, VA, 147

Allen, John W., 193

Ames, Adelbert, 86, 89

Ames, Nelson, 119

Amsden, Frank P., 77, 80

Anderson, George T., 34, 37

Anderson, Richard H., 122, 168, 187

Annandale, VA, 213

Antietam, battle of, 48-53

Appomattox River, VA, 180, 189, 212

Aquia Creek, VA, 32, 36, 59, 71, 213

Archer, James J., 41

Arnold, William, 119, 120, 122, 124, 127

Ashby, Turner, 15, 16, 17

Auburn, VA, 117, 118

Avery, Isaac E., 90, 93, 96

Avery House, VA, 196

Bailey's Creek, VA, 186-87, 190

Baltimore, MD, 6, 146, 214

Baltimore & Ohio Railroad, 11, 12, 15

Baltimore & Wilmington Railroad, 145

Bank's Ford, VA, 66, 76, 112

Banks, Nathaniel P., 7, 15, 17, 23, 24, 25, 29, 30, 31

Barlow, Francis C., 156, 170, 177, 178, 180, 186

Barry, John P., 22

Barry, William F., 61

Battery F–recruitment of, 2-5; Gettysburg monument of, 2 n5, 220-24; mustered into service, 2, 6; drilling of, 5; type of armament, 5, 9, 15, 48, 56, 150; elections in, 9; lack of clothing, 10-11; feelings toward Matthews, 10-11; action at Dam #5, 11; at Hancock, MD, 12; in Shenandoah Valley 1862 campaign, 15-18, 24-28; in Fredericksburg area, 19-24; target practice of, 23-24, 150; reviews of, 24, 54, 60, 71, 111, 151, 206; paid, 6, 24, 68, 78, 111, 113, 203, 214; at Cedar Mountain, 31-32; at Rappahannock Station action, 33-34; at Thoroughfare Gap, 37; at Second Manassas battle, 38-44; in

Maryland Campaign, 48-54; at Antietam, 49-53; in Fredericksburg Campaign, 60-63; in Fredericksburg battle, 62-63; Mud March, 65-66; in winter camp, 1862-1863, 68-71; in Chancellorsville Campaign, 71-76; transferred to Artillery Reserve, 77; Battery G consolidated with, 80-81; in Gettysburg Campaign, 82-108; transferred to Second Corps, 106; in Bristoe Station Campaign, 113-125; in Mine Run Campaign, 126-29; in winter camp, 143-52; reenlisted, 144; furlough of, 144-45; in winter camp again, 147-52; Battery G detached, 150; in Wilderness battle, 155-61; at Spotsylvania, 162-66; reduced in size, 165; in North Anna battle, 167-68; at Totopotomoy Creek, 170-71; in Cold Harbor battle, 171-72; in first attacks on Petersburg, 176-77; in Weldon Railroad battle, 180-81; in Deep Bottom operations, 103-5; Second Deep Bottom operations, 189-90; increased in size, 191; votes in 1864 election of, 196; inspection report of, 197; transferred to Artillery Reserve, 209; march to Washington, DC, of, 212-13; turned in cannon, 212; mustered out of service, 216; postwar reunions of, 220-222, 223-25

Bayard, George D., 23, 29

Bealton Station, VA, 60, 115, 117

Beckham, Robert F., 119, 120

Beem, David E., 100 n43

Beidelman, William, 224

Belle Plain, VA, 72, 76

Benham, Henry W., 72

Berlin, MD, 57

Berry Hill, VA, 125

Berryville, VA, 17, 18

Bingham, Henry W., 144

Birney, David B., 159, 165, 166-71, 177-79, 181-82, 190-92

Blair, Frank P., Sr., 201

Bloomfield, VA, 58, 107

Bolton, William J., 203

Bowling Green, VA, 213

Boydton Plank Road, VA, 204

Brady, James, 1, 2, 64-65, 68-69

Brandy Station, VA, 82, 109, 113, 115, 143, 147

Bristoe Station, VA, 36, 37, 121, 125; battle of, 121-24

Broad Run, VA, 121, 122, 124

Broadway Landing, VA, 213

Brockway, Charles B., 5 n6, 6, 9, 10, 15, 17, 21-22, 25, 31, 32, 37, 38, 40-41, 43-45, 47, 54, 63, 66, 68, 77-78, 82, 89, 90, 93, 96, 97, 99, 100, 103, 120, 124, 125, 127-28, 144, 157-59, 164, 180, 182, 193, 204, 207, 217

Brockway, Frank, 159, 199-02, 204-5, 206-09, 212-15, 217, 224 n12

Brooke, John R., 119, 121

Brooks Station, VA, 61

Brown, T. Fred, 122

Bryan, Thomas M., Jr., 21-22

Bull Run Mountains, 27, 36

Bunker Hill, VA, 16, 106

Index

Burkittsville, MD, 57

Burnside, Ambrose E., 48, 58, 59, 60, 62, 65, 68, 151, 163, 170, 178

Burton, John E., 192

Butler, Benjamin F., 147

Butterfield, Francis, 161

Caines, E. H. C., 100

Caldwell, John C., 113, 119

Camp Barr, 213

Camp Barry, 150

Camp Curtin, PA, 2, 5

Camp Parole, 45

Camp Return, 214

Campbell, Charles T., 2

Campbell, John A., 201

Campbell, John F., 144, 196, 201-03, 206, 209-10, 216

Carroll, Samuel S., 43, 99-101, 102, 121, 161

Case, Truman L., 2, 40, 43, 47, 54, 65, 68

Catlett's Station, VA, 23, 24, 118, 119, 121

Cedar Mountain, VA, 30-32, 113, 114

Cedar Run, VA, 117-20

Centreville, 19, 117, 118, 119, 121, 125

Chancellorsville, VA, battle of, 71-76

Chester Gap, VA, 107

Chester Hospital, PA, 145-46

Chesterfield Bridge, VA, 167-68

Chickahominy River, VA, 173, 175

Christian, John H., 6, 9

Christian, William A., 52

Clark, A. Judson, 189-90, 196

Cold Harbor, VA, battle of, 170-73

Cole's Hill, VA, 127, 143

Cooke, John R., 122

Cooper, James, 86, 89, 120, 121, 147, 182

Coulter, Richard, 52, 224

Coulter, William, 172

Cox's Farm, VA, 212

Crawford, Samuel W., 181

Culpeper, VA, 30, 57, 112, 113, 114, 115, 125, 128

Curry, Patrick, 204

Curtin, Andrew G., 1, 9, 69, 149

Danforth, Henry T., 2

Darnestown, MD, 7-8

Dawson, Thomas R., 151-52

De Russy, Gustavus A., 62, 63

Deep Bottom, VA, actions at, 186-88, 189-91

Denning, C. R., 56

Deserted House, VA, 182

Dow, Edwin B., 162, 163

Dranesville, VA, 84

Dumfries, VA, 25, 61, 82, 213

Duryee, Abram, 25, 28, 38, 40, 41, 49, 52

Eakin, Chandler P., 86

Early, Jubal A., 73, 90, 118, 127, 175, 185

Eddy, U. D., 184

Edgell, F. M., 83

Edwards' Ferry, 10, 84

Ellis Ford, VA, 60

Ely's Ford, VA, 155-56

Eustis, Henry L., 158

Ewell, Richard S., 24, 49, 86, 90, 107, 118, 126, 147, 157, 166, 168

Evans, Nathan G., 34

Executions, military, 111, 114, 151-52

Fairfax Court House, VA, 83, 84, 213

Falmouth, VA, 23, 60, 65, 66

Fayetteville, VA, 117

Featherston, Winfield S., 41, 43

Fillebrown, James S., 58 n25

Fisher's Hill, VA, 17

Five Forks, VA, 207

Fort Morton, VA, 196

Fort Rice, VA, 209

Fort Stedman, VA, 192, 199, 200, 203, 207

Fort Warren (Davis), VA, 192

Franklin, William B., 43, 60, 62, 63, 65, 68

Frederick, MD, 48, 84

Fredericksburg, VA, 21, 23, 30, 59, 60-63, 76, 213

Fremont, John C., 24, 27, 29

French, Myron, 97

French, William H., 107, 117, 122, 125, 127

Front Royal, VA, 24, 27, 28, 29

Funkstown, MD, 106

Fussell's Mill, VA, 190

Gainesville, VA, 36, 37, 125

George, Frank, 159 n10

Germanna Ford, VA, 126, 156

Getty, George W., 156, 159, 160

Gettysburg, PA, 220, 224; battle of, 85-105

Gibbon, John, 58, 60, 63, 99, 168, 170, 180, 181, 186

Gillespie, W. C., 61-62

Give, John M., 102 n45

Godbold, Henry L., 2, 21, 22, 34, 54

Goose Creek, VA, 18

Gordon, John B., 90, 120, 180, 207

Gordonsville, VA, 30, 32, 44

Grant, Lewis A., 158

Grant, Ulysses S., 151, 154, 161, 165, 173, 175-189

Graves, James, 206

Greenwich, VA, 117, 118, 121

Gregg, David M., 117, 119, 120, 121, 189, 191

Griffinsburg, VA, 114

Hall, James A., 31

Index

Halleck, Henry W., 59, 60, 68

Hamilton, Charles S., 15, 16, 17

Hancock, MD, 10, 12

Harman, Jacob M., 200

Hancock, R. J., 93

Hancock, Winfield S., 85, 99, 149, 150, 155, 156, 157, 162, 164, 166, 167, 175, 177, 185-87, 189, 190, 191

Harper's Ferry, VA, 9-10, 27, 48, 57, 106

Harris, Andrew L., 96

Harrisburg, PA, 214, 216

Harris House, VA, 165

Harrison, H. C., 184

Hartsuff, George L., 23, 28, 33, 52, 54

Hatcher's Run, VA, 203-4, 206, 208

Haymarket, VA, 37, 44

Hays, Alexander, 119, 120, 121, 122, 147, 158

Hays, Harry, 90, 93, 96

Hays, William, 107-8, 109, 111, 212

Hazard, John G., 111, 122, 124, 126, 149, 182, 184, 186, 189, 192, 193, 195, 196 n49, 206-07

Heinbach, George E., 220, 221

Heintzelman, Samuel P., 43

Heth, Henry, 85, 106, 121, 122, 158

Hill, Ambrose P., 30, 41, 85, 86, 121-22, 126, 157, 178, 180, 191

Hill, William F., 111

Hoke, Robert F., 177

Hood, John B., 53

Hooker, Joseph, 47, 48, 53, 59, 63, 68, 70, 71, 75, 77, 78, 80, 81, 84, 113

Hughes, Mason B., 220

Humphreys, Andrew A., 105, 207

Hunt, Henry J., 56, 62, 70, 72, 75, 77, 165

Huntington, James F., 83, 85, 86, 103

Hunter, R. M. T., 201

Indiana troops–14th Infantry, 100, 102, 161; 16th Infantry, 19; 27th Infantry, 48

Jacobs, Michael, 145

Jackson, Thomas J., 11-12, 16, 18, 24, 27-28, 30, 36, 38, 48, 49, 57, 59, 60, 62-63, 73, 75

James River, VA, 175, 185

Jerusalem Plank Road, VA, 180-81, 192

Johnson, Edward, 89-90, 103, 118, 164

Jones House, VA, 192

Jones Neck, VA, 186

Kearny, Phil, 38

Kelly's Ford, VA, 125

Kemper, James L., 167

Kennedy, James F., 224

Kernstown, VA, 18

Kershaw, Joseph B., 186

Kilpatrick, Hugh J., 112, 114, 117

Kimball, Nathan, 18

King, Rufus, 23, 29, 30, 38, 47

Kirkland, W. W., 122

Landrum House, VA, 164

Larrabee, Oscar G., 102 n45

Latimer, Joseph W., 86

Lawton, Alexander R., 49

Lee, Robert E., 32, 34, 36, 40, 48, 57, 59, 60, 86, 106-7, 113, 118, 125

Lee, Stephen D., 40, 52

Leonard, Samuel H., 11, 12

Leppien, George F., 31, 57, 60

Lewis, Alfred E., 2

Libby Prison, 45

Lincoln, Abraham, 24, 54, 60, 68, 71, 195, 201, 203, 210

Linden Station, VA, 107

Littlestown, PA, 105

Longstreet, James, 32, 33, 34, 36, 37, 40, 48, 57, 59, 60, 71-72, 73, 86, 106

Loudoun Valley, VA, 106

Louisiana troops–5th through 9th Infantry, 90; 9th Infantry, 93

Lovettsville, VA, 57

Lucas, Thomas J., 19, 21

Lyle, Peter, 52

Madison Court House, VA, 114

Maine troops–2nd Battery, 31; 5th Battery, 31, 57, 61, 70, 86, 93; 6th Battery, 41, 162, 181, 196; 1st Cavalry, 21; 10th Infantry, 58 n25

Manassas, second battle of, 38-44

Manassas Gap, VA, 27, 107

Manassas Gap Railroad, 17, 18, 29, 107

Manassas Junction, VA, 19, 25, 29, 36, 37-38

Markham Station, VA, 107

Martinsburg, VA, 15, 16

Massachusetts troops–10th Battery, 206; 12th Infantry, 21; 13th Infantry, 11, 15, 18; 19th Infantry, 124

Mattapony River, VA, 166, 168, 213

Matthews, Charles G., 210

Matthews, Ezra W., 2, 9, 12, 16, 21, 38, 41, 43-44, 47, 48-52, 53, 54, 69, 71, 77, 80, 145, 217-18, 222

McCall, George W., 5, 23

McClellan, George B., 15, 17, 19, 29, 30, 31, 47, 48, 54, 56, 58, 59, 195

McConkey, Elbridge, 2, 3, 9

McDowell, Irvin, 19, 23, 27, 29, 31, 36, 38, 40, 47

McFarland, John A., 209

McGilvery, Freeman, 84, 85

McGowan, Samuel, 159, 161

McIntosh, David G., 124

McLaws, Lafayette, 76

Meade, George G., 47, 48, 53, 54, 62-63, 84, 109, 113, 115, 117, 121, 126, 149, 155, 156, 157, 161, 165, 173, 186, 212

Middleburg, VA, 18, 83

Miles, Nelson A., 195

Index

Milford Station, VA, 66

Miller, David R., farm, 49

Mine Run, VA, campaign of, 126-29

Minnesota troops–1st Infantry, 121

Mississippi troops–Madison Light Artillery, 158-59; 16th Infantry, 43

Mitchell, C. H., 125, 144, 147

Mitchell, William G., 170

Monroe, John A., 126, 147

Montgomery, D. W., 145

Morrisville, VA, 60, 108, 109

Morton's Ford, VA, 147

Mott, Gershom, 156, 158, 162, 163, 166, 180, 184, 186-87, 190, 192

Mount Vernon, VA, 216

Mowrer, George W., 200, 201, 204, 214, 225

Muddy Branch, MD, 10

Need, Francis, 102 n45

New Hampshire troops–1st Battery, 72, 77, 80, 83, 182

New Jersey troops, Battery B, 189, 190, 191; 3rd Battery, 196; 1st Cavalry, 37

New Market Heights, VA, 182

New York troops–4th Heavy Artillery, 196; Battery G, 1st Artillery, 119, 196; Battery I, 1st Artillery, 86, 89; Battery L, 1st Artillery, 70, 86, 89; 11th Battery, 181, 192; 28th Infantry, 18; 41st Infantry, 96; 54th Infantry, 96; 68th Infantry, 96

Nicholson, John P., 220, 222

North Anna River, VA, battle of, 166-68

North Carolina troops–1st Cavalry, 120; 6th, 21st, 57th Infantry, 90

Ny River, VA, 165, 166

Occoquan River, VA, 83

Ohio troops–Battery H, 1st Artillery, 83; 4th Infantry, 100; 8th Infantry, 100, 161; 75th Infantry, 96

Orange & Alexandria Railroad 19, 33, 36, 37, 117, 118, 119, 121

Orange Plank Road, VA, 126, 128, 155, 156, 157, 159

Orange Turnpike, VA, 126, 127, 155, 157

Ord, Edward O. C., 23, 25-28

Paris, VA, 107

Parke, John G., 203, 207

Patrick's Station, VA, 206

Patterson, William P., 65, 69, 71, 76, 78, 109, 111, 114, 117, 125 n37

Pender, William D., 41, 43

Pennsylvania troops–Battery A, 1st Artillery, 64, 69; Battery B, 1st Artillery, 64, 69, 86, 89, 150, 180, 214; Battery G, 1st Artillery, 61, 64, 69, 77, 150; Battery C, 21, 22, 31, 33, 34, 37, 38, 40, 41, 49, 58, 72, 126; Battery F, 224; 11th Infantry, 224; Reserves, 1, 6, 47, 62-63, 68, 69; 2nd Reserves, 65; 28th Infantry, 18; 46th Infantry, 16; 48th Infantry, 183; 51st Infantry, 201; 53rd Infantry, 119; 90th Infantry, 52, 146;

107th Infantry, 31, 34; 121st Infantry, 69; 142nd Infantry, 69; 148th Infantry, 191; 149th Infantry, 182; 153rd Infantry, 96, 224

Petersburg, VA, campaign against, 173-207

Philadelphia, PA, 145

Pickett, George, 207

Pleasonton, Alfred, 115, 151

Poague, William T., 121, 122, 159 n10

Pollock's Mill, VA, 62, 72

Poolesville, MD, 10

Pope, John, 29, 30, 31, 32, 40, 47

Port Conway, VA, 112

Price, M. F., 80

Purcellville, VA, 57

Raccoon Ford, VA, 32

Rake, Isaac, 225

Rapidan River, VA, 65, 71, 109, 126, 147

Rappahannock River, VA, 32, 60, 65, 71, 81, 109, 112, 115

Rappahannock Station, VA, 33-34, 60, 113, 115, 117, 125

Reading, PA, 220

Reams' Station, VA, 191

Rectortown, VA, 58

Reynolds, John F., 54, 56-57, 72, 73, 85

Rhode Island troops–Battery A, 1st Artillery, 119, 120; Battery B, 1st Artillery, 122, 149; Battery C, 1st Artillery, 77, 80

Richmond, VA, 212-13

Richmond, Fredericksburg & Potomac Railroad, 59, 166

Ricketts, James B., 23, 28, 29, 30, 31, 33, 36, 38, 40-41, 43, 47, 49, 52, 53, 54, 58

Ricketts, Robert Bruce, 2, 9, 11, 12, 16-17, 19-20, 23-24, 25, 28, 30, 54, 56, 58, 60, 61, 63, 64, 66, 68, 70, 71, 72, 75, 76, 77, 83, 86, 89, 93, 96, 99, 102, 105, 108, 109, 111, 112, 115, 119, 120, 124, 126, 145, 146, 150, 156, 157, 159, 162, 163, 167, 168, 170-72, 177, 180, 181, 187, 189, 193, 195-96, 199, 200, 207, 209, 212, 213, 216, 218-22, 224

Riggin, James H., 97, 99

Robertson River, VA, 114

Robertson's Tavern, VA, 127, 128

Robinson, John C., 63

Rodes, Robert, 90, 118, 119, 120, 121, 127

Rudisill, Abraham, 80-81, 82, 83, 84, 105

Rush, Richard H., 2

Salem, VA, 36

Sandy Hook, MD, 106

Schmehl, Joel H., 220, 221

Schurz, Carl, 97

Sedgwick, John, 73, 76, 115, 117, 125, 128, 147, 151, 162

Seeley, Francis W., 75

Index

Seiders, Luther, 225

Seward, William H., 203

Seymour, Isaac, 93

Sharpsburg, MD, 106

Shenandoah River, VA, 17, 28, 106

Shields, James, 16, 17, 23, 25, 27

Shoemaker, William M., 184 n17

Sickel, Horatio G., 65

Smith, John, 111

Smith, William, 90

Smith, William F., 68, 170, 172, 177

Snicker's Gap, VA, 57

Snickersville, VA, 58

Snider, Francis H., 47, 89, 107-8, 129, 159 n12

South Mountain, MD, 48, 57, 105

Spence, Belden, 81, 89, 125, 126, 144, 145, 147

Spotsylvania, VA, battle of, 161-65

Stafford Court House, VA, 25, 60, 82

Stephens, Alexander, 201

Stevens, Greenleaf T., 61

Stevens, Isaac I., 40

Stewart, Thomas J., 222

Stewart, William, 206

Stiles, John, 37, 38

Strasburg, VA, 24, 28

Stratford, Richard S., 97, 99

Strong, Joseph, 206

Stuart, James E. B., 32, 56, 112, 113, 114, 118, 119, 120

Sweet, Oney F., 97

Sykes, George, 85, 121, 128

Taneytown, MD, 84, 85

Taylor, Nelson, 54, 63

Tenallytown, MD, 6, 7

Thoburn, James, 38

Thomas, James B., 31

Thompson, James, 21, 31, 49, 52, 56, 127

Thoroughfare Gap, VA, 27, 36, 37, 44

Thurston, William H., 53 n13, 97 n37, 144, 146, 147, 150, 151-53, 159 n12, 165, 169, 172, 178, 178, 181, 182, 185, 190, 195, 196, 199, 201, 203, 204, 208, 210, 212, 214

Tidball, John C., 150, 155, 164, 169, 180, 182, 207, 213

Tilghman's Wharf, VA, 186

Tillson, Davis, 23, 33-34

Todd's Tavern, VA, 156, 162

Tompkins, John A., 77, 80

Torbert, Alfred T. A., 166

Totopotomoy Creek, Va, 169

Tower, Zealous B., 34, 38

Truman, John C., 54

Trump, William H., 2, 221

Tyler, Robert O., 77, 85, 167

Unger's Store, VA, 12

United States Ford, VA, 75

United States Military Railroad, 206

United States Regular Army troops–Battery H, 1st Artillery, 86; Battery I, 1st Artillery, 126; Battery K, 4th Artillery, 75; Battery C, 5th Artillery, 64, 126; Batteries C&I, 5th Artillery, 184, 196

United States Sanitary Commission, 182, 196

Urbana, VA, 112

Verdiersville, VA, 128

Virginia Central Railroad, 186

Virginia troops–Purcell Artillery, 31; 7th Cavalry, 15

von Gilsa, Leopold, 96

Wadsworth, James, 72-73, 85, 93

Wainwright, Charles P., 56, 57, 58, 60, 66, 70 n30, 72, 73, 75, 77, 86, 89, 96, 100, 102, 224

Wapping Heights, VA, 107

Ward, J. H. H., 158

Warren, G. K., 111, 112, 115, 117, 120, 121, 122, 126, 127, 128, 151, 156-57, 158, 168, 208

Warrenton, VA, 30, 34, 36, 58, 108, 125

Warrenton Junction, VA, 19

Washington Arsenal, 6-7

Washington, DC, 6, 145, 146

Waterloo Bridge, VA, 30

Waterman, Richard, 80, 83

Webb, Alexander S., 112, 119, 120, 121, 122

Weldon Railroad, VA, 178-79, 180, 191

West, Robert M., 70

West Virginia troops–Battery C, 100; 7th Infantry, 77, 80

Wheaton, Frank, 158

White Oak Church, VA, 63, 76, 78, 81

White Oak Road, VA, 208

White Plains, VA, 108

Whittier, Edward, 86, 96

Wiedrich, Michael, 86, 96-97, 100, 102

Wilcox, Cadmus M., 122, 159, 180

Wilderness, VA, battle of, 155-61

Wilkes-Barre, PA, 218, 224

Williams, Alpheus S., 15, 16, 17, 18

Williamsport, MD, 10, 15, 106

Winchester, VA, 12, 16-17, 24

Windmill Point, VA, 175

Wireman, Henry, 52, 144, 195, 199, 200, 201, 204, 206, 214, 225

Wisconsin troops–36th Infantry, 199

Wolf Run Shoals, VA, 213

Wood, John T., 111-12

Woodborough, MD, 105

Wright, Horatio G., 162, 180, 185

Yordy, Jacob S., 225